The Ul

More than 4300 Real Estate Terms
Explained with
Clear and Concise Definitions
For
Real Estate Investors, Homeowners,
Agents and Brokers

By Allan Susoeff, Jr. PE, PhD

AskAlHow.com
Arkansas | California

ISBN 978-0-578-63128-8 (Paperback)

Library of Congress Control Number: 2020900120

First Printed Edition

Published by Think Tank Green, LLC, Little Rock, AR

Printed by LuLu.com, in the United States of America

www.AskAlHow.com

Table of Contents

Foreword

Years ago, when I was working on my engineering degree, I had a professor who was asked why so many roads and bridges did not seem to fit the design criteria that he was teaching us. His reply was, *"Some roads are actually planned but most simply evolved over time"*. The same could be said for this work. It was never my intention to write a dictionary. I started out putting a few terms together for one of my Real Estate Investing Classes; I wanted to create a glossary for that class. Then I added a few more words and terms due to another class. Pretty soon, I realized that I needed something a bit more "all encompassing" in order to avoid constantly having to stop teaching so as to define some bit of jargon that has evolved within the building and real estate industries. And thus, you now have this book in your hands.

First of all I want to put caveat in here about my being this book's author. That's a something of a misnomer. I'm more of a compiler, editor, and perhaps collaborator. I have gathered the definitions contained in this book from all over the Internet, from other books that I personally own by other authors, and from my experience having been in the building business, engineering business, and real estate business to date; some 30 plus years. I want to make it clear that in no way, shape, or form have I intentionally plagiarized anybody. However, when we are trying to define any given term, it becomes awfully challenging to not use the same words in the description that others have used before me. That being said, you will likely find definitions that bear a striking resemblance or may even be pretty close to verbatim to other definitions you may have read in other books or online. There is no intent to defraud anybody, rather I picked the best definitions whether they were 100% my words, a combination of my words and other people's words, or simply some other author's words. This first edition has more than 4300 terms in it so I daresay it's the most exhaustive volume of its type on the market today; I personally have not seen a bigger one yet. I hope that I can add a few hundred words as well as some examples and illustrations in upcoming editions.

All that being said, I want this book to be a living dictionary, not a static one. This is the first edition. I'm hoping that approximately every year or two, I have this book updated for you because real estate and building are both ever-changing industries, and words go in and out of service regularly. In fact, what I'd really like to ask is that you, the reader partner with me. I have set up a webpage at www.AskAlHow.com/dictionary where you can suggest edits, point out omissions, and add in any words or terms you feel need to be included. In future editions I would also like to have some examples and some illustrations and will be keeping an eye out for somebody to partner with me on that as well. Give the webpage a visit when you have time and feel free to leave feedback there. Also, I don't believe in charging people money twice for the same thing, so if you go on the webpage and upload me proof of purchase, I will be happy to send you a download link for an Epub, Pdf, or Mobi version of this work as well. This way you can keep it on your tablet or reader as well as your bookshelves.

I would also like to take a moment to acknowledge a few people who have helped me along the way with this book and with life in general. First of all my spouse Liz Williams. Here is an example of a truly patient woman. I know I'm not an easy guy to live with, particularly when I'm tunneled into the computer, deeply embedded in "work mode". I am moody. I am impatient. And sometimes I'm a grouch for no apparent reason at all. Thank you for your patience and belief in me.

I also want to thank my business coach, Dan Mangena, at www.dreamwithdan.com. Dan has been instrumental in my bringing my expertise to the market. He pointed out to me one day that not only is teaching what a person knows a great way to build income, it is also a fantastic way to serve mankind. To use his words, *"There comes a point at which, if you don't give back in some way, such as teaching and sharing your knowledge and experience, so that the next group of people coming up can learn from your victories but more often from your mistakes, then you just spit in the face of all humanity"*. Strong words. But I think he's probably right. Sharing information enriches all of us.

Finally there are my many mentors and teachers. In real estate that would be Steve, Ron, Tim, Cameron, and BJ. In life I would like to mention Wayne, Joe, Liz Dawn, Amber, and Tom. All you folks have contributed immensely whether you realize it or not.

Past that, enjoy this handy reference and Good Luck to you in all you do and attempt to do.

~Allan~

A

Abacus The flat slab on top of a capital, supporting the architrave.

Abandonment The voluntary and permanent cessation of use or enjoyment with no intention to resume or reclaim one's possession or interest. Most often pertains to an easement of a property.

Abatement Often referred to as free rent or early occupancy and may occur outside or in addition to the primary term of the lease. Can also mean to lessen something , like in "Noise Abatement".

Above Building Standard Upgraded finishes and specialized designs necessary to accommodate a tenant's requirements.

Abrasive Paper Heavy paper coated on one side with sand or other abrasive material and used for smoothing surfaces. Sandpaper.

Abrasive Surface Tile Floor tile roughened to avoid being slippery when damp.

Absentee Landlord A Landlord that does not live on the premises.

Absentee Owner An owner who does not personally manage or reside at property owned. See Absentee Landlord.

Absolute Auction An auction in which the subject property is sold to the highest bidder regardless of the amount of the winning bid. An Absolute Auction has no reserve price.

Absolute Net Absolute net is a lease that requires the tenant to pay all costs associated with the operation, repair, and maintenance of the building in addition to base rent. . See Triple Net Lease.

Absolute Title A title that is without any liens or judgments. A clear title.

Absorption Rate The rate at which rentable space is filled with tenants.

Abstract of Judgment An abstract of judgment is a document that summarizes the outcome of a lawsuit and spells out precisely the amount of money, penalties, interest, and attorney's fees that is owed to the winning party by the party that lost.

Abstract of Title A condensed version of the history of a title for a particular parcel of real estate as recorded in the county clerk's records; typically consists of a summary of the original grant and all subsequent conveyances and encumbrances affecting the property. A simplified Chain of Title.

Abstract Update Documents recorded at the county clerk's office to correct or make current and existing abstract of title.

Abut See Abutting.

Abutment A structure made to hold an arch.

Abutting The joining, reaching, or touching of adjoining land. Abutting parcels of land have a common boundary.

ABX Index A synthetic tradable index referencing a basket of 20 subprime mortgage-backed securities.

AC Condenser A condenser unit used in central air conditioning systems typically has a heat exchanger section to cool down and condense incoming refrigerant vapor into liquid.

AC Disconnect The main source of power beside the A/C Condenser. Typically has a circuit breaker and throw switch.

AC The short form of the phrase air conditioner or air conditioning.

Accelerated Amortization When an owner pays extra principal in excess of the minimum required by the note and mortgage.

Accelerated Cost Recovery System An accelerated cost recovery system is a way of calculating tax depreciation. It provides greater depreciation in the early years of property ownership instead of spreading it out over several years. It allows recovery of the value of the property faster than other depreciation options.

Accelerated Depreciation A method of calculating for tax purposes the depreciation of income property at a faster rate than would be achieved using the straight-line method. Any depreciation taken in excess of what would be claimed using the straight-line rate is subject to recapture as ordinary income to the extent of the gain resulting from the sale. See Accelerated Cost Recovery System.

Acceleration Clause Also known as an acceleration covenant, this is a contract provision requiring the borrower to repay all of their outstanding loan to a lender if certain requirements are not met.

Acceleration Covenant See Acceleration Clause.

Accelerator Something which brings about acceleration in the curing process; in particular: concrete, mortar, grout, or plaster hydration.

Acceptance A seller's written statement that approves a buyer's offer.

Access Right The right of an owner to enter and/or exit their property.

Access The means of entry to a piece of property.

Accessibility This term has to do with the extent at which a disabled person is provided ease of entry into and throughout the confines of a building or property. See ADA.

Accession Title to improvements or additions to real property is acquired as a result of the accretion of alluvial deposits along the banks of streams or as a result of the annexation of other fixtures.

Accessory Apartment A separate living quarters created within a single family home. Sometimes called a Mother-In-Law Quarters.

Accommodating Party The intermediary in a section 1031 exchange, used especially in a delayed exchange, also known as a Tax-Free Exchange, who holds money or property for a short time to facilitate the exchange. See Qualified Intermediary.

Accommodation Party One who has signed an agreement without receiving value for it, for the purpose of lending his or her name so that another person can secure a necessary loan or other arrangement. See Co-Signer.

Accretion An increase or addition to land by the deposit of sand or soil washed up naturally from a river, lake, or sea.

Accrual Method A method of accounting that requires income or expense to be entered when the amount is earned, or the obligation is payable. Distinguished from Cash Method in which amounts are posted when paid or received.

Accrue
1. To accumulate or increase.
2. To enter in financial records an amount that has not been paid or received.

Accrued Depreciation The actual depreciation that has occurred to a property at any given date; the difference between the cost of replacement new as of the date of the appraisal, and the present appraised value.

Accrued Expense Costs that have been incurred but not paid during an accounting period.

Accrued Interest Accrue; to grow; to be added to. Accrued interest is interest that has been earned but not due and payable.

Acknowledgment A formal written declaration before a duly authorized officer by a person who has executed an instrument that such execution is the person's act and deed.

Acoustical Plaster A substance which contains fibers or aggregate designed so that it absorbs sound.

Acquisition An act or process by which a person procures property.

Acquisition Loan Money borrowed for the purpose of purchasing a property.

Acre A measure of land equaling 43,560 square feet; or in surveying terms, 160 square rods or 10 square chains.

Acre Foot Typically used to describe bodies of water such as lakes, rivers and ponds, an acre-foot is a volume occupied by one acre of land with a depth of one foot. Volume for an acre-foot is equivalent to 43,560 cubic feet.

ACRS See Accelerated Cost Recovery System.

Act Of God An unpreventable destructive occurrence of the natural world.

Action for Specific Performance A court action to compel a defaulting principal to comply with the provisions of a contract.

Action To Quiet Title See Quiet Title.

Active Contingent When a seller accepts an offer from a buyer, the offer is contingent upon the buyer's ability to meet certain conditions before finalization of the sale.

Active Income All salaries, tips, wages, and commissions the taxpayer earns from actually performing a duty or service.

Active Participation Type of investor position that determines how rental income is taxed. Requirements for active participation are less stringent than for material participation. An investor may have a manager for rental real estate and still be considered an active participant. Indicators of active participation in real estate are:

1. One who approves new tenants
    a. Decides on rental terms
    b. Approves capital or repair expenditures
2. Active participation excludes owners with a 10% interest or less.

Active Solar Heating A system that uses energy from sunlight to heat a structure and/or provide hot water. Installation of active solar heating equipment is eligible for certain income tax credits.

Active Under Contract A home is listed as active under contract when the seller has accepted an offer with contingencies, but still wants the house to be listed as active. In this situation, the seller is also likely to be accepting backup offers in case their current offer fails to meet its contingencies.

Actual Age When buying or selling a home, it's important to know and consider the house's actual age. The actual age of a building simply refers to how long the dwelling has been standing. Often it can be found by investigating county real estate data.

Actual Cash Value (ACV) Cost to replace an item of personal property, minus the depreciation. Actual cash value represents the value that the item could currently be sold for, which is often less than what it would cost to replace it. Insurance companies sometimes use actual cash value to determine what to pay a policyholder after loss or damage to insured property.

Actual Eviction The result of legal action originated by a lessor, by which a defaulted tenant is physically ousted from the rental property pursuant to a court order.

Actual Notice Express information or fact; that which is known; actual knowledge.

Actual Possession See Possession.

Actualage In appraisal, the chronological age of an improvement, as contrasted with its effective age.

ACV See Actual Cash Value.

Ad Valorem Tax Meaning *"according to value"*, A tax levied according to value; generally used to refer to real estate tax.

ADA See Americans With Disabilities Act.

Addendum An Addition to a contract. If a buyer or seller want to change an existing contract, they might add an addendum outlining the specific part of the contract they'd like to adjust and the parameters of that change. The rest of the contract stays the same, regardless of the addendum.

Additional First-Year Depreciation Tax provision that allows up to $20,000 of depreciable personal property purchased each year to be expensed, rather than depreciated, provided that not more than $200,000 is purchased in a year. The $20,000 is phased out, dollar for dollar, when purchases exceed $200,000 in a given year.

Additional Principal Payment An additional principal payment describes the portion of a monthly payment that is above the minimum amount and is applied specifically towards the principal of the loan.

Additional Rent Additional rent refers to any monetary obligations that a tenant is responsible for in addition to the base rent or the minimum monthly rent. Base rent is the agreed-upon cost that a tenant pays to the landlord, property owner or property manager for the right to possess a property. See Triple-Net-Lease.

Add-On Interest Add-on interest refers to the interest paid by the borrower on the principal for the life of the loan.

Adjacent Lying near to but not necessarily in actual contact with.

Adjoining Contiguous; attaching, in actual contact with. See Abutting.

Adjoining Contiguous Attaching; sharing a common border. See Abutting.

Adjudication The legal process by which an arbiter or judge reviews evidence and argumentation including legal reasoning set forth by opposing parties or litigants to come to an official decision which determines rights and obligations between the parties involved. Three types of disputes are resolved through adjudication:

1. Disputes between private parties, such as individuals or corporations.
2. Disputes between private parties and public officials.
3. Disputes between public officials or public bodies.

Adjustable-Rate Mortgage (ARM) The interest rate for an adjustable-rate mortgage changes periodically. Typically the borrower would start with lower monthly payments than they would with a fixed-rate mortgage, but fluctuating interest rates will likely make those monthly payments rise in the future.

Adjusted Basis The property value for income tax purposes, which is figured by taking the original basis (or cost) plus improvements minus depreciation.

Adjusted Tax Basis See Adjusted Basis.

Adjusted Cost Basis Adjusted cost basis is a cost valuation basis used in tax accounting in which the historical cost of an asset undergoes various adjustments to arrive at the adjusted cost basis. The adjusted cost basis is necessary to determine potential gains and losses resulting from the sale of real estate in subsequent periods.

Adjusted Funds From Operations (AFFO) A measure of REIT performance or ability to pay dividends used by some analysts with concerns about quality of earnings as measured by funds from operations, (FFO). The most common adjustment to FFO is an estimate of certain recurring capital expenditures needed to keep the property portfolio competitive within its marketplace.

Adjusted Sales Price In an appraisal, the adjusted sales price is the indicated price of a comparable property after adjustments have been made to account for differences between comparable and subject properties.

Adjustment Date This is the date your mortgage begins to accrue interest. The adjustment date usually falls on the first day of the month after mortgage funds are advanced or dispersed to the borrower.

Adjustment Period The adjustment period refers to how often interest rate adjustments occur in an adjustable rate mortgage. Most adjustment periods are one, three, or five years in length.

Adjustments (In Appraisal) Dollar value or percentage amounts that, when added to or subtracted from the sales price of a comparable, provide an indicator of the value of a given property. Since no two homes are exactly alike, adjustments are necessary to compensate for variation in the features of the comparable relative to the subject.

Administrative Deed An administrative deed is a property deed that is in the name of someone who died, who did not have a will.

Administrative Fee An Administrative Fee is typically stated as a percentage of assets under management or as a fixed annual dollar amount.

Administrator The party appointed by a county court to settle the estate of a deceased person who died without leaving a Will.

Administrator's Deed A deed conveying the property of one who died without a Will. See Intestate.

Adobe House An early-twentieth-century house that is made of adobe brick or some other material made to look like adobe brick. Adobe is mud and straw mixed together and dried to make a strong brick-like material. Pueblo peoples stacked these bricks to make the walls of the house. The characteristic projecting roof beams are called vigas. Modern versions use stick construction and cover it with stucco or some other durable finish.

ADR See Asset Depreciation Range.

Adult A person who has attained the age of majority. This is age 18 or 21, depending on the state.

Advances Payments made by the servicer when the borrower fails to make a payment.

Adverse Possession A means of acquiring title where an occupant has been in actual, open, notorious, exclusive, and continuous occupancy of property under a claim of right for the required statutory period. See Squatter's Right.

Adverse Use Adverse use describes the process by which a person can illegitimately obtain the title to a property without the consent or permission of the property owner. A person typically obtains title through adverse possession. See Squatter's Right.

Adviser Any broker, consultant or investment banker who represents an investor in a transaction. Advisers may be paid a retainer, commission, and/or a performance fee upon the close of a financing or sales transaction.

Aerator The round screened screw on tip of a sink spout. It mixes water and air for a smooth flow.

Affidavit A statement or declaration reduced to writing and sworn to or affirmed before some officer who is authorized to administer an oath or affirmation. See Acknowledgement.

Affidavit of Title A written document specifying under oath that a seller is the actual possessor of the title of a property.

Affirm To confirm, to ratify, to verify.

Affirmative Lending An attempt to make the demographic distribution of loan recipients more closely match that of area residents or depositors. Required of federally chartered lending institutions under the community reinvestment act. See Community Reinvestment Act.

AFFO See Adjusted Funds From Operations.

Affordability Index The affordability index is a measurement of housing affordability compiled by the National Association of Realtors® and other groups.

Affordable Housing A general term applied to both public and private sector efforts to help low and moderate-income people purchase homes. Typically these sorts of programs offer lower cash down payments, eased loan-qualifying rules, and/or below-market interest rates.

A-Frame A post-World War II style house with a frame in the shape of one or more *"A's."* A-frame houses many times provide less living space than traditional homes, as they tend to be compact, and have **a** smaller footprint on the first floor.

AFTC See After Tax Cash Flow.

After Acquired Clause A provision in a mortgage loan that includes a property subsequently purchased as security on the existing mortgage.

After Repaired Value (ARV) This is an estimate, based on comparable properties near the subject property of the value of the home after it has been repaired and remodeled.

After Tax Cash Flow (ATCF) This is commonly referred to as *"profit".* It is the amount left after paying all expenses and taxes from an investment.

After-Tax Equity Yield The rate of return on an equity interest in real estate, after considering financing costs and income tax implications of the investor.

After-Tax Income See After-Tax Cash Flow.

After-Tax Proceeds From Resale The amount of money left after taxes for the investor

Agency The relationship between principal and agent which arises out of a contract either expressed or implied, written, or oral, wherein a person employs an agent to do certain acts on the person's behalf in dealing with a third party. See Real Estate Agency.

Agency Disclosure A written explanation, to be signed by a prospective buyer or seller, which explains to that prospective buyer or seller the role that the broker and or agent plays in the transaction. The purpose of disclosure is to explain whether the broker and their agents represents the buyer or seller or is a dual agent or a subagent. This disclosure explains to whom the broker owes loyalty.

Agent One who represents or has the power to act for another person; who is referred to as the principal. Legally speaking, the authorization may be express, implied, or apparent. A fiduciary relationship is created under the Law Of Agency when a property owner, as the principal, executes a listing agreement or management contract authorizing a licensed real estate broker to be her or his agent.

Aggregate
1. A material or structure formed from a mass of fragments or particles loosely compacted together.
2. A terms used to describe crushed stone.
3. To form or group into a class or cluster.

Aggregation Risk The risk associated with warehousing mortgages during the pooling process for future securitization.

Agreed Boundary An agreed boundary is a boundary that is chosen by the owners of adjacent land where the property line is in dispute or where the true property line is not easily ascertained due to man-made or natural causes.

Agreement of Sale A written agreement between seller and purchaser in which the purchaser agrees to buy certain real estate and the seller agrees to sell upon terms and conditions set forth therein.

Air Handler (AHU) An air handler, or air handling unit is a device used to regulate and circulate the air as part of a heating, ventilating, and air-conditioning (HVAC) system. Also Abbreviated: AHU.

Air Lot A designated airspace over a piece of land. Air lots, like surface property, may be transferred. See Air Rights.

Air Rights The right to use the open space above a piece of property. Contrast with Mineral Rights.

Air Space The spot that is in-between an insulation facing an interior of exterior wall coverings. Also called Air-Gap.

Allowance The amount put aside for extra items that are not included inside an original construction contract. Typically 5-10% of the overall bid.

Alienation A transferring of property form one to another; the transfer of property and possession of lands, or other things, from one person to another

Alienation Clause The clause in a mortgage instrument that does not all the borrower to sell without lender approval on assumption or contract-for-deed. If an attempt is made to do so without prior approval, all of the mortgaged balance becomes due on the sale of the property. See Due on Sale Clause.

Alienation The act of transferring property to another. Alienation may be voluntary, such as by sale, or involuntary, such as through eminent domain.

Allodial System A legal system that allocates full property ownership rights to individuals. The allodial system is the basis for property rights in the United States.

Allowances When a person purchases a home that has been recently built, he or she might ask for allowances. An allowance is a bit of money that the builder offers to the home buyer. This money might be used by the buyer for things like carpet, furniture, or anything else that they need to outfit the home. Not to be confused with Allowance.

Alluvion The actual soil increase resulting from accretion.

Alpha An alpha is a risk adjusted statistical measure of performance. Alpha takes the price risk volatility of a managed portfolio of equities, or alternative assets and contrasts its risk-adjusted performance to some benchmark index. The excess return of the fund relative to the return of the benchmark index is a fund's alpha.

ALTA See American Land Title Association.

Alteration Agreement A document outlining the shareholder's responsibilities to the corporation when renovating his or her dwelling unit. Typically used in Co-op and Condominium arrangements.

Alteration A word used in describing a partial construction project or remodeling work.

Alternate Bid An amount which is added to or subtracted from the quoted price if alternate methods and materials are chosen.

Alternative Minimum Tax (AMT) A type of flat-rate tax that applies to taxpayers who have certain types of income. See TAX

Alternative Mortgage An alternative mortgage is any mortgage that is not a traditional, fixed-rate mortgage. The alternative mortgage might be an adjustable-rate mortgage or an interest-only mortgage.

Alternative Mortgage Instrument (AMI) Any mortgage other than a fixed interest rate, level payment amortizing loan. Various examples of AMI's are:
1. Variable Rate Mortgages
2. Rollover Loans
3. Graduated Payment Mortgages
4. Shared Appreciation Mortgages
5. Adjustable Rate Mortgages
6. Growing Equity Mortgages

Alternative Or Specialty Investments Any property types that are not considered conventional institutional-grade real estate investments. Some examples might include mobile homes, timber, congregate care facilities, self-storage facilities, agriculture, and parking lots.

Amendments Changes to previously approved and adopted written agreements are amendments.

Amenities Neighborhood facilities and services that enhance a property's value. By definition, they are always outside of the property. Swimming pools, three-car garages, decks, etc., that are on the property are features that could be considered amenities.

American Bankers Association A trade organization for officers of commercial banks. Publishes the monthly *ABA Banking Journal* and several other specialized banking periodicals.

American Council Of Life Insurance (ACLI) A life insurance related trade association that offers historical data on interest rates and loan terms for commercial property mortgages.

American Institute Of Architects A professional organization of architects, designers, and developers. Publishes the monthly *AIA Journal* and other periodicals.

American Institute Of Real Estate Appraisers (AIREA) See Appraisal Institute.

American Land Title Association (ALTA) A national association of title companies, abstractors, and attorneys established to promote uniformity and quality in title abstract and insurance policies.

American Mansard A nineteenth-century-style, the Mansard Style is often called *"Second-Empire Style"* and *"French Second Empire Style"* in the United States. The word *"Mansard"* refers to the ornate Continental roof, originally employed in Paris in the 19th Century. Homes are designed around the large reception hall beneath a rounded, cupola style roof. The best-known example of this style is the Philadelphia City Hall, built in 1871-1881.

American Motel Hotel Brokers Network An association for real estate brokers who specialize in the sale of hotels and motels.

American Partnership Board A company that trades Real Estate Limited Partnerships.

American Planning Association (APA) A professional organization of regional and urban planners for the purpose of promoting professional standards, research, and education. APA was formed by the merger of the American Institute of Planners *(AIP)* and the American Society of Planning Officials *(ASPO)*. APA publishes a monthly magazine, *Planning*, and a quarterly journal, *Journal of the APA*.

American Real Estate Exchange A global online listing, trading, and information source for real estate professionals.

American Real Estate Society (ARES) An organization of scholars, researchers, and practitioners who are mainly concerned with solving business problems related to real estate. Publishes the *Journal of Real Estate Research*, *Journal of Real Estate Literature,* and *Journal of Real Estate Portfolio Management*.

American Society Of Appraisers (ASA) A professional organization of appraisers *(not restricted to real estate)*. ASA publishes the biannual journal *Valuation*. It offers the professional designations FASA and ASA.

American Society Of Farm Managers And Rural Appraisers Professional association whose members are experts in the appraisal or management of farms and rural property.

American Society Of Home Inspectors (ASHI) Professional organization of home inspectors in the United States and Canada. Formed in 1976 as a not-for-profit organization to build public awareness of home inspection and to enhance the technical and professional performance of home inspectors.

American Society Of Real Estate Counselors (ASREC) A professional organization of real estate investment counselors and consultants. Affiliated with the National Association Of Realtors®. Awards the designation of Counselor of Real Estate *(CRE)*. Publishes the journal *Real Estate Issues*.

Americans with Disabilities Act (ADA) A federal law, effective in 1992, designed to eliminate discrimination against individuals with disabilities.

AMI See Alternative Mortgage Instrument.

AML See Adjustable Mortgage Loan.

Amortization Of Deferred Charges A procedure that does for intangible assets what Depreciation Accounting does for tangible assets. Under Generally Accepted Accounting Principles (GAAP), the cost of an intangible asset is to be written off, usually over the life of the asset. This typically applies to costs incurred to arrange loans and leases; these costs are written off over the term of the loan or lease.

Amortization Schedule See Amortization Tables

Amortization Tables Amortization tables are mathematical charts that are used by lenders and borrowers to calculate the monthly payment on a loan or mortgage. The tables are generally created by an amortization calculator that considers the total amount of a loan, the interest rate that is charged and the loan's lifespan.

Amortization Term The time it takes to retire, that is to pay off, a debt through periodic payments. Also known as the full amortization term.

Amortization The amortization is the schedule of mortgage payments spread out over time. In real estate, a buyer's amortization schedule is usually one monthly payment scheduled over a 15, 20 or 30 year period of time. Also means, the liquidation of a financial burden by installment payments, which include principal and interest.

Amortized Loan A loan in which the principal and interest are payable in monthly or other periodic installments over the term of the loan.

Amortized Mortgage T he payments during the life of the loan remain the same. Each month the payment is applied to the interest earned and the remainder reduces the principal amount. See Amortized Loan.

Amount Of One Per Period See Compound Amount Of One Per Period.

Amount Of One See Compound Amount Of One.

Anchor Bolts Bolt used to attach objects or structures to concrete

Anchor Stores A major store that is found in a shopping mall creating drawing power to the location. See Anchor.

Anchor The tenant that serves as the predominant draw to a commercial property, usually the largest tenant in a shopping center. See Anchor Stores

Ancillary Tenant A shopping center tenant that occupies less space and is of lesser importance in generating shopping center traffic than an anchor tenant. Typically pays higher rental rates relative to anchor tenants.

Annexation The process by which an incorporated city expands its boundaries to include a particular area. The rules of annexation are established by state law and typically require a public ballot within the city and the area to be annexed. Other incorporated areas are generally protected from annexation by an adjacent city.

Annual Cap A limit on the amount of adjustment in the interest rate on an Adjustable Rate Mortgage over a twelve-month period. See Cap.

Annual Mortgage Constant The amount of Annual Debt Service divided by the principal; expressed as a dollar amount.

Annual Mortgagor Statement An annual mortgager statement is a summary that borrowers receive once a year from their lender. This statement provides details as to how much of the borrower's monthly payments went to insurance and property taxes and any other deductions from the payment. It gives details about how much of the principal balance has been paid and how much is outstanding.

Annual Percentage Rate (APR) The annual percentage rate *(APR)* is the amount of interest charged on your loan every year.

Annual Debt Service Annual Debt Service is the required annual principal and interest payments for a loan.

Annuity An annuity is a payment of a fixed sum of money to an individual at set intervals that are decided at the start of the annuity. Primarily used as an income stream.

Annuity Due See Ordinary Annuity.

Annuity Factor A mathematical figure that when multiplied by a periodic amount, shows the present value or future value of an income stream. Annuity factors are based on the number of years involved and the applicable percentage rate.

Annuity In Arrears See Ordinary Annuity.

Anticipation A substantial amount of the value in real estate is in the anticipation of occupancy, possible income, and/or the sale of the property afterwards. It represents long-term monetary considerations.

Anticipatory Breach Anticipatory breach is a contract law term that refers to a situation when a party lets the other party know that it will not be honoring the obligations of a contract.

Antitrust Laws The laws were originally designed to preserve the free enterprise of the open marketplace by making illegal certain private conspiracies and combinations formed to minimize competition. Violation of antitrust laws in the real estate business typically involves either price fixing which is brokers conspiring to set fixed compensation rates, or allocation of customers or markets; which can be regarded as Steering, where brokers agree to limit their trade or dealing to certain areas, people, or properties.

APA American Planning Association.

Apartment (Building) A dwelling unit within a multifamily structure, almost always provided as rental housing. An apartment building is a structure with individual apartment units, but a common entrance, hallway, and typically other common areas and amenities. See Multifamily Housing.

Appeals Board An Appeals Board is a body empowered with the ability to overturn decisions of the local government permitting agency and/or code enforcement agency based on an appeal by an aggrieved petitioner.

Application An application is the information that you will submit to a bank, mortgage company, or other lender, that offers specific details about your income, family, and any bills that you owe.

Application Fee The application fee is the non-refundable charge that a lender or a landlord may or may not choose to assess in order to process a mortgage application.

Application For Payment A written document requesting payment.

Apportion To set funds apart for a special purpose and/or distribute according to a plan.

Apportionment Adjustment of the income, expenses and/or carrying charges of real estate usually computed to the date of closing in such a way that the seller pays all expenses to that date. The buyer assumes all expenses moving forward from the date the deed is conveyed to that buyer.

Appraisal An appraisal is an estimate considered to be professional, expert, and unbiased as to how much a home is worth. When buying a home, the lender requires at least one appraisal by a third party to be sure the loan amount requested is less than or equal to the value of the home. If the home's appraised value is below what the buyer has offered, the lender may request the buyer pay the difference in cost or may deny the loan.

Appraisal Approach the use of one of 3 methods to estimate the value of a given property. See Cost Approach, Income Approach, and Market Comparison Approach.

Appraisal By Cost Approach The concept of adding together all parts of a property separately appraised in order to form a whole. Typically the value of the land considered as vacant added to the cost of reproduction of the building minus any depreciation.

Appraisal By Income Capitalization Approach An estimate of value using capitalization of productivity and income.

Appraisal By Sale Comparison Approach Comparability with the sale prices of other similar properties sold within a reasonable period, usually no more than 6 month.

Appraisal By Summation See Cost Approach.

Appraisal Date In an Appraisal Report, this is the date to which the value applies.

Appraisal Fee The appraisal fee is the amount of money that a professional appraiser will charge in order to produce the appraisal and determine the Fair Market Value of a property.

Appraisal Foundation An organization that came into existence in the late 1980s in an effort to encourage uniform requirements for appraisal qualifications and reporting standards. This foundation has two principal boards, the Appraiser Qualifications Board, which establishes and publishes qualifications for state licensing and certification of appraisers, and the Appraisal Standards Board, which produces and promotes the Uniform Standards Of Professional Appraisal Practice *(USPAP)*.

Appraisal Institute An organization of professional appraisers that was formed in 1991 by the merger of the American Institute Of Real Estate Appraisers and the Society Of Real Estate Appraisers. It offers MAI and SRA designations. The MAI is qualified to appraise any property, while the SRA is primarily qualified for residences. Both designations require high standards of education and experience for membership. See MAI, SRA.

Appraisal Institute Of Canada. The Canadian National Society Of Professional Real Estate Appraisers,; the Canadian version of the American Appraisal Instituted, founded in 1938; dedicated to serving the public interest through continually advancing high standards for the appraisal profession by granting use of the CRA *(Canadian Residential Appraiser)* and AACI *(Accredited Appraiser Canadian Institute)* designations. See CRA, AACI.

Appraisal Report An appraisal report gives a detailed description of the property. The information on the appraisal report is used to estimate the market value of a home.

Appraised Value The estimate of a property's present worth.

Appraiser One qualified and licensed to estimate the value of real property. See Certified General Appraiser, Certified Residential Appraiser, Licensed Appraiser, and various organizations and designations.

Appreciation The increase in the worth or value of a property, due to economic or related causes. Appreciation may be either temporary or permanent, typically fluctuating in a range of value.

Appreciation Return The portion of the total return generated by the change in the value of the real estate assets during the current quarter, as measured by both appraisals and sales of assets.

Approach See Appraisal Approach.

Appropriation Money set aside, typically by some formal, written action for a specific purpose.

Approved Assessing Unit An assessing unit specific to New York State, which has been certified by the New York State Board as having completed a revaluation program implementing a system of real property tax administration, which is eligible for state assistance.

Appurtenance Something which is outside the property itself however belongs to the land and adds to its greater enjoyment such as a right-of-way or a barn or a dwelling.

Appurtenant Belonging to; incident to; annexed to.

APR See Annual Percentage Rate

Apron A panel or board installed beneath the Windowsill.

Arbitrage The simultaneous purchase and sale of a security with the purpose of obtaining a higher yield from the differential between its acquisition and selling price. The Securities version of Flipping.

Arbitration A means of settling a controversy between two parties through the medium of an impartial third party not via litigation, whose decision on the controversy will be final and binding.

Architect A person who designs buildings and, in many cases, also supervises their construction.

Architectural Drawing A technical drawing of a building *(or building project)*.

Architecture The manner in which a building is constructed, including the layout, floor plan, style and appearance, materials used, and the building technology used.

Architrave The molded frame around a doorway or window, or the main beam resting across the tops of a set of columns.

Area A two-dimensional space defined by boundaries; such as floor area, area of a lot, and market area.

Area Wells A barrier wall that is made of metal or concrete around a basement or cellar window. A Window Well.

AREUEA See American Real Estate And Urban Economics Association.

ARGUS A computer program widely used by institutional investors that allows an analyst to simulate expected property performance, including that of multitenant office buildings and shopping centers.

ARM Adjustable-Rate Mortgage.

Arms-Length Transaction A sale between two unrelated parties, each acting in their own best interest.

Arrears Generally means to be behind on a payment:
1. At the end of a term.
2. Sometimes used to signify default; overdue in payment.

Artesian Well A deep-drilled shaft that upon reaching water see a rise in that water level due to natural underground pressure.

Artificial Intelligence The ability of any computer program to evaluate information.

ARV See After Repair Value.

AS IS See As Is Condition

ASA
1. American Society Of Appraisers.
2. A senior professional designation offered by the American Society of Appraisers.

Asbestos Abatement A method by which asbestos is removed from a building.

Asbestos Insulation material which was frequently used in older buildings as pipe wrap, boiler insulation, floor tile, and ceiling coating. As it ages, asbestos may become friable. As this happens, it may crumble and release particles which, as a dust, become airborne. Breathing asbestos particles has been linked to several serious lung illnesses. Removal and encapsulation of asbestos in buildings is known to be expensive but necessary to prevent illness. The discovery of asbestos in a building is likely to cause a significant value loss, due to cost of mitigation.

As-Is Condition The acceptance by the tenant or buyer of the existing condition of the premises at the time a lease is consummated, including any physical defects.

Asked The amount a property owner sets as a selling price for his property.

Asking Price The initial selling price of a property, determined by the seller.

ASREC See American Society Of Real Estate Counselors.

Assemblage Combining of two or more parcels of land. See Plottage Value.

Assessed Valuation See Assessed Value

Assessed Value An assessment is used by a state, county, or municipality, to determine how much in taxes the owner of a property will pay. The assessor calculates the assessment of a home's value by looking at comparable homes in the area and reviewing an inspection of the home in question.

Assessing Unit A municipality such as a city, town, county, or village with the authority to assess real property

Assessment A charge against real estate made by a unit of government, *(state, county, or municipality)*, to cover a proportionate cost of an improvement such as a street or sewer.

Assessment Ratio The ratio of assessed value to Market Value.

Assessment Review Board An independent board whose primary function is to hear tax appeals from taxpayers who believe that their properties are incorrectly assessed. Also known as Grievance Boards.

Assessment Roll A list of all taxable property in a municipality, which shows the assessed value of each parcel, and is used to establish the tax base. An assessment roll is also known as a *"Tax Roll"*.

Assessor An official who has the responsibility of determining assessed values.

Asset Management Fee The fee charged to investors based on the amount invested into real estate assets for the fund or account.

Asset Management Asset management refers to the systematic approach of the governance and realization of value from the things that a group or entity is responsible for, over their whole life cycles. The term is commonly used in the financial sector to describe both individuals and companies who manage investments on behalf of others.

Asset Turnover Calculated as total revenues for the trailing 12 months divided by the average total assets.

Assets An asset is defined as any possession that carries value.

Assets Under Management The current market value of real estate assets for which a manager has investment and asset management responsibilities.

Assign To transfer one's property rights or contract rights to another. Contracts commonly assigned Include Leases, Mortgages, And Deeds of Trust.

Assignee Name The individual or entity to which the obligations of a lease, mortgage or other contract have been transferred.

Assignee The person to whom an agreement or contract is assigned.

Assignment An assignment is when the seller of a property signs over rights and obligations to that property to the buyer before the official closing.

Assignment Liens These are liens that were not bid on at a tax sale and still have option for purchase. They can then be purchased usually at the county Clerk's office through the mail or in person. Using the principle of caveat emptor, typically, the liens left over from a sale were not purchased because there was something negative about the property or they were not worth the investment.

Assignment of Agreements An assignment of rights under specifically identified agreements such as construction contracts, architect's agreements, or a contract to purchase real estate.

Assignment of Leases An assignment of rights under specifically identified leases.

Assignment Of Rents A contract that assigns rents from and income generated by the tenant of a property to the mortgage lender in a case of a default on the mortgage.

Assignment The method by which a right or contract is transferred from one person to another. Contracts commonly assigned include Leases, Mortgages, and Deeds of Trust.

Assignor A party who assigns or transfers an agreement or contract to another

Associate Broker An associate broker is qualified to be a real estate broker but still works for and is supervised by another broker. Associate brokers are sometimes called broker-associates, broker-salespersons, or affiliate brokers.
1. In some states, a licensed broker whose license is held by another broker.
2. In Alabama, a real estate licensee whose status is that of a salesperson in other states.

Associated Builders And Contractors (ABC) A national construction trade association representing more than 21,000 members.

Assumable Loan A loan in which the lender is willing to *"transfer"* from the previous owner of the home to the new owner, sometimes at the same interest rate, sometimes at a new rate. An assumable loan can make your home more attractive to buyers when you want to sell.

Assumable Mortgage Assumption is when a seller transfers all terms and conditions of a mortgage to a buyer. The buyer takes on the seller's remaining debt instead of taking out a new mortgage of their own.

Assumed Name Statute The law, in effect in most states, that requires that no person shall conduct a business under any name other than his or her own individual name, unless such person files the desired name with the county clerk in each county where the business is conducted. In the case of brokers and salespeople, statement of such filing should be submitted to the state's real estate commission.

Assumption Gives a buyer the permission to take over and take responsibility for an existing mortgage instead of getting a new one. See Assumable Loan.

Assumption Clause Some lenders will offer an assumption clause as part of a mortgage note. In effect, an assumption clause gives the homeowner an opportunity to sell their home with the mortgage already taken care of.

Assumption Fee The assumption fee is the charge paid by a buyer who assumes a mortgage on a property. This fee most commonly occurs when someone buys a property that has not been completely paid off to the bank at the time of sale.

Assumption of Mortgage The transfer of title to property to a grantee, by which the grantee assumes liability for payment of an existing note secured by a mortgage against the property. Should the mortgage be foreclosed, and the property sold for a lesser amount than that due, the grantee/purchaser who has assumed and agreed to pay the debt secured by the mortgage is personally liable for the deficiency. Before a seller may be relieved of liability under the existing mortgage, the lender must accept the transfer of liability for payment of the note. See Assumable Mortgage, Assumable Loan.

Astragal A moulding or wooden strip of semicircular cross section.

At-Risk Rules Tax laws that limit the amount of tax losses an investor, particularly a Limited Partner, can claim. At-risk rules were extended to real estate by the 1986 tax act and apply to property placed in service after 1986. losses on real estate investments put in service after this time will be deductible only to the extent of money the equity investor stands to lose.

Attachment Legal seizure of property to force payment of a debt. A Lien.

Attest To witness by observation and signature.

Attic Access A space found directly below the pitched roof of a house or other building.

Attic Ventilators A ventilation system which regulates the heat level of a building's attic by exhausting hot air.

Attorn To agree to recognize a new owner of a property and to pay that individual or entity rent.

Attorney-in-fact The holder of a power of attorney.

Attorney's Opinion Of Title A written statement by an attorney, after examination of Public Records and/or Abstracts Of Title, that in his or her judgment the title to a particular property is good.

Attornment The agreement by a tenant to recognize a replacement or successor landlord in the event of a foreclosure or other enforcement of rights under an assignment of leases or agreement of similar effect.

Attractive Nuisance An appealing but potentially hazardous feature or characteristic of a piece of real estate that may lure trespassers who could suffer harm; in law, the owner of an attractive nuisance must take extraordinary precautions to avoid liability for harm to trespassers.

Auction A way of marketing property to the highest bidder. bids are taken verbally, simultaneously through mail or telegrams, or via some online means, and the property is sold to the highest bidder. Auctioning real estate may require both an auctioneer's license and a real estate license depending on the state.

Auctioneer One who conducts an auction.

Audit An inspection of the books, records, and procedures used by a business or individual, conducted by a CPA or other person qualified to do so.

Automated Mortgage Underwriting Loan processing that is entirely or predominantly handled via unattended computer connection See Automated Underwriting.

Automated Underwriting is a technology-driven underwriting process that provides a computer generated loan decision. The lending industry is broadly migrating to the use of new technology-driven loan underwriting platforms to improve the processing time for all types of loans.

Average Common Equity Calculated by adding the common equity for the five most recent quarters and dividing by five.

Average Downtime Expressed in months, the amount of time expected between the expiration of a lease and the commencement of a replacement lease under current market conditions.

Average Free Rent Expressed in months, the rent abatement concession expected to be granted to a tenant as part of a lease incentive under current market conditions.

Average Occupancy The average occupancy rate of each of the preceding 12 months.

Average Rate Of Return The measure of an investment's profitability. Total net earnings are divided by the number of years the investment was held, then by the investment's initial acquisition cost, to derive the annual income rate. A drawback is that it does not consider the timing of earnings.

Average Total Assets Calculated by adding the total assets of a company for the five most recent quarters and dividing by five.

Aviation Easement An aviation easement is a stipulation that restricts owners of properties situated near an airport from having structures or trees that exceed a certain height. Aviation easements exist to maintain the safety of both residents near an airport as well as the safety of the aircrafts that fly into the airport.

Avulsion A sudden tearing away of land by the action of natural forces.

B

Back Taxes Unpaid and therefore late property taxes.

Back Title Letter A back title letter is a document given by a title insurance company to an attorney representing a buyer or seller that describes the history of the title. See Title Search.

Backfill The replacement of excavated earth into a hole or against a structure.

Backflow The unintentional flow of water into the supply pipes of a plumbing system.

Backflow Preventer A backflow prevention device is used to protect potable water supplies from contamination or pollution due to backflow. The simplest, most reliable way to provide backflow prevention is by use of an air gap. Also referred to as a Reduced Pressure Zone device, or RPZ.

Backing Frame This a lumber set-up in-between the wall studs to provide extra support for handrail brackets, cabinets, and towel bars. This method allows items to be screwed and installed into solid wood instead of a dry wall that is weak, which may let items fixed into this wall to fall from the wall.

Backout Work carried out by a framing contractor used to prepare for a Rough Frame Inspection.

Backup Block Concrete block used as a non-exposed structural wall and backs a finished surface used in providing a wall system.

Backup Contract A contract to buy real estate that becomes effective if a prior contract fails to be consummated.

Backup Offer A backup offer is a seller's secondary option in case the first offer does not go through.

Bad Title A condition where complete real estate ownership is impaired by unsettled claims and liens and may prevent an owner from selling. See Cloud On Title.

Bailment Describes a legal relationship in common law where physical possession of personal property, or a chattel, is transferred from one person *(the 'bailor')* to another person *(the 'bailee')* who subsequently has possession of the property.

Balance Sheet A balance sheet is a financial document that details the assets, liabilities, and net worth of an individual. Balance sheets are commonly used in sole proprietorships, business partnerships and corporations.

Balance The amount left over after subtracting, as, for example, the amount owed on a loan *(also called principal balance)* or the amount in an account.

Balance, Principle Of In Real Estate Appraisal, In an appraisal, there is an assumed optimal mix of inputs that, when combined with land, will result in the greatest land value. Inputs, or factors of production, include labor, capital, and entrepreneurship.

Ballast A type of transformer used to regulate the current to fluorescent lamps and provides sufficient voltage to start the lamps.

Balloon Frame Wall This is a lay out and construction methods for framing a gable wall.

Balloon Framing A wooden framework extending the full height of the building from foundation plate to rafter plate, as oppose to platform framing, in which each floor is framed separately.

Balloon Loan A type of loan with a maturity that is shorter than the amortization period. See Balloon Mortgage.

Balloon Mortgage Instead of a traditional fixed-rate mortgage in which the owner pays on the loan in installments, a balloon mortgage is paid in one lump sum *(See Balloon Payment)*. It's typically associated with investment or construction projects that are issued for the short term and don't require collateral.

Balloon Mortgage Payment See Balloon Payment.

Balloon Payment The final payment of a balloon mortgage loan that is considerably larger than the required periodic payments, because the loan amount was not fully amortized.

Balloon Risk The risk that a borrower may not be able to make a balloon payment at maturity due to a lack of funding.

Balloon See Balloon Mortgage, Balloon Payment.

Balusters Any of a number of closely spaced supports for a railing. various symmetrical supports, as furniture legs or spindles. They are typically lathe-turned.

Band Of Investment The phrase *"Band of Investments"* refers to a method used by commercial appraisers and/or investors to calculate the overall capitalization rate. This rate is then used to convert the net income produced by a given property into an indication of value.

Bankrupt The state of an entity that is unable to repay its debts as they become due.

Bankruptcy Judicial proceedings under federal statutes to relieve a debtor who is unable or unwilling to pay its debts. After addressing certain priorities and exemptions, the bankrupt entity's property and other assets are distributed by the court to creditors as full satisfaction for the debt, or renegotiated. See Chapter 7, Chapter 11, Chapter 13.

Bankruptcy-Remote An entity created to be a borrower in a commercial loan which is less likely to put itself into or be entangled in a federal bankruptcy or state insolvency proceeding.

Bargain and Sale Deed A deed that carries with it no warranties against liens or other encumbrances but that does imply the grantor has the right to convey title. The grantor may add warranties to the deed at his or her discretion. Many tax deeds are deeded in this fashion.

Barge Beam rafter usually horizontal that gives support to shorter rafters.

Bargeboard A decorative board covering the fly rafter of the gable end.

Barring The Right Of Redemption A phrase used in Tax Sales, If the owner has failed to pay off the lien and the redemption period has expired, the lien holder may then foreclose on the property.

Base And Meridian Imaginary lines used by surveyors to find and describe the location of land. The baseline is east-west; the meridian line is north-south.

Base Fee A determinable fee estate that may be inherited.

Base Line Part of a rectangular survey. One of a set of imaginary lines running east and west and crossing a principal meridian at a specific point. Base lines are used by surveyors for reference in locating and describing land under the rectangular survey system. See Property Description, and Base and Meridian

Base Period A point of time that serves as a benchmark for reflecting the change in an index. The *base period* is usually set equal to 1, 100%, or 100.

Base Principal Balance The original mortgage amount adjusted for subsequent fundings and principal payments, without regard to accrued interest or other unpaid debt.

Base Rent A set amount used as a minimum rent with provisions for increasing the rent over the term of the lease.

Base Year See Base Period.

Baseboard A board forming the foot of an interior wall, and typically decorative.

Basement Window The window frame and glass unit that is in the window buck.

Base Shoe A Type of molding use to cover gaps between the flooring and baseboard. Typically ¼ round moulding or similar.

Basic Industry Multiplier In economic base analysis, basic industry multiplier refers to the ratio of total population in a local area to employment in basic industry. Basic industry is considered to be any concern which attracts income from outside the local area. The jobs added in basic industry may also contribute to the need for local service jobs; and, if the workers have families, additional new people may be brought to the area.

Basic Rent The minimum rent a tenant must pay under a HUD-subsidized housing program.

Basis Typically used by accountants, the original cost of a property, including not only the purchase price, but also commissions and other fees typically associated with a transaction. This is the number used to figure other versions of the basis such as the adjusted basis.

Basis The point from which gains, losses, and depreciation deductions are computed. Generally the cost or purchase price of an asset.

Basis Point 1/100 of 1 percent.

Bat A brick divided into two equal part.

Batt A slab-shaped piece of insulating material used in building houses.

Batten A small board or strip of wood used for various building purposes, as to cover joints between boards, reinforce certain doors, or supply a foundation for lathing.

Batter Board One of a number of boards set horizontally to support strings for outlining the foundation plan of a building.

Bay Window An alcove of a room, projecting from an outside wall and having its own window . Beam: A horizontal structural member usually to support the roof or floor above.

Bearer Instrument A security that does not indicate the owner; payable to whoever presents it.

Bearing Header in framing construction:

1.   A beam placed perpendicular to joists and to which joists are nailed in framing for a chimney, stairway, or other opening.
2.   A wood lintel.
3.   The horizontal structural member over an opening.

Bearing Partition A wall built to give support to heavy loads.

Bearing Point This is a situation where the structural weight is concentrated and transferred to the foundation at a certain point.

Bearing Wall A wall that gives support to more loads.

Bedrock Unbroken solid rock, overlaid in most places by soil or rock fragments.

Bedroom Community A residential community in the suburbs, often near an employment center, but itself providing few employment opportunities.

Before Tax Cash Flow (BTCF) The cash flow before an adjustment for income tax is made. This includes debt service which is the amount paid to retire the mortgage.

Before-And-After Rule In an Eminent Domain award, many jurisdictions appraise the property value before the taking, then the property value after the taking, considering enhancement or injury to the property that was the result of condemnation. See Federal Rule.

Before-Tax Cash Flow Cash flow prior to deducting income tax payments or adding income tax benefits. See Cash Throw-Off.

Before-Tax Equity Reversion See After-Tax Proceeds From Resale, except it does not consider income taxes.

Below-Grade Any structure or portion of a structure located underground or below the surface grade of the surrounding land.

Below-Market Interest Rate (BMIR) In some government-subsidized housing, the owner is charged a low interest rate with the requirement that savings be passed on to tenants in the form of reduced rent.

Benchmark A permanent reference mark or point established for use by surveyors when measuring differences in elevation.

Beneficiary The person for whom a trust operates or in whose behalf the income from a trust estate is drawn. A lender who lends money of real estate and takes back a note and deed of trust from the borrower.

Bequeath To give or hand down by will; to leave by will. See, Bequest.

Bequest That which is given by the terms of a will. See Bequeath.

Berm A raised earthen shoulder constructed as a barrier to water runoff or to screen from view an unsightly area.

Beta Also referred to as *"The Beta Coefficient,"* Beta is a statistical term used by money managers operating in the tradable equities securities market. Essentially, Beta is a measure of the volatility, or systematic risk, of a particular security or a portfolio in comparison to the market as a whole.

Betterment The improvement made to real estate.

Biannual Occurring twice a year. See Semiannual. Contrast with Biennial.

Bid An offer, stated as a price or spread, to purchase a product or service.

Bid Bond A bid bond guarantees compensation to the bond owner if the bidder fails to begin a project. Bid bonds are often used for construction jobs or other projects with similar bid-based selection processes.

Bid Down the Interest In a tax lien auction the state will start the bidding at a set interest rate. The bidders then may *"bid down"* from the original interest rate to something lower, typically in ¼% increments. This will proceed until no one is willing to go lower and there is a winning bid.

Bid Down The Ownership In a tax lien auction, an investor can buy the lien for only a percentage of the property. This is usually a less desirable method since this makes it harder for an investor to enforce the lien or foreclose on it, due to not having full recourse. Very few investors want less than 100% ownership, and most counties avoid this method.

Bid Security Funds Bond submitted with a bid as a guarantee to the recipient of the bid that the contractor, if awarded the contract, will execute the contract in accordance with the bidding requirements of the contract documents.

Bid Shopping This is the practice of divulging a contractor's or subcontractor's bid to other prospective contractor in order to convince that c0ntractor to lower their bid as well.

Bid
1. A formal offer by a contractor, to carry on a specific project at a particular price with the terms and conditions stated in the offer.
2. A formal offer by an investor or other potential owner, to purchase real property at a particular price with the terms and conditions stated in the offer.

Bidder's Package The Bidder's Package explains to the bidder the outline of the tax sale that is particular to that jurisdiction. The information provided, will explain how the auction will be run and how to make payments on winning bids.

Bidding Requirements The terms and condition for the submission of a bid document.

Biennial Occurring every 2 years.

Bifold Door Doors with openings so that it can be folded into two parts usually used for closet doors.

Bilateral Contract A contract in which each party promises to perform an act in exchange for the other party's promise to perform.

Bi-Level .A house built on 2 levels in which the main entrance is situated above the lower level but below the upper level. Popular in the mid to late seventies. See Tri-Level.

Bill Of Assurance The name given, in some states, to the total collection of Restrictive Covenants that apply to a group of contiguous lots.

Bill of Sale -A written instrument given to pass title of personal property from vendor to vendee.

Binder An agreement to cover the down payment for the purchase of real estate as evidence of good faith on the part of the purchaser. Similar to Earnest Money.

Binder Deposit The part of the total amount of a property paid to a seller by a buyer to have the option to purchase the property. See Binder, Earnest Money.

Bi-pass Doors Typically closet doors which slide one behind the other and are often used for closets. Also spelled Bypass Doors.

Biweekly Loan A mortgage which requires principal and interest payments at two week intervals. The payment is exactly half of what a monthly payment would be. Over a year's time, the 26 payments are equivalent to 13 monthly payments on a comparable mortgage loan, however, as a result of the payment structure, the loan will amortize much faster than loans with monthly payments.

Bi-Weekly Mortgage See Bi-Weekly Loan.

Black Book The final acceptance of the offering plan by the attorney general allowing shares in a co-op to be sold. See Prospectus.

Black's Guide A data source for office buildings in certain major cities. Offers rental information on multitenant office buildings in the cities and suburban areas it covers.

Blanket Covering two or more similar properties.

Black Mold Also called Toxic Mold. There is no single type of mold called "black mold" Many molds are black in color. When people use the term, they may be referring to a type called *Stachybotrys chartarum* or *S. chartarum*, also known as *Stachybotrys Atra*. There is no scientific evidence to suggest that exposure to *S. chartarum* is more dangerous than exposure to any other type of mold, however, some people have an allergy to molds in general.

Blanket Mortgage A mortgage that covers more than one parcel of real estate and provides for each parcel's partial release from the mortgage lien on repayment of a definite portion of the debt.

Blanket Fiberglass Insulator used for the special handling and the lengths and widths needed for metal building which comes in long rolls 15 or 23 inches wide.

Bleeding A Project In construction:
1. In new construction, overstating expenses and fees so as to divert a larger than normal amount of the project costs to the developer's profit.
2. Managing an existing piece of real estate so as to obtain the highest possible current income from it, to the extent that many normal

operating expenses are forgone. Usually this results in rapid deterioration and loss of property value.

Blended Rate An interest rate, when applied to a refinanced loan, that is higher than the rate on the old loan but lower than the rate offered on new loans. A blended rate is generally offered by the lender to induce home buyers to refinance existing, low-interest rate loans as an alternative to assuming the existing loan.

Blighted Area A section of a city in which a majority of the structures are dilapidated. Typically used in urban areas as opposed to suburban or rural areas. A slum.

Blind Pool A commingled fund accepting investor capital without prior specification of property assets.

Block Out To put a barrier within the wall of a foundation so that concrete would not enter into the arena.

Blockbusting The practice of inducing homeowners in a particular neighborhood to sell their homes quickly, often at below market prices, by creating the fear that the entry of a minority group or groups into the neighborhood will cause a precipitous decline in property values. Illegal by Federal Law.

Blocked Door Wood shims used between the door frames used to keep doors in a semi open position allowing controlled access & egress to the shaft.

Blocked Rafters Used at the bearing points of rafters and ceiling joists to keep rafter from twisting.

Blocking A number of small pieces of wood for spacing, joining, or reinforcing members.

Blown Insulation Is used to insulate existing walls and ceilings where framing members are not exposed.

Blueprint Is a reproduction of a technical drawing, documenting architecture or an engineering design.

Blue Stake Another phrase for Utility Notification. It is used to notify underground facility owners and operators.

Blue-Sky Laws State laws requiring the offeror of securities to give full disclosure, and register the offering as required by federal and state law.

Board Approval A condition in cooperative sales contract which state that a buyer must be accepted by the board of directors as one of the requirement to completing the sale.

Board Foot A specialized unit of measure for the volume of lumber. It is the volume of a one-foot length of a board one foot wide and one inch thick.

Board Of Directors People elected by stockholders to govern the corporation.

Board Of Equalization A government entity whose purpose is to assure uniform property tax assessments.

Board Of Realtors® A local group of real estate licensees who are members of the state and National Association Of Realtors®.

Board Of Zoning Appeals See Appeals Board.

Board Package A collection of financial, character, and disclosure documentation that a potential purchaser compiles and submits to a co-op board for review.

Boilerplate Standard language found in contracts. Preprinted material.

BOMA See Building Owners And Managers Association.

BOMA Measurements Standards offered by the Building Owners And Managers Association for measuring the leasable square footage of an office building.

Bona Fide In good faith, without fraud.

Bond The evidence of a personal debt, which is secured by a mortgage or other lien on real estate.

Bond Market Is a financial market where participants ca buying and sell treasury bonds.

Bonding Is debt instrument that a government or a company issues to raise money in order to secure a contractor's license.

Book Depreciation See Depreciation *(Accounting)*.

Book Value Also referred to as common shareholder's equity, this is the total shareholder's equity as of the most recent quarterly balance sheet minus preferred stock and redeemable preferred stock.

Boom
1. In construction, a device use to lifting or lowering a load.
2. In finance, an economic time of easily flowing capital, low unemployment, and large profits.

Boot The term used for any property, object, or money a person receives in addition to the like/kind property in a 1031 exchange. While a straight like/kind *(property-for-property)* exchange is usually tax-deferred, if you get more boot than you give in the transaction, that extra cash, property, or object will be taxable.

BOQ A bill of quantities. This is a document used in tendering in the construction industry in which materials, parts, and labor and their costs are itemized.

Bottom Chord The lowest longitudinal member of a truss. It is usually horizontal but may be at an incline depending on truss design.

Bottomland See Wetlands.
1. Low land near a river, lake, stream, which is often flooded. See Flood Plain.
2. Land in a valley or dale.

Bottomplate The horizontal beam on which the studs of a partition are installed. Also called the 'sole plate'.

Boundary See Property Line.

Box Crib A wooden tool used to hold heavy objects during construction.

BOY Beginning Of Year.

Boycotting Two or more businesses conspiring against other businesses, usually to reduce competition.

Brace An inclined piece of framing lumber use as a support to wall or floor to make the structure strong.

Branch Office A secondary place of business apart from the principal or main office from which real estate business is conducted. A branch office generally must be run by a licensed real estate broker, broker salesperson, or associate broker working on behalf of the broker operating the principal office.

Breach of Contract The failure, without legal excuse, of one of the parties to a contract to perform according to the contract. See Default.

Breaker Box See Breaker Panel.

Breaker Panel A distribution board use as a component of an electricity supply system which divides an electrical power feed into subsidiary circuits, while providing a protective fuse or circuit breaker for each circuit in a common enclosure. Also known as Breaker Box.

Breakeven Point The point at which there is sufficient potential income to cover expenses. The point at which an investor has neither lost nor gained money.

Brick Ledge A section of a foundation wall for bricks to rest.

Brick Lintel A structural member placed over an opening in a wall metal brick rests on.

Brick Mold A strip of material used to close the gap between a brick wall and a door or window in the wall.

Brick Row House Also called Brownstone, or Eastern Townhouse. A nineteenth century-style house, usually having 4 or 5 stories with a stoop leading up to the first floor. There are common side walls with a house on either side.

Brick Tie A small, corrugated metal strip long nailed to wall sheeting or studs.

Brick Veneer A vertical facing of brick laid against and fastened to sheathing of a framed wall or tile wall construction.

Brickmold See Brick Mold.

Brick And Mortar The physical property; often contrasted with intangibles, sometimes contrasted with cyberspace.

Bridal Registry Mortgage An innovation, sponsored by the Federal Housing Administration, in which a couple who plan to be married may establish a registry through which friends and relatives may contribute to a fund that can be used as a down payment on a home. The portion of the Down Payment coming from the fund is considered a substitute for cash contributed by the borrowers, when application is made for a mortgage insured by the FHA.

Bridge Loan A bridge loan is a short-term loan a homeowner takes out against their property to finance the purchase of another property. It's usually taken out for a period of a few weeks to up to three years. See Gap Loan, Swing Loan.

Bridging A brace or an arrangement of braces fixed between floor or roof joists to keep them in place.

British Thermal Unit The British thermal unit *(Btu or BTU)* is a non-SI, traditional unit of heat which is defined as the amount of heat required to raise the temperature of one pound of water by one degree Fahrenheit.

Broker One who buys and sells for another for a commission. A broker has passed a broker's license exam and received education beyond what the state requires of real estate agents. They understand real-estate law, construction, and property management. Real estate agents are required to work under the supervision of a broker.

Broker/Salesperson A person who has passed the broker's licensing examination but is licensed to work only on behalf of a licensed broker and who may be allowed to manage an office. In many states, known as and licensed as an associate broker or broker/associate.

Brokerage The business of buying and selling for another for a commission.

Broom Clean A description of the condition of property that is to be turned over to the buyer or tenant; the floors are to be cleared of trash and swept, but any sort of deep cleaning has not been performed.

Brownfields Deserted, defunct, and derelict toxic industrial sites in need of renewal. Federal legislation has diminished the innocent landowner's liability exposure and provided the landowner the opportunity to expense cleanup costs rather than capitalize them. See Superfund.

Brownstone Also called Brick Row House, or Eastern Townhouse.
1. A nineteenth century-style house, usually having 4 or 5 stories with a stoop leading up to the first floor. There are common side walls with a house on either side.
2. Sandstone which was once a popular building material.

BTCF See Before Tax Cash Flow.

BTU See British Thermal Unit.

Buck Rough frame opening members.

Budget An itemized list of expected income and expenses prepared weekly, monthly, or annually. See Pro-Forma.

Budget Loan A loan in which the monthly payments made by the borrower cover not only interest and a payment on the principal, but also $\frac{1}{12}$ of such expenses as taxes, insurance assessments, private mortgage insurance premiums, and similar charges.

Budget Mortgage A Mortgage that requires monthly payments for taxes and insurance in addition to interest and principal.

Buffer Zone A strip of land that separates one land use from another.

Build To Suit An arrangement whereby a landowner offers to pay to construct on his or her land a building specified by a potential tenant, and then to lease land and building to the tenant.

Buildable Acres The area of land that is available to be built on after subtracting for roads, setbacks, anticipated open spaces and areas unsuitable for construction.

Builder Warranty A guarantee on the quality of construction offered by the developer or building contractor. See Homeowners' Warranty Program.

Builder's Risk Insurance A special type of property insurance usually for general contractors and builder, which indemnifies against damage to buildings while they are under construction.

Builders And Sponsors Profit And Risk Allowance (BSPRA) The amount above the cost of apartments that is allowed to be included in the project cost for purposes of determining the loan amount in certain government-sponsored programs.

Building And Loan Associations See Savings And Loan Associations.

Building Capitalization Rate In appraisal, the Capitalization Rate is used to convert an Income Stream into one lump sum value. The rate for the building may differ from that for the land because the building is a wasting asset.

Building Code Regulations which protect the public by imposing structural, material, design, and other requirements on residential, commercial, and industrial buildings

Building Efficiency Ratio See Efficiency Ratio.

Building Inspection The physical review of property as it proceeds under construction to ensure that each major component meets building codes: foundation, plumbing, electrical wiring, roofing, materials. Typically performed by an inspector employed by the local municipality. Also, periodic inspection of existing public buildings for health and safety considerations.

Building Insurance A special type of property Insurance covering the property from risks such as fire, landslip, etc.

Building Line A line fixed at a certain distance from the front and/or sides of a lot beyond which no structure can project; a setback line used to ensure a degree of uniformity in the appearance of buildings and unobstructed light, air, and view. Also called a setback.

Building Loan Agreement An agreement whereby the lender advances money to an owner primarily in the erection of buildings. Such funds are commonly advanced in installments as the structure is completed.

Building Owners And Managers Association (BOMA) See BOMA.

Building Paper This is a long roll material sheet used in buildings, it is thick kraft paper often impregnated with a waterproofing agent such as asphalt.

Building Permit Written governmental permission for the construction, renovation, or substantial repair of a building.

Building Residual Technique An Appraisal technique whereby income to land is subtracted from Net Operating Income to result in the building income.

Building Restrictions The limitations on the size or type or style of property improvements established by zoning acts or by deed or lease restrictions. Building restrictions are considered encumbrances and violations may render the title unmarketable.

Building Standard Plus Allowance The landlord lists, in detail, the building standard materials and costs necessary to make the premises suitable for occupancy. A negotiated allowance is then provided for the tenant to customize or upgrade materials.

Build-Out Space improvements put in place per the tenant's specifications. Takes into consideration the amount of tenant finish allowance provided for in the lease agreement.

Build-To-Suit A method of leasing property whereby the developer or landlord builds to a tenant's specifications.

Built-Ins Appliances, machinery, and other equipment that are constructed as part of a building rather than left freestanding and moveable.

Built-up Roof A roofing composed of three to five layers of asphalt felt laminated with coal tar, pitch, or asphalt. The top is finished with crushed slag or gravel.

Bulk Sale The sale of a group of real estate assets, typically dissimilar properties in different locations. This sales technique was used by the RTC in the early 1990s to dispose of multiple assets at one time, forcing a buyer to accept the bad ones with the good.

Bull Nose Rounded corners in lumber or drywall.

Bullet Loan See Balloon Loan

Bundle Of Legal Rights The theory that land ownership involves ownership of all legal rights to the land, such as possession, control within the law, and enjoyment, rather than ownership of the land itself. See Bundle of Rights Theory.

Bundle Of Rights Theory The theory that ownership of realty implies a group of rights such as occupancy, use and enjoyment, and the right to sell, bequeath, give, or lease all or part of these rights.

Bundle A package of shingles. Usually there are 3 bundles per square and 27 shingles per bundle.

Bungalow A small, early-twentieth-century-style, 1-story house that usually has an open or enclosed front porch.

Bureau Of Land Management (BLM) An agency of the United States. Department of the Interior that oversees the management of much of the land owned by the U.S. government, particularly national forests, and other relatively undeveloped land.

Burned-Out Tax Shelter A real estate investment that was originally intended to provide large income tax deductions but no longer does. A Tax Shelter generally becomes less effective over time because deductions for accelerated depreciation are smaller in the later years of an asset's life and nonexistent when assets are fully depreciated, and interest deductions are smaller in the later years of mortgage life when most of the payment applies to principal.

Business Day The part of a day during which most businesses are operating, generally accepted to be from 9 am to 5 pm Monday through Friday. Often, this term is defined in the relevant document as a day other than a Saturday, Sunday, or national holiday.

Business Plan A three to five year blueprint for an organization or individual real estate practitioner.

Business Value

1.   The intangible value in a business, above the value of its tangible assets, which include buildings, land, and fixtures.

2.   The entire value of a business; the summation of all of its parts, both tangible and intangible.

Butt Edge The lower edge of the shingle tabs.

Butt Hinge A hinge in which one leaf attaches to the door's edge, the other to its jamb.

Butt Joint The junction where the ends of two timbers meet, and also where sheets of drywall meet on the 4 foot edge.

Buy Down See Buydown.

Buy-Back Agreement A provision in a contract under which the seller agrees to repurchase the property at a stated price upon the occurrence of a specified event within a certain period of time.

Buydown A payment made, usually by the seller, to help the buyer qualify for the loan. A buydown is a mortgage-financing technique lowering the buyer's interest rate for anywhere from a few years to the lifetime of the loan. Many times this is used to help close a deal in that the property seller or contractor makes payments to the mortgage lender lowering the buyer's monthly interest rates, which, in turn, lowers their monthly payments.

Buyer's Broker An agent hired by a prospective purchaser to find an acceptable property for purchase. The broker then represents the buyer and negotiates with the seller in the purchaser's best interest.

Buyer's Market When there are more sellers than buyers. A situation where buyers have a wide choice of properties and may negotiate lower prices. Often caused by over-building, local population decreases, or economic slump.

Buyout Arrangement by the owner of a building to acquire the remaining lease term of a tenant in a different building. This frees the tenant from the old lease obligations and permits them to negotiate a lease in the new building.

Buy-Sell Agreement A pact among partners or stockholders under which some agree to buy the interests of others upon some event.

By Laws The rules for a co-op's or condominium's governing structure, including the functions and power of the board, election guidelines, amendment guidelines, etc.

Bi-Fold Doors Doors that are hinged in the middle for opening in a smaller area than standard swing doors. Often used for closet doors.

Bylaws See By Laws.

Bypass Doors Doors that slide by each other and commonly used as closet doors. See Bi-pass Doors.

C

CACI Consolidated Analysis Center Incorporated. CACI is a service provider of demographic information. Given a location, it can identify the population and income level around the subject property.

CAD See Cash Available For Distribution, Central Appraisal District, Computer-Aided Design.

Cadastre See Cadastral Map.

Cadastral See Cadastral Map.

Cadastral Map A legal map for recording ownership of property. The map describes boundaries and ownership.

Cadastral Survey In the United States, a Cadastral Survey within the Bureau of Land Management (BLM) maintains records of all public lands.

CAI Community Associations Institute.

Caisson Part of a foundation. A hole drilled into the earth and embedded into bedrock 3-4 feet.

California Bungalow A 1-story, small, compact, early-twentieth-century house. See bungalow.

California Ranch A post-World War II style, 1-story, ground-hugging house with a low, pitched roof.

Call Date Periodic or continuous rights given to the lender to cause payment of the total principal balance prior to the maturity date.

Call Provisions Clauses in a loan that give the lender the right to accelerate the debt upon the occurrence of a specific event or date. See Acceleration Clause.

CAM See Common Area Maintenance.

Cancellation Clause A provision in a lease or other contract which confers upon one or more of all of the parties to the lease the right to terminate the party's or parties' obligations thereunder upon an occurrence of the specific condition or contingency set forth in the clause.

Cant An angled line or surface which cuts off a corner.

Cantilever An overhang where one floor extends beyond and over a foundation wall.

Cantilevered Void Material used in unusually expansive soils conditions.

Cap Flashing A water repelling L shaped weatherproofing material installed to stop water from entering behind the base flashing.

Cap
1. In Finance: An adjustable rate mortgage which has a limit placed on adjustments to protect the borrower from large increases in the interest rate or the payment level. See Annual Cap, Life-of-Loan Cap, Payment Cap.
2. In Construction: The upper member of a column, pilaster, door cornice, molding, or fireplace.

Cap Rate See Capitalization Rate.

Capacity Of Parties One of the requirements for a valid contract. Parties with less than full capacity include minors, the mentally insane, and those who are intoxicated may not sign or be legally held to the conditions or a contract.

Cape Cod See Cape Cod Colonial

Cape Cod Colonial An early-American-style 1 1/2-story compact house that is small and symmetrical with a central entrance. The roof is the steep gable type covered with shingles. The authentic types have low central chimneys, but end chimneys are very common in the new versions. Bedrooms are on the first floor. The attic may be finished into additional bedrooms and a bath. A vine-covered picket fence is traditional. Also called Cape Cod.

Capital
1. A sum of money used to purchase long-term assets.
2. Stocks, bonds, or mortgages that were sold to raise money to purchase assets, as well as retained earnings.
3. Assets, other than land, used to generate income.
4. In architecture the capital *(from the Latin caput, or "head")* forms the topmost member of a column or a pilaster.

Capital And Interest This is a type of loan where the borrower pays back a certain sum of money on a monthly basis until the final payment is made plus the interest charge on it.

Capital Appreciation The appreciation accruing to the benefit of the capital improvement to real estate.

Capital Asset Any asset of a permanent nature used for the production of income.

Capital Calls Additional money to be invested by equity owners to fund any deficits in construction costs or operating costs.

Capital Expenditure One time major purchase that extends the economic life of the asset.

Capital Expense Expenses required for the standard upkeep of a building as well as for any changes or improvements to any of the building's systems. Examples of these are expenses for heating and air-conditioning, water systems, parking lots, interior or exterior paint and carpets.

Capital Gain Income that results from the sale of an asset not in the usual course of business.

Capital Improvement Any structure erected as a permanent improvement to real estate, usually extending the useful life and value of a property. The replacement of a roof would be considered a capital improvement, but the painting of a bathroom would not.

Capital Loss A loss from the sale of an asset not in the usual course of business.

Capital Market The portion of the market for investment funds where equities, mortgages, and bonds are traded.

Capital Recovery See Recapture Rate.

Capital Reserve Budget A type of account contained in a company's balance sheet that is reserved for long-term capital improvement projects or any other large and anticipated expenses that will be made in the future. This type of fund is set aside, *(reserved),* to make sure that the company or municipality has enough funding to finance the project at least partially.

Capital Reserves Funds set aside for capital expenditures.

Capitalization

1. In finance, a process whereby anticipated future income is converted to one lump sum capital value. A Capitalization Rate is divided into the expected periodic income to derive a capital value for the expected income. Sum of Interest Rate and Recapture Rate.
2. In accounting, setting up an Asset on the financial records, rather than deducting it currently.

Capitalization Rate Net operating income divided by the sales price. The way an investor would ascertain whether the investment is acceptable to him.

Capitalize To estimate the present lump sum value of an Income Stream.

Capitalized Value The value estimated by converting an Income Stream into a lump sum amount.

Capital Structure The composition of capital invested in a property, reflecting the interests of those who contributed both debt and Equity Capital.

Capped Rate A capped rate is an interest rate that is allowed to fluctuate, but which cannot surpass a specifically stated interest cap. A capped rate loan issues a starting interest rate that is usually a specified spread above a benchmark rate, such as LIBOR.

Capture Rate The sales or leasing rate of a real estate development Contrasted to the sales or leasing rate of all developments in the market area.

Carbon Monoxide A colorless, odorless gas, dangerous and potential lethal to humans and animals which is a natural byproduct of Hydrocarbon fuel combustion.

Carpenter Gothic A nineteenth-century-style house with exposed framing members, high steep roofs, complex silhouettes, diagonal braces, and a large amount of ginger-bread trim.

Carry-Cost Rule It is an instrument use by banks to assess borrowers for mortgages.

Carrying Charges Expenses necessary for holding property, such as taxes and interest on idle property or property under construction.

Carrying Cost See Carrying Charges.

Carryover Basis In a tax-deferred exchange, carryover basis is the Adjusted Tax Basis of the property surrendered which is used to determine the tax basis of the property acquired.

Casement Frames The enclosing part of a window sash.

Casement These are windows that are hinged on the side and open outward to the left or right.

Cash Available For Distribution (CAD) Derived from the amount earned by a Real Estate Investment Trust. It is Funds From Operations *(FFO)*, less the cost of recurring capital expenditures such as replacing building roofs, resurfacing parking lots, and major repairs to HVAC equipment.

Cash Equivalent Cash equivalents, also known as "cash and equivalents," are one of the three main asset classes in financial investing, along with stocks and bonds. These securities are characterized by a low-risk, low-return profile and include U.S. government treasury bills, bank certificates of deposit, and money markets.

Cash Flow Analysis See Discounted Cash Flow.

Cash Flow Mortgage Debt instrument under which all or nearly all the cash flow generated by the rental income is paid to the lender. There is no stated interest rate.

Cash Flow The actual cash an investor will receive after paying operating expenses and debt service *(mortgage payment)* from the gross income.

Cash Flow/Before/After Tax The net income the property generates which is calculated both before and after tax considerations.

Cash Method A method of accounting based on cash receipts and disbursements.

Cash On Cash Return Can be determined by using the annual before tax cash flow and the amount of cash used to purchase the property. Annual cash flow divided by total cash required for purchase.

Cash Reserve Is a specified minimum fraction of the total deposits of customers, which commercial banks have to hold as reserves with the central bank.

Cash Throw-Off See Cash Flow.

Cash-On-Cash See Equity Dividend Rate.

Cash-On-Cash Yield The relationship, always expressed as a percentage, between the net cash flow of a property and the average amount of invested capital during an operating year.

Cash-Out Refinance A cash-out refinance, also known as a cash-out refi, is when a homeowner refinances their mortgage for more than it's worth and withdraws the difference in cash. To be eligible for this kind financing, a borrower usually needs at least 20% in equity, and have an above average credit score.

Casing Wood Are generally used to trim around doors and windows, as well as for decoration.

Casualty Insurance A type of insurance policy that protects a property owner or other person from loss or injury sustained as a result of theft, vandalism, or similar occurrences.

Catslide An early-American-style, 2- or 2 1/2-story house that is square or rectangular with a steep gable roof that extends down to the first floor in the rear.

Caulking The processes and material also called sealant use to seal joints or seams in various structures and some types of piping.

Caveat Emptor A Latin phrase meaning, *"let the buyer beware".* The buyer must examine the goods or property and buy at the buyer's own risk.

Caveat Subscriptor *"Let the seller beware."* Doctrine governing the sale of something for which the seller could be liable if it is found to be defective.

Caveat Venditor See Caveat Subscriptor.

Caveat A warning. A Caveat is often written to a potential buyer, to be careful; often offered as a way for the seller or broker to minimize liability for what otherwise might be a deceptive trade practice. See Caveat Emptor, Due Diligence.

CBD Central Business District.

CCA Chromated Copper Arsenate. A chemical wood preservative used to protect wood from termites.

CCIM Certified Commercial Investment Member, a professional designation of the Realtors® National Market Institute *(RNMI)*.

CCRs See Covenants, Conditions, & Restrictions.

CD Certificate Of Deposit.

Cease And Desist List Once the Secretary of State establishes a Cease And Desist Zone, this is a list of homeowners who have filed owner's statements expressing their wish not to be solicited by real estate brokers or salespersons. Soliciting of listed homeowners by licensees is then prohibited. Violators of such prohibition can be subject to licensure suspension or revocation. See Cease and Desist Zone.

Cease And Desist Zone A rule adopted by the Secretary of State which prohibits the direct solicitation of homeowners whose names and addresses appear on a Cease And Desist List maintained by the Secretary. Such rule may be adopted upon the Secretary's determination that some homeowners within a defined geographic area have been subject to intense and repeated solicitation by real estate brokers and salespersons. See Cease and Desist List.

Ceiling Joist A Ceiling Joist ties the walls of a structure together and supports the ceiling of a room.

Celotex™ A producer of a roofing and insulation materials.

Cement Cement is a binder, a substance that sets and hardens and can bind other materials together. Cement is not concrete. Concrete is a mixture of cement aggregates, and water.

Census Tract Geographical area mapped by the U.S. government for which

Central Appraisal District (CAD) A government organization that appraises the value of property for tax assessment purposes. Its costs and results of its appraisal and collection efforts are shared by other government entities to avoid inconsistencies and duplication of effort. See Assessor.

Central Business District (CBD) The downtown section of a city, generally consisting of retail, office, hotel, entertainment, and governmental land uses with some High Density Housing.

Ceramic Tile Material used as a finishing of a floor or wall of a house.

CERCLA See Comprehensive Environmental Response Compensation And Liability Act.

Certificate of Completion The official document issued by the building department, which is proof that a remodeling or renovation project was done in compliance with the law.

Certificate Of Deposit (CD) A type of savings account that carries a specified minimum deposit and term and generally provides a higher yield than passbook-type savings accounts.

Certificate Of Eligibility During the VA loan process, lenders will require a veteran to show proof they've met the minimum service requirement to qualify for a VA loan.

Certificate Of Estoppel See Estoppel Certificate.

Certificate Of Insurance A document issued by an insurance company that verifies the coverage.

Certificate Of No Defense See Estoppel Certificate.

Certificate Of Occupancy (CO) A document presented by a local government agency typically the building department within a city or county level municipality, certifying that a building and/or the leased area has been satisfactorily inspected and is in a condition suitable for occupancy.

Certificate Of Reasonable Value A Certificate Of Reasonable Value *(CRV)* is issued by the Department of Veterans Affairs and is required for veterans to receive a VA loan. It establishes the maximum value of the property and therefore the maximum size of the loan.

Certificate Of Sale The document generally given to a purchaser at a tax foreclosure sale. A certificate of sale does not generally convey title. It is an instrument certifying that the holder may receive title to the property after some redemption period has passed and that the holder paid the property taxes for that interim period.

Certificate Of Title The statement of opinion on the status of the title to a parcel of real property, based on an examination of specified public records. Typically produced by a title attorney or title company after a title search.

Certified Commercial Investment Member (CCIM) A designation awarded by the Commercial Investment Real Estate Institute, which is affiliated with the National Association Of Realtors®.

Certified General Appraiser One qualified and licensed to appraise any property, under the Appraiser Certification Law recently adopted by most states. Usually requires at least two years of general appraisal experience, 165 hours of education, and the passing of a state examination.

Certified Historic Structure See Historic Structure.

Certified Property Manager (CPM) A professional designation awarded to real estate managers by the Institute Of Real Estate Management, an affiliate of the National Association Of Realtors®.

Certified Residential Appraiser One qualified and licensed to appraise residences and up to 4 units of housing, under appraiser certification law. Standards call for less education, less experience, and less comprehensive exam than for General Certification.

Certified Residential Broker (CRB) A Designation Awarded By The Residential Sales Council, which is affiliated with the National Association Of Realtors®.

Certified Residential Specialist (CRS) A professional designation awarded by the Residential Sales Council, based on education and experience in residential sales. Candidates must hold the GRI designation.

Certiorari A legal term referring to the judicial review of a property's assessment.

Cession Deed Is the assignment of property to another entity.

CFM Cubic Feet Per Minute a measurement of the volume at which air flows into or out of a space.

Chain A linear unit of land measurement used in land surveying: 66 feet in length. Each *chain* consists of 100 links.

Chain Of Title Like the *"car fax"* of homes, the chain of title is the documentation of all past ownership of a property. It runs from the present owner to the very first owner of the property. The succession of conveyances from some accepted starting point by which the present holder of real property derives his or her title.

Chair Rail Chair Rail is a type of moulding fixed horizontally to the wall around the perimeter of a room. A Dado Rail.

Chalk Line In construction, a line produced with chalk and string for alignment purpose.

Change Order Instructions to revise construction plans after the work has been started. Change orders can be costly.

Chapter 11 That portion of the federal bankruptcy code that deals with personal and business reorganizations.

Chapter 13 That portion of the federal bankruptcy code that deals with personal liquidations.

Chapter 7 That portion of the federal bankruptcy code that deals with business liquidations.

Charrettes Community planning tool that welcomes and improves public participation in discussions about a community's future growth and development.

Chase
1. A channel made in a wall for something to pass through.
2. A geographical term (usually British) designating an area of privately owned land for hunting

Chattel Mortgage A pledge of personal property as security for a debt.

Chattels Personal property.

Check Tracts of land located repetitively every 24 miles from a principal meridian and 24 miles from a defined base line. Guide meridians and correction lines define a checks' boundaries, consisting of 16 townships.

Chink A way used to fix fiberglass insulation all around exterior frames, corners in the exterior wall.

Chip Board Wood panel normally used to substitute plywood in the roofing sheathing and exterior wall. Also called OSB or Strand Board.

Circuit Breaker An automatic switch that stops the flow of electric current in a suddenly overloaded or otherwise abnormally stressed electric circuit.

Circuit A path in which electrons from a voltage or current source flow. Electric current flows in a closed path called an electric circuit. The point where those electrons enter an electrical circuit is called the *"source"* of electrons.

Circulation Factor The interior space required for internal office circulation not accounted for in the net square.

City Planning Commission A local government organization designed to direct and control the development of land within a municipality. Typically, building inspectors work within a City Planning office which is directed by a City Planning Commission

Cladding A protective or insulating layer fixed to the outside of a building or another structure.

Claim Of Right Used as a factor in determining adverse possession claims. Adversely occupying another's real estate for a statutory period of time may create a claim of right.

Clapboard Long, narrow boards with one edge thicker than the other, overlapped horizontally to cover the walls of frame houses; a type of SIDING.

CLARITAS A company providing a household segmentation tool that concisely describes and categorizes people by their age, income level, and social preferences. It is a sister company of National Decision Systems.

Class "A" A real estate rating generally assigned to properties that will generate the highest rents per square foot due to their high quality and/or superior location.

Class "B" Good assets that most tenants would find desirable but lack attributes that would permit owners to charge top dollar.

Class "C" Buildings that offer few amenities but are otherwise in physically acceptable condition and provide cost-effective space to tenants who are not particularly image-conscious.

Class (Of Property) A subjective division of buildings by desirability among tenants and investors. Criteria include age, location, construction quality, attractiveness of style, level of maintenance, and so on. See Class "A", Class "B", & Class "C".

Clear Title Also known as a *"just title," "good title,"* or a *"free and clear title";* a clear title doesn't have any kind of lien or levy from creditors. It means there's no question of legal ownership of the property such as building code violations or bad surveys.

Clear-Span Facility A building, most often a warehouse or parking garage, with vertical columns on the outside edges of the structure and a clear span between columns.

Client The one by whom a broker is employed.

Clip Ties A cut metal wires that is sharp that extend out of a concrete foundation wall.

Closed Period The term during which a mortgage cannot be Pre-Paid. Often found in mortgages on commercial property, but seldom in residential mortgages. The mortgage is usually assumable by subsequent buyers of the property.

Closed-End Fund A commingled fund that has a targeted range of investor capital and a finite life.

Closed-End Mortgage A mortgage loan whose principal amount cannot be increased during the payout period. Contrast with Open-End Mortgage.

Closing Costs Closing costs are usually comprised of between 2-5% of the total purchase price of the home. According to a recent survey by Zillow, the average homebuyer pays approximately $3,700 in closing costs. These fees are paid on or by the closing date.

Closing Date The date upon which the property is conveyed by the seller to the buyer.

Closing Statement An accounting of funds from a real estate sale, made to both the seller and the buyer separately. Most states require the broker to furnish accurate closing statements to all parties to the transaction.

Closing The closing is the final stage of the real estate transaction. The date is agreed upon when both the buyer and seller go under contract on the home. On the closing date, the property is legally and officially transferred from seller to buyer.

Closure Document A letter written by a state environmental agency indicating the successful remediation of a site.

Cloud On The Title An outstanding claim or incumbrance which, if valid, would affect or impair the owner's title.

Clouded Title See Cloud on the Title

CLUE (C.L.U.E.) An insurance company repository owned by LexisNexis for reported claim activity and previous property damage. CLUE is an acronym for Comprehensive Loss Underwriting Exchange. Insurers use the report to ascertain patterns of possible future claims and adjust their insurance premiums according to risk.

Cluster Housing A subdivision design technique in which detached dwelling units are grouped relatively close together, leaving open spaces as common areas.

Cluster Zoning A type of zoning which permits residential uses to be clustered more closely together than normally allowed. This leaves substantial land area to be devoted to open space or recreational use. See Cluster Housing.

CMBS A Mortgage-Backed Security that is collateralized by a pool of commercial properties.

CMO See Collateralized Mortgage Obligation.

CMO REIT A type of Real Estate Investment Trust *(REIT)* that principally invests in Collateralized Mortgage Obligations *(CMOS)*.

CO See Certificate of Occupancy.

Co-Borrower A Co-Signer. If a buyer is having trouble getting approved for a loan, they can elicit the help of a co-borrower. This person is usually a family member or friend who's added to the mortgage and guarantees the loan. They're listed on the title, have ownership interest, sign loan documents, and are obligated to pay monthly mortgage payments if the buyer is unable to pay.

Code Of Ethics A statement of principles concerning the behavior of those who subscribe to the code. Realtors, Architects, and Engineers are all subject to an industry specific Code of Ethics.

Code See Building Code, Code Of Ethics, Housing Code.

Codicil A testamentary disposition subsequent to a will that alters, explains, adds to, or confirms the will, but does not revoke it.

COFI See Cost of Funds Index.

Cognovit Note A promissory note which contains a provision by which the borrower agrees to let the lender, without notice to the borrower or guarantor, file an answer on behalf of the borrower confessing judgment in favor of the lender, which then allows a court to issue a judgment immediately rather than through the normal, lengthier process of litigation.

Coinsurance See Coinsurance clause.

Coinsurance Clause The clause in insurance policies covering real property which requires the policyholder to maintain fire insurance coverage that is generally equal to at least 80% of the property's actual replacement cost.

Co-investment Co-investment occurs when two or more pension funds or groups of funds share ownership of a real estate investment. In co-investment vehicles, relative ownership is always based on the amount of capital contributed. It also refers to an arrangement in which an investment manager or adviser co-invests its own capital alongside the investor.

Co-investment Program An investment partnership or insurance company separate account that enables two or more pension funds to co-invest their capital in a single property or portfolio of properties. The primary appeal for investors is to achieve greater diversification or invest in larger properties typically outside the reach of small- to mid-sized tax-exempt funds, with a greater measure of control than is afforded in typical commingled fund offerings.

COLA Cost Of Living Adjustment. See Index, Consumer Price Index.

Cold Air Return A vent that pulls cold air into a furnace so it can be heated and pushed back to a room by the air handler within a heating and air system.

Cold Canvass The process of contacting homeowners in an area in order to solicit listings.

Collapsible Corporation The term which applies to some corporations that are dissolved within 3 years. The IRS treats gain on the sale or liquidation of the corporation as ordinary income to the stockholder.

Collar Beam A collar beam is a horizontal member between two rafters and is very common in domestic roof construction.

Collar the flange that is preformed to be placed on top of a vent pipe so as to seal the roofing that is above the vent pipe opening.

Collateral Anything of value given or pledged to a lender as a security for a debt or other obligation.

Collateralized Mortgage Obligation (CMO) A type of security backed by a pool of mortgages bundled together and sold as an investment.

Color of Title Used as factor in an adverse possession claim when the occupying party actually received title but by a defective or incorrect deed.

Column A pillar in architecture and structural engineering is a structural element that supports loads.

Combination The act of converting two different structures into one large unit.

Combustion Air The duct work installed to bring fresh, outside air to the furnace and/or hot water heater. Normally 2 separate supplies of air are brought in: One high and One low.

Combustion Chamber The area in a furnace, boiler, or woodstove where fire happens; this area is lined with firebrick or molded or sprayed insulation.

Commercial Bank A financial institution authorized to provide a variety of financial services, including consumer and business loans (generally short-term), checking services, credit cards and savings accounts. The Federal Deposit Insurance Corporation insure most commercial banks. Commercial banks may be members of the Federal Reserve System.

Commercial Broker One who is licensed to list and sell Commercial Property, which may include shopping, office, industrial, and apartment projects.

Commercial Investment Real Estate Institute An affiliate of the National Association of Realtors® whose members are mainly concerned with commercial and investment properties. Offers educational courses leading to the CCIM Designation.

Commercial Mortgage Financing Different from residential in that not only the credit and Debt to income ratios of the borrower are examined, but also the assets of the business can be taken into consideration

Commercial Mortgage Loan See Commercial Mortgage Financing.

Commercial Property A classification of real estate that includes income-producing property, such as office buildings, restaurants, shopping centers, hotels, and stores.

Commercial Real Estate See Commercial Property.

Commercial Zones An area that is used for commercial purposes such as hotels, retail stores, restaurants, and different other service businesses.

Commercial Mortgage Banker One in the business of making Commercial Mortgage Loans.

Commingle To mingle or mix, such as the deposit of another's money in a broker's personal account.

Commingled Fund A pooled fund vehicle that enables qualified employee benefit plans to commingle their capital for the purpose of achieving professional management, greater diversification and/or investment positions in larger properties.

Commingled Property The property of a married couple that is so mixed or commingled that it is difficult to determine whether it is separate of community property. Commingled property becomes community property.

Commingling The illegal act of a real estate broker who mixes the money of other people with that of his or her own; brokers are required by law to maintain a separate trust account for other parties' funds held temporarily by the broker. See Fiduciary.

Commission A sum due a real estate broker for services in that capacity.

Commission Split The arrangement of sharing commissions earned between a sales agent and sponsoring broker, and/or between the selling broker and listing broker.

Commissioner
1. The head administrator of a state Real Estate Commission.
2. A person appointed to a role on or by a commission.
3. A person elected to regulate a particular part of government.

Commitment A pledge or a promise or affirmation agreement.

Commitment Fee A charge required by a lender to lock in specific terms on a loan at the time of application.

Commitment Letter An official notification to a borrower from a lender indicating that the borrower's loan application has been approved and stating the terms of the prospective loan.

Commodity Pool A commodity pool is an enterprise in which funds contributed by a number of persons are combined for the purpose of trading futures contracts, options on futures, or retail off-exchange or to invest in another commodity pool.

Commodity Pool Operator (CPO) A CPO is an individual or organization which operates a commodity pool and solicits funds for that commodity pool.

Common Area For lease purposes, the areas of a building and its site that are available for the non-exclusive use of all its tenants. Hallways, pools, and parks within an apartment complexes are all common areas.

Common Area Assessments A Fee, usually assed monthly, towards a Homeowners Association (HOA). Part of that fee likely goes toward a common area assessment to maintain an area open to the community.

Common Area Maintenance Rent charged to the tenant in addition to the base rent to maintain the common areas. .

Common Elements In a condominium, those portions of the property not owned individually by unit owners but in which all unit owners hold an indivisible interest. Generally includes the grounds, parking areas, recreational facilities, and external structure of the building. See community association, CCRs, Common Area.

Common Law A body of law based on custom, usage, and court decisions.

Community Association General name for any organization of property owners to oversee some common interest. In a condominium or planned unit development, the association has the responsibility of managing the common elements in the project. A homeowners' association may be established in a subdivision to enforce deed covenants.

Community Property A system of property ownership based on the theory that each spouse has an equal interest in the property acquired by the efforts of either spouse during marriage. Community property refers to property acquired by a married couple and owned equally by both spouses.

Community Shopping Center See Shopping Center.

Community Associations Institute (CAI) A non-profit educational and research organization concerned with the problems of managing homeowners' associations and other community associations (such as condominium owners associations). CAI sponsors educational seminars and publishes various handbooks and brochures.

Community Reinvestment Act A federal law that requires federal regulators of lending institutions to encourage lending within the local area of the institution, particularly to low- and moderate-income residents and those residing in inner-city neighborhoods. See Redlining.

Co-Mortgagor One who signs a mortgage contract with another party or parties and is thereby jointly obligated to repay the loan. Generally a co-mortgagor provides some assistance in meeting the requirements of the loan and receives a share of ownership in the encumbered property. See Co-signer.

Comparable (Comps) The sold properties, listed in an appraisal report, which are substantially equivalent to the subject property. See Comparable Sales.

Comparable Sales Comparable sales are used by an appraiser to establish how much a home is worth based on what other similar homes in the area have sold for recently. Only homes that have legally closed count as a comp and most lenders and insurance providers require appraisers to use at least three closed sales. See Comparable (Comps).

Comparative Market Analysis (CMA) An estimate of the value of property using only a few indicators taken from sales of comparable properties, such as price per square foot. These value estimates are not appraisals and do not meet the standards of appraisal as defined by USPAP, however, they can give a general idea as to the value of a property based on past sales and presenting listed property.

Comparative Sales Approach See Market Comparison Approach.

Comparative Unit Method An appraisal technique to establish relevant units as a guide to appraising the subject property.

Comparison Method See Market Comparison Approach.

Competent Parties Persons who are recognized by law as being able to contract with others. Two requirement of competent parties are those of legal age and sound mind.

Complete Appraisal A professional opinion of value without invoking the Departure Provision of USPAP. All relevant appraisal approaches are included.

Completion Bond A bond used to guarantee that a proposed subdivision development will be completed.

Composite Depreciation A method of determining the depreciation of a multi-building property using the average rate at which all the buildings are depreciating.

Compound Amount Of One Per Period The amount that a series of deposits of $1.00 per period would grow to if left on deposit with interest allowed to compound.

Compound Interest The interest paid on the original principal and also on the unpaid interest that has accumulated.

Comprehensive Environmental Response, Compensation, and Liability Act (CERCLA) A piece of federal legislation passed in 1980 requiring owners of contaminated properties to bear the cleanup costs.

Compressed Buy-Down A Buy-Down loan for which the extent of rate reduction is changed at 6-month intervals. Many buy-downs feature a deep discount in the first year that is reduced gradually each year. The compressed buy-down is a variation of this type with accelerated gradations.

Compression Web Part of a truss system linking the bottom and top chords and providing downward support.

Compressor A mechanical device used to increase the pressure of a gas so as to turn the gas into a liquid.

Comps See Comparable and Comparable sales.

Computerized Loan Origination (CLO) A computer-based network of lenders that allows affiliated real estate brokers, builders, or advisors to originate loans at the site of the home. Provides a streamlined process whereby a person can buy a home and apply for a loan at the same place and time.

Concessions Cash or cash equivalents expended by the landlord in the form of rental abatement, additional tenant finish allowance, moving expenses or other monies expended to influence or persuade a tenant to sign a lease.

Concrete Block A brick made of concrete.

Concrete Board Panel created from concrete and fiberglass that is utilized as a tile backing material.

Concrete Cover The space that is in-between the top of embedded reinforcement and the outside of the concrete that is measured using a cover meter.

Concrete Slab Concrete structure normally used for roofs, floors, and bridge decks.

Concrete Slump A test carried out to analyze the effectiveness of a fresh concrete.

Concrete The combination of cement, sand, gravel, and water. Normally used for the construction of sidewalk, garage, basement floors, patios, foundation, etc. steel rods are also part of the mixture.

Condemnation
1. The process of taking private property, without the consent of the owner, by a governmental agency for public use through the power of eminent domain.
2. A judicial or administrative proceeding or process to exercise the power of eminent domain.

Condensation Water droplet that is found on the exterior covering of a building mostly during the cold period. Louvers or attic ventilators reduces the amount of moisture condensation in attics.

Condensing unit A part of cooling system kept outside the building. It is a combination of compressor and condensing coil to give off heat.

Condition Provision in a contract that some or all terms of the contract will be altered or cease to exist upon a certain event.

Conditional Commitment The agreement by a lender to provide a loan to a qualified borrower, within a specified time period, but without stating who the borrower will be.

Conditional Offer A purchase contract tendered to the seller that stipulates one or more requirements to be satisfied before the purchaser is obligated to buy.

Conditional Sales Contract The contract for the sale of property stating that delivery is to be made to the buyer, title to remain vested in the seller until the conditions of the contract have been fulfilled.

Conditional Use Permit (CUP) The Variance granted to a property owner that allows a use otherwise prevented by zoning.

Condominium Conversion See Conversion.

Condominium Declaration See Declaration.

Condominium Hotel A condominium used for hotel/motel purpose.

Condominium Owner's Association An organization of all unit owners in a condominium to oversee the common elements and enforce the bylaws.

Condominium A form of real estate ownership of a multifamily residential dwelling. Each occupant has 100% ownership of his own apartment and partial ownership of common elements such as hallways, elevators, plumbing, etc.

Condop A situation in which one part of a building is a condominium, while the other is run by the co-op corporation. Typically, this happens in a property that has both commercial space *(condo)* and a residential space *(co-op)*.

Conduction Transfer of heat or electricity through a substance, resulting from a difference in temperature between different parts of the substance.

Conductivity A measure of material ability to transfer heat.

Conduit
1. An alliance between mortgage originators and an unaffiliated organization that acts as a funding source by regularly purchasing loans, usually with a goal of pooling and securitizing them.
2. A metal pipe through which wire is installed.

Conduit Tax Treatment The income passing through an entity without taxation. Certain entities are preferred as real estate ownership vehicles because they pass income and losses through to underlying owners without paying a tax or changing the nature of their earnings. See Limited Liability Company.

Conflict Of Interest The situation in which a person is faced with a possible decision in an official or fiduciary capacity from which he or she stands to benefit personally because of another relationship. To avoid this, the decision maker may step down from one role or the other.

Conforming Loan See Conforming Mortgage

Conforming Mortgage These are securitized mortgages sold on the secondary market that meet specific requirements established by Fannie Mae and Freddie Mac.

Conformity Principle A type of appraisal principle that holds that property tends to reach maximum value when the neighborhood is reasonably homogeneous in social and economic activity.

Conformity The usage of land area within a particular area which leads to maximization of land value.

Congregate Housing Congregate Housing is housing in which residents share common areas, particularly the dining facility.

Consent Decree A judgment whereby the defendant agrees to stop the activity that was asserted to be illegal, without admitting wrongdoing or guilt.

Consideration
1. Something of value that induces one to enter into a contract. Consideration may be *"valuable" (meaning money or commodity)* or *"good" (meaning love and affection)*.
2. Also, an act of forbearance, or the promise thereof, given by one party in exchange for something from the other. Forbearance is a promise not to do something.

Consignment In real estate finance, the process in which the FSLIC replaces the management of an insolvent savings and loan association but allows the association to continue operating.

Consolidated Metropolitan Statistical Area (CMSA) See Primary Metropolitan Statistical Area.

Consolidation Loan New loan that pays off more than one existing loan, generally providing easier repayment terms.

Constant Annual Percent See Mortgage Constant.

Constant Payment Loan A loan on which equal payments are made periodically so as to pay off the debt when the last payment is made. See Level-Payment

Constant See Mortgage Constant.

Construction Contract An agreement between the owner and contractor in which the contractor agrees to construct the owner's building *(or other described project)* in accordance with the contract documents and within a specified time, for a mutually-agreed upon consideration to be paid by the owner.

Construction, Drywall A construction type where the sheet material or wooden panel is applied in a dry condition. Usually refers to the installation of Sheetrock, also known as drywall.

Construction Exchange Also known as an *"improvement exchange"*, this is a situation in which an investor buys a property with the intent to build on it or construct improvements, before taking it as a replacement property.

Construction, Frame A construction pattern where the structural parts are wood or when wooden frame is used in supporting the building.

Construction Industry Manufacturers Association A United States based international trade group serving the business needs of construction equipment manufacturers and construction service providers.

Construction Lenders These are lenders that specialize in construction loans.

Construction Loan A construction loan or *"Self-Build Loan"* is a short-term loan used to finance the construction of a home or real estate project. This type of loan covers project costs before long-term funding can be financed.

Construction Management The act of ensuring the various stages of the construction process are completed in a timely and seamless fashion.

Construction The creation of a structure.

Constructive Eviction A purchaser's inability to obtain clear title. Or, acts by the landlord that so materially disturb or impair the tenant's enjoyment of the leased premises that the tenant is effectively forced to move out and terminate the lease without liability for any further rent.

Constructive Notice The notice given to the world by recorded documents. All persons are charged with knowledge of such documents and their contents, whether or not they have actually examined them. Possession of property also is considered constructive notice that the person in possession has an interest in the property.

Constructive Receipt
1. For tax purposes, the right to receive money that would be taxable and is taxable, even if receipt is postponed.
2. In real estate exchanges, the receipt of cash or other non-like-kind property or the acquisition of the right to use or benefit from such cash or property during an exchange transaction.

Consultant Any company or individual that provides the following services to institutional investors:
1. Definition of real estate investment policy;
2. Adviser and /or manager recommendations
3. Analysis of existing real estate portfolios
4. The monitoring of and reporting on property asset
5. Commingled fund and portfolio performance
6. Review of specified property and portfolio investment opportunities.

Consultants are distinguished from investment advisers or investment managers in that a consultant does not source or execute transactions and does not directly manage assets.

Consulting   The act of providing information, analysis, and recommendations for a proposed real estate decision. See Consultant.

Consumer Credit Counseling Service (CCCS)   The Consumer Credit Counseling Service, (CCCS), is a nationally recognized non-profit agency chartered with the goal of helping consumers out of debt. Consumers who get into debt and may need help getting out of it. For those with such a need, the CCCS provides counseling services to help the consumer stop creating more debt and start paying down their debt.

Consumer Price Index (CPI)   Measures inflation in relation to the change in the price of goods and services purchased by a specified population during a base period of time. The CPI is usually used to increase the base rent periodically as a means of protecting the landlord's rental stream against inflation and/or to provide a cushion for operating expense increases for a landlord unwilling to undertake the record-keeping necessary for operating expense escalations.

Consumer Reporting Agency (CRA)   See Credit Rating Service.

Contaminant   A substance, element, or compound that may harm humans or other forms of life if released into the environment. Refers to concentrations that are above acceptable levels and/or are in a location where they should not be found.

Contemporary Style   A contemporary style home is a type of architecture that features what many would call a *"modern"* look. It focuses primarily on streamlined angles, clean edges, and a diverse collection of shapes. In contemporary style, sharp edges and lines are essential. Another marker of contemporary style is the windows, which tend to be large, often floor to ceiling, and unadorned.

Contiguous   Actually touching; contiguous properties have a common boundary.

Contiguous Space   Multiple suites/spaces within the same building and on the same floor that can be combined and rented to a single tenant, or a block of space located on multiple adjoining floors in a building.

Contingencies   A provision or condition in the purchase of real estate requiring a certain act to be done or an event to happen before the contract becomes binding.

Contingency   If a property is contingent, or the contract contains a contingency, certain events must transpire, or the contract can be considered null. A contingency might be that the home must past an appraisal or receive a clean inspection, or that the buyer must sell their current home in order to be able to purchase the home they are offering to buy.

Contingent Fee   A fee that someone must pay if and when a certain event happens based on the verbiage of a contract

Contingent Interest Payment on a loan that is due only if certain conditions are met.

Contingent vs. Pending When a property is contingent, it means the owner has accepted an offer however, certain contractual expectations must be met, or the offer will be void. When all contingencies are met, the property changes status to pending. While contingent offers are still considered active listings, pending offers are taken off the market and other offers will not be entertained. The sale of a home could also be contingent on the buyer selling their home by a specified date. If either the buyer or seller fail to meet the expectations of the contingency, either party can exit the contract.

Continuity Tester An instrument used to tell if a circuit is able to conduct electricity.

Continuous Occupancy Clause A provision frequently included in a retail store's shopping center lease, requiring the store to remain open. See Continuous Operations Clause.

Continuous Operations Clause A provision in a shopping center lease which requires a store to maintain certain situational aspects such as minimum inventory levels, remaining open certain hours, be adequately staffed, and keeping the store name for a certain period of time.

Contour Map A map that displays the topography of the site. A map with contour lines that indicate various elevations.

Contract An agreement entered into by two or more legally competent by the terms of which one or more of the parties, for a consideration, undertakes to do or to refrain from doing some legal act or acts. A contract may be either unilateral which means only one party is bound to act, or bilateral where all parties to the instrument are legally bound to act as described by the verbiage of the contract.

Contract Documents The complete set of design plans and specifications for the construction of a building.

Contract For Deed A contract for the sale of real estate under which the sale price is paid in periodic installments by the purchaser, who is in possession and holds equitable title, although actual title is retained by the seller until final payment.

Contract For Exchange Of Real Estate A contract for sale of real estate in which the consideration is paid wholly or partly in property.

Contract Of Sale See Agreement Of Sale.

Contract Price (Tax) In an Installment Sale, for tax purposes, generally the selling price minus existing mortgages assumed by the buyer.

Contract Rate See Face Interest Rate.

Contract Rent The rental obligation, expressed in dollars, as specified in a lease. Also known as face rent.

Contract Sale This is a sale where you have ownership of the property and therefore, you have claim over the title until the contract amount is paid. This gives you leverage over whether you would like to accept the offer or not.

Contractor One who contracts to supply specific goods or services, generally in connection with development and/or construction of a property.

Contractual Lien The legal name given to the ownership interest that a particular party has in a property, on the basis of some contract.

Contribution Will improvements offset their cost and increase profitability

Contributory Value An appraising principle where the value of a property's component parts is measured by their effect on the selling price of the whole. Appraisers use sold properties as "paired sales" to isolate component parts and to identify their monetary contribution to the whole.

Control Joint Straight grooves used to determine the place the concrete should cracked

Control Premium An amount paid to gain enough ownership to set policies, direct operations, and make decisions for a business.

Controlled Business Arrangement (CBA) A real estate brokerage office that provides related services through subsidiary companies that operate within the brokerage office. The arrangement allows a broker to provide financing, title and hazard insurance, and other ancillary services without violating the Real Estate Settlement Procedures Act *(RESPA)*.

Controlled Growth Controlled growth is a general blanket term for various situations that occur when restrictions are placed on real estate expansion in a certain area. See Zoning.

Convection Currents made as a result of heating air, which rises and pulls cooler air behind it.

Conventional Loan A loan that is not insured or guaranteed by a government agency. Often these are in house loans that are kept by the lender, not sold on the secondary market. See Conventional mortgage. See Conventional Mortgage.

Conventional Mortgage A conventional mortgage is a loan not guaranteed or insured by the federal government. These borrowers usually make larger down payments of at least 20%, don't require mortgage insurance, and are at a lower risk of defaulting on their home loan payment. See Conventional Loan

Conversion To change from one character or use to another.

Convertibility The ability of a loan to be changed from an adjustable rate schedule to a fixed rate schedule.

Convertible Apartment A bedroom apartment with space enough to build one more bedroom.

Convertible ARM A Convertible Adjustable Rate Mortgage (ARM) allows buyers to take advantage of low interest rates by receiving a loan at a *"teaser loan interest rate"*. Their monthly mortgage payment stays the same, but interest rates fluctuate; usually every six months or 12 months. The borrower has the option of converting their ARM to a fixed-rate mortgage, but there are generally fees for such a switch.

Convertible Debt A mortgage position that gives the lender the option to convert to a partial or full ownership position in a property within a specified time period.

Convertible Preferred Stock Preferred stock that is convertible to common stock under certain formulas and conditions specified by the issuer of the stock.

Convey To deed or transfer title to another.

Conveyance
1. Most commonly refers to the transfer of title to property between parties by a deed. The term may also include most of the instruments with which an interest in real estate is created, mortgaged, or assigned.
2. The written instrument that evidences transfer of some interest in real estate.

Cooling Load The rate usually measured in Cubic Feet per Minute (CFM) of cool air needed to balance the temperature of a structure.

Co-Op
1. An arrangement between two real estate agents that generally results in splitting the commission between them.
2. A type of housing in which each tenant is a shareholder in a corporation that owns the building. also termed cooperative.

Cooperating Broker One who agrees to share the commission with another broker.

Cooperative A residential multi-unit building whose title is held by a trust or corporation that is owned by, and operated for, the benefit of persons living within the building. These persons are the beneficial owners of the trust or the shareholders of the corporation, each having a proprietary lease. See Co-op.

Coped Joint A joint between two or more pieces of trim which has been modified, traditionally with a coping saw, to have an irregular surface such that one piece fits exactly into the other piece.

Cope A way of taking away the top and bottom flange of the end of a metal I-beam. This practice is for allowing it to fit within, and fixed to, the web of another I-beam in a "T" shape.

Corbel A decorative supports to hold a mantel or horizontal shelf.

Core Typically includes the four major property types, specifically:
1. office
2. retail
3. industrial and
4. multifamily.

Core assets are high-quality, multi-tenanted properties typically located in major metropolitan areas and built within the past five years or recently renovated. They are substantially leased at 90 percent or better, with higher-credit tenants and have well-structured, long-term leases with the majority of those tenants, fairly early in the term of the lease. Core investments are either unleveraged or very low leveraged and generate good, stable income that, together with potential appreciation, is expected to generate total returns in the 8 percent to 10 percent range.

Core Properties See Core.

Core Space The central areas of a building that usually contain elevator banks, restrooms, stairwells, electrical services, janitorial closets, and similar spaces.

Core-Plus These investments possess similar attributes to core properties, providing moderate risk and moderate returns but these assets offer an opportunity for modest value enhancement, typically through improved tenancy/occupancy or minor property improvements. This strategy might employ leverage in the range of 30 to 50 percent with return expectations of 9 percent to 12 percent. See Core.

Corner Bead Formed sheet metal that covers the outside corners of drywall before drywall mud is applied. The bead both reinforces the corner and lends to its shape. Corner bead comes in several varieties, however the most popular is a squared corner which provides a 90 degree angle and a rounded corner which provides a ¾ radius .

Corner Board A trim used for external corners of a frame structure where the ends of the siding are finished. Also called a corner batten.

Corner Brace Braces that are in diagonal form of the framed structure used for stiffening and strengthening the wall.

Cornice Horizontal decorative molding that crowns a building or furniture element.

Corporation An entity or organization created by operation of law whose rights of doing business are essentially those of an individual. The entity has continuous existence until dissolved according to legal procedures.

Corporeal Visible or tangible real or personal property.

Correction Lines The horizontal provisions in the rectangular survey system made to compensate for the curvature of the earth's surface. Every fourth township line is used as a correction line on which the intervals between the north and south range lines are remeasured and corrected to a full six miles.

Corrective Maintenance A type of maintenance that is done when a system, equipment, or a machine is faulty. This type of maintenance includes detecting and/or isolating the problem as well as taking the necessary steps to fix the problem. Corrective maintenance is different from preventative maintenance.

Cosigner See Accommodation Party.

Cost Amount paid for property plus closing costs and improvements

Cost Approach The process of estimating the value of a property by adding the appraiser's estimate of the reproduction or replacement cost of the building, minus the depreciation, to the estimated land value.

Cost Basis Used mostly as an accounting term, the original cost of a building, land, or piece of equipment. With modifications for subsequent capital improvements and depreciation, this becomes the adjusted (tax) basis.

Cost Estimating In construction, the act of predicting the total costs of labor, materials, capital, and professional fees required to construct a proposed project.

Cost Of Funds Index (COFI) A cost of funds index is the average of the regional interest expenses acquired by financial institutions. It's used to calculate variable rate loans.

Cost Of Living Adjustment A change in payments, such as the amount of rent, based on a change in an index that measures inflation.

Cost Of Living Index An indicator of the current price level for goods and services related to some base year.

Cost-Approach Improvement Value The current cost to construct a reproduction of, or replacement for, the existing structure less an estimate for accrued depreciation.

Cost-Approach Land Value The estimated value of the fee simple interest in the property as if vacant and available for development to its highest and best use.

COSTAR A data provider that offers information on lease rates, absorption, and construction for many geographic real estate markets. Merged with COMPS.COM in November 1999.

Cost-Benefit Analysis A decision-making process, often used in public finance, that forces the decision maker to consider all direct and indirect positive and negative effects of the proposed decision on an objective basis, usually in dollars. Benefits must exceed costs in order to justify the project or adopt the policy.

Cost-Of-Sale Percentage An estimate of the costs to sell an investment representing brokerage commissions, closing costs, fees, and any other necessary disposition expenses.

Cost-Plus-Percentage Contract An agreement on a construction project in which the contractor is provided a specified percentage profit over and above the actual costs of construction. These contracts are generally considered poor business practice because the contractor has little incentive to hold down costs.

Co-tenancy Any of a number of forms of multiple ownership such as Tenancy In Common and Joint Tenancy.

Counseling The business of providing people with expert advice on a subject, based on the counselor's extensive, expert knowledge of the subject.

Counselor Of Real Estate (CRE) A member of the American Society Of Real Estate Counselors (ASREC). Membership is based on experience and professional conduct as a real estate counselor.

Counter Flashing A flashing that is used on chimneys to cover shingle flashing and to stop moisture entry and /or migration.

Counterfort A buttress built against or integral with a wall such as a retaining wall or dam, built on the back or thrust-receiving side.

Counteroffer A new offer made as a reply to an offer received, having the effect of rejecting the original offer.

County Clerk A government official who records and files items such as deeds, mortgages, and other official records.

Coupon The nominal interest rate charged to the borrower on a promissory note or mortgage.

Coupon Book A booklet given by a mortgage lender to a borrower with a set of preprinted tickets known as coupons which shows the account number, the required payment amount, and the payment due date. Each month a coupon is to be detached and sent in with a check for the mortgage payment.

Course A continuous horizontal layer of similarly-sized building material, in a wall. Usually used in connection with masonry.

Court
1. A government institution or facility used to decide civil conflicts and disputes or to try criminal prosecution cases brought before it.
2. A place to play a sport, which may be placed within a subdivision or apartment complex.
3. An open area next to or within buildings or other structures; courtyard.

Cove Moulding A moulding that has a concave face utilized to finish interior corners. Also spelled *"Molding"*.

Covenant A covenant is a written promise.

Covenant Not To Compete A clause in an agreement where one party promises not to work for the other parties direct competition for a specified amount of time.

Covenant of Quiet Enjoyment Insurance for a homeowner or tenant against being disturbed of his or her right to possess a property.

Covenant of Right to Convey The time grantor possesses the legal power to convey the title.

Covenant of Seisin Making sure the grantee that the grantor possesses the title being conveyed.

Covenant of Warranty A deed's pledge that the grantor is going to defend the title against lawful claimants.

Covenant Running With The Land A covenant restricting or limiting property

Covenants Agreements written into deeds and other instruments promising performance or nonperformance of certain acts or stipulating certain uses or nonuse's of the property.

Covenants, Conditions, and Restrictions (CC&Rs) Condominium documents that serve as the operational procedures describing the rights and prohibitions of the co-owners in a condominium association.

CPI See Consumer Price Index.

CPM A Certified Property Manager. A professional designation of the Institute Of Real Estate Management (IREM).

CPO See Commodity Pool Operator.

CPS1 The test-marketing phase of a condominium project in which a sponsor gauges public demand for a particular community. Before beginning this phase of a project, the sponsor must submit an application and any proposed advertising materials to the attorney general for approval.

Cram Down In Bankruptcy, this is the reduction of various classes of debt to a lower amount, with acceptance by the bankruptcy court.

Crawl Space A shallow area under the living quarters of a building, that is enclosed by the foundation wall and has an exposed dirt at its floor.

CRB A Certified Real Estate Brokerage Manager. A professional designation of the Realtors® National Marketing Institute *(RNMI)*.

CRE A Counselor Of Real Estate. A member of the American Society Of Real Estate Counselors *(ASREC)*.

Creative Financing Any financing arrangement other than a traditional mortgage from a third-party lending institution.

Credit
1. In finance, the availability of money. Example: When money and credit are readily available, it is easier to buy real estate. credit policy is determined to a large extent by the federal reserve system.
2. In accounting, a liability or equity entered on the right side of the ledger.

Credit Bureau See Credit Rating Service, Consumer Reporting Agency.

Credit Enhancement The credit support needed in addition to the mortgage collateral to achieve a desired credit rating on mortgage-backed securities. The forms of credit enhancement most often employed are subordination, over-collateralization, reserve funds, corporate guarantees, and letters of credit.

Credit Life Insurance A policy that retires a debt upon the death or disability of the borrower. Contrast mortgage insurance.

Credit Rating (Report) An evaluation of a person's capacity of debt repayment. Generally available for individuals from a local retail credit association; for businesses by companies such as Dunn & Bradstreet; and for publicly held bonds by Moody's, Standard & Poor's, and Fitch's. Individuals have access to their own files.

Credit Rating Service A Credit Bureau. An organization that provides information regarding the creditworthiness of a prospective borrower. See Consumer Reporting Agency *(CRA)*.

Credit Rating A report that a lender obtains from a credit agency so as to know the credit habits of a loan or credit applicant. See Credit Score.

Credit Score A number that reflects the borrower's credit risk level, typically with a higher number indicating lower risk. Credit scores are generated through statistical models using elements from the borrower's credit history report and change over time to reflect changes in the borrower's credit history.

Cricket Another roof constructed over the main roof so as to elevate the slope of the roof or valley. So as to allow water to drain away from the chimney joint.

Cripple A 2 x 4 or 2 x 6 piece of short vertical frame lumber fixed over a window or door.

Cross Bridging A bracing that is diagonal in shape fixed between adjacent floor joists, which is placed beside the center of the joist span so as to avoid joists from twisting.

Cross Tee A metal beam that is in a *"T"* shape used in suspended ceiling systems to ensure the spaces that are between the main beams.

Cross-Collateralization A grouping of mortgages or properties that serves to jointly secure one debt obligation.

Cross-Defaulting Allows the trustee to call all loans in a group into default when any single loan is in default.

Crown Molding Crown Molding includes a large family of moldings which are designed to gracefully flare out to a finished top edge, typically installed where a wall meets a ceiling. Also spelled *"Moulding"*.

CRS A Certified Residential Specialist

Cubic Foot Method Process used to calculate the cost of reproduction or replacement through the volume of the structure.

Cul-De-Sac A dead-end street that widens sufficiently at the end to permit an automobile to make a U-turn.

Culvert A corrugated drainpipe about 15inches or 18inches in size installed under a driveway and parallel to and near the street.

Cumulative Discount Rate Expressed as a percentage of base rent, it is the interest rate used in finding present values that considers all landlord lease concessions.

Cumulative Use Zoning A zoning type, which permits a higher priority use, although it is not the type of use typically designated for given the area.

Cupping A warping type that allow boards to curl up at their edges.

Curable Depreciation A type of depreciation or deterioration that can be corrected at a cost less than the value that will be added.

Curb Appeal The attractiveness or lack thereof, of a house or other land improvement as viewed from the street.

Curb Stop In a water-service pipe, a control valve for the water supply of a building, normally placed between the sidewalk and curb; used to shut off the water supply in case of emergency.

Curb
1. A short elevation of an exterior wall above the deck of a roof to which a skylight is attached.
2. a stone or concrete edging to a street or path.
3. a check or restraint on something.

Cure Period Time during which borrow can correct a default

Current Occupancy The current leased portion of a building or property expressed as a percentage of its total area or total units.

Current Value The value usually sought to be estimated in an appraisal.

Current Yield For CMBS, the coupon divided by the price.

Curtesy A life estate, usually as a fractional interest, given by some states to the surviving spouse in real estate owned by his/her deceased spouse. Most states have abolished curtesy.

Custom Builder One who builds unique houses. Contrast with Tract House.

Cut-In Brace Nominal 2" thick members, typically 2 by 4's, cut between each stud in a diagonally form.

Cycle A recurring sequence of events that regularly follow one another, generally within a fixed interval of time.

D

Dado
1. The lower part of a wall, below the dado rail and above the skirting board.
2. A groove cut in the face of a board, into which the edge of another board is fixed.

Dado Rail See Chair Rail.

Damages The indemnity recoverable by a person who has sustained an injury to his/her person, property, or relative rights, through the act, the negligence, or fault of another.

Damp Proof Course (DPC) A layer that is water-tight, laid underneath masonry walls to stop moisture.

Damper A door made of metal placed around the fireplace chimney.

Dampproofing A type of moisture control applied to building walls and floors to prevent moisture from passing into the interior spaces.

Data Enhanced Lists Marketing Lists used for advertising, solicitation, and other purposes. Typically include home data, ownership data, description of property, and the like.

Date Of Appraisal See Appraisal Date.

Date Of Closing See Closing Date.

Datum A horizontal plane from which heights and depths are measured.

Daylight The terminal end of a pipe not fixed to anything.

DBA See Doing Business As

DCR See Debt Coverage Ratio.

Dead Bolt A locking mechanism distinct from a spring bolt lock as a deadbolt cannot be moved to the open position except by rotating the lock cylinder with the key.

Dead Light The non-operable section of a window unit that is fixed.

Deal Structure With regard to the financing of an acquisition, deals can be unleveraged, leveraged, traditional debt, participating debt, participating/convertible debt, or joint ventures.

Dealer (Tax) One who buys and sells for his or her own account. The merchandise is inventory, consequently any gain on the sale is ordinary income.

Debenture A note or bond given as evidence of debt and issued without security.

Debit The amount charged as due or owing. See Debt.

Debt Capital Money borrowed for a particular business purpose.

Debt Capital Money loaned usually on a long-term basis and used to buy an investment such as real estate. See Capital Structure.

Debt Consolidation Replacing several loans with one loan, usually with a lower monthly payment and a longer repayment period.

Debt Coverage Ratio The relationship between Net Operating Income (NOI) and Annual Debt Service (ADS). Often used as an underwriting criteria for income property mortgage loans.

Debt Service The outlay necessary to meet all interest and principal payments during a given period.

Debt Service Constant See Mortgage Constant.

Debt Service Coverage Ratio (DSCR) The annual net operating income from a property divided by annual cost of debt service. A DSCR below 1 means the property is generating insufficient cash flow to cover debt payments.

Debt Something owed to another and not yet paid in full. An obligation to pay or return something.

Debt/Equity Ratio (D/E Ratio) D/E Ratio is a measure of the degree to which a company is financing its operations through debt versus wholly-owned funds. The debt-to-equity D/E ratio is calculated by dividing the company's total liabilities by its shareholder's equity.

Debtor In Possession The situation arising in a bankruptcy proceeding when the party who owes money remains in control of the use of property.

Debtor A person obligated to repay a debt; opposite of creditor. See Debt.

Debt to Equity Ratio See Debt/Equity Ratio.

Debt To Income Ratio All monthly expenses dived by gross monthly income.

Decedent One who is dead.

Deck, Decked To install plywood, OSB, or wafer board sheeting on a floor or roof.

Declaration An initial deed document for a condominium community that describes the property in detail, including plans and proposed pricing.

Declaration Of Condominium Ownership A Declaration Of Condominium Ownership also referred to as a declaration of condominium is a recorded document that typically includes a legal description of the condominium property, a description of the various units and common areas, the percentage interest and voting rights of each unit owner, and all the CC&Rs.

Declaration Of Restrictions An instrument recorded with the county which describes restrictive covenants for a given area such as a neighborhood or subdivision.

Declaration Of Trust A written statement by a trustee to acknowledge that the property is held for the benefit of another.

Declaration Master deed that contains legal descriptions and important information about a condominium facility.

Declining Balance Depreciation A method of depreciation, often used for income tax purposes, whereby a rate is applied to the remaining balance to derive the depreciation deduction. Contrast accelerated depreciation.

Declining Balance Method An accounting method of calculating depreciation for tax purposes designed to provide large deductions in the early years of ownership.

Decree An order issued by one in authority; a court order or decision.

Decree Of Foreclosure And Sale An announcement by a court that establishes the amount of outstanding mortgage and requires the property to be sold to pay off the debt.

Dedicate To appropriate private property to public ownership for a public use.

Dedicated Circuit An electrical circuit for just a single appliance.

Dedication A grant and appropriation of land by its owner to some municipality for some public use, accepted for such use, by an authorized public official on behalf of the public.

Deductible The amount an insured person must contribute towards a loss before an insurance company will pay the balance due.

Deductible Expenses The amount connected with business operations and management used in business.

Deed A written legal instrument that when executed and delivered conveys title to, or an interest in, real estate. A housing deed is the legal document transferring a title from the seller to the buyer. It must be a written document and is sometimes referred to as the vehicle of the property interest transfer.

Deed Books The books, files, or record storage of the Public Records in which county governments keep the deeds and other real estate-related documents that have been filed.

Deed In Lieu Of Foreclosure A deed-in-lieu of foreclosure is a document transferring the title of a property from a homeowner to the bank that holds the mortgage. Also refers to one type of process by which the mortgagor can avoid foreclosure. Under that scenario, the mortgagor gives a deed to mortgagee when mortgagor is in default according to terms of mortgage.

Deed Of Reconveyance The instrument used to reconvey title to a trustee under a deed of trust once the debt has been satisfied.

Deed Of Release A document, in the form of a deed, in which one who has limited rights to a piece of real estate, typically a mortgagee or lienholder, abandons those rights back to the owner of the real estate; often takes the form of a quitclaim deed.

Deed Of Trust An instrument used to create a lien by which the mortgagor conveys her or his title to a trustee, who holds it as security for the benefit of the noteholder.

Deed Restrictions The clauses in a deed limiting the future users of the property. Deed restrictions may impose a variety of limitations and conditions, such as limiting the density of buildings, dictating the types of structures that can be erected, and preventing buildings from being used for specific purposes or from used at all.

Deed To Secure Debt A type of mortgage used in many states whereby property is deeded to a lender to secure a debt.

Deed-In-Lieu See Deed In Lieu Of Foreclosure.

Default The nonperformance of a duty, whether arising under a contract or otherwise; failure to meet an obligation when due. If a homeowner defaults on their loan, it means they have not paid the sum they agreed to. Typically, a mortgage default means the homeowner hasn't made a home loan payment in 90 days or more.

Defeasance Clause A clause used in leases or mortgages that cancels a specified right on the occurrence of a certain condition, such as cancellation of a mortgage on repayment of the mortgage loan.

Defeasible Fee Estate A qualified estate in which the grantee could lose his or her interest upon the occurrence or non-occurrence of a specified event. There are two types of defeasible fee estates:

1. Those known as a condition subsequent where the possibility of re-entry takes place, and
2. A qualified limitation, where the grantee's ownership automatically ends with the possibility of reverter *(otherwise known as a fee simple determinable).*

Defeasible Fee A title subject to being revoked under some situations.

Defect In Title Any recorded instrument that would prevent a grantor from giving a clear title.

Defendant The party sued in an action at law.

Deferred Charges Deferred charges are nontangible costs that are expected to provide value over a number of years. For accounting or tax purposes, these are to be amortized over the life to which they are expected to provide value.

Deferred Gain In a Tax-Deferred Exchange, the amount of Realized Gain that is not recognized.

Deferred Maintenance Account An account a borrower is required to fund that provides for

Deferred Maintenance In appraisal, a type of physical depreciation owing to lack of normal upkeep.

Deferred Payments Payments to be made at some future date.

Deficiency In mortgage finance, the shortfall of funds recovered through the sale of property securing a foreclosed loan is a deficiency.

Deficiency Judgment A judgment given when the security for a loan does not entirely satisfy the debt upon its default.

Defined-Benefit Plan An employee's benefits are defined, either as a fixed amount or a percentage of the beneficiary's salary at the time of retirement. Pension plans, Health and Welfare plans, and some Keogh plans are established as defined benefit plans.

Defined-Contribution Plan An employee's benefits at retirement are determined by the amount contributed by the employer and/or the employee during his or her employment tenure, and by the actual investment earnings on those contributions over the life of the fund. Examples include 401(k), thrift plans and profit sharing plans.

Dehumidistat A system used to operate a mechanical ventilation system built on the relative humidity of the home.

Delamination When the panel plies separate due to a bad adhesive.

Delayed (Tax-Free) Exchange A transaction in which a property is traded for the promise to provide a replacement Like-Kind Property in the near future. See Tax-Free Exchange, Starker.

Delayed Exchange Also known as a *"Starker Exchange"*, this is when an investor gives up his or her investment property and then receives the replacement property at a later date.

Delinquency A mortgage is considered delinquent when a scheduled payment is not made. Usually the period prior to being considered delinquent is 30 days. If a payment is more than 30 days late, a lender might begin collection or foreclosure proceedings.

Delinquency List This is a list of delinquent properties usually held by a county , but not to be confused with a tax sale list. These are not always a good list to search for properties since, often times the owners will end up paying the delinquent taxes and the property will not end up going to a tax sale.

Delinquency Rate Statistically, the number of loans with delinquent payments divided by the number of loans held in a portfolio. Sometimes, the rate is based on the total dollar volume of the loans instead of number. Generally, delinquency rate includes only loans where payments are 3 or more months past due.

Delinquent Taxes Unpaid taxes that are past due.

Delivery And Acceptance The transfer of a title by deed from the grantor to the grantee.

Delivery In Escrow Delivery of a deed to a third person until the performance of some act or condition by one of the parties.

Delivery The legal act of transferring ownership. Documents such as deeds and purchase agreements must be delivered and accepted to be valid. Usually happens at closing by a title company or title attorney.

Demand The amount of opportunity to sell something in a given location at a given price. The lower the demand, the lower the price!

Demand Loan See Demand Note.

Demand Note A note which is payable on demand of the holder.

Demised Premises Property subject to lease.

Demising Clause A clause found in a lease whereby the landlord (lessor) leases and the tenant (lessee) takes the property.

Demising Partition A separation between two tenants or between a tenant and the corridor. See Demising Wall.

Demising Wall The partition wall that separates one tenant's space from another or from the building's common areas.

Demographic Pertaining to characteristics of the population, such as race, sex, age, household size, and to population growth and density.

Demography The study of the characteristics of people residing in an area, including age, sex, income.

Demolition The act of completely destroying a building.

Demolition Permit Approval by a municipality to bring down and demolish an existing structure.

Density The intensity of a land use.

Density Zoning The zoning ordinances that restrict the average maximum number of houses per acre that may be built within a particular area, generally a subdivision.

Dep See Depreciation.

Department of Housing and Urban Development Regulates FHA and GNMA.

Departure Provision (USPAP) Section of the Uniform Standards Of Appraisal Practice *(USPAP)* that allows an appraiser to deviate from a Complete Appraisal, thus providing a Limited Appraisal under certain conditions. The departure provision is allowed only in situations where it would not cause a user to be misled or confused.

Depletion A tax deduction to account for reduced land value due to removing minerals.

Deposit Account An arrangement whereby an individual or organization may place cash under the safekeeping of a financial institution. It is to be understood, though not always expressly said, that the institution may invest the cash and pay the depositor a specified amount of interest and that the depositor can reclaim the full value of the account according to the agreed upon procedures governing the account.

Deposit Money paid in good faith to assure performance of a contract. Deposits are commonly used with sales contracts and leases. If the person who put up the deposit fails to perform, the deposit is forfeited, unless conditions in the contract allow a refund. brokers are to put deposits in a separate checking account pending completion of the contract. See Earnest Money, Binder.

Depository Institutions Deregulation And Monetary Control Act The federal law that represents significant decontrol of federally regulated banks and savings institutions, including gradual phase out of limits on interest rates paid on passbook accounts. See Regulation Q.

Depreciable Basis See Basis *(Tax)*, Adjusted Tax Basis.

Depreciable Life
1. For tax purposes, the number of years over which the cost of an asset may be spread.
2. For appraisal purposes, the estimated useful life of an asset.

Depreciable Real Estate (Tax) Real Estate that is subject to deductions for depreciation. It generally includes property used in a trade or business, or an investment, subject to an allowance for depreciation under section 167 of the internal revenue code.

Depreciated Cost See Book Value or Adjusted Tax Basis.

Depreciation Generally, the reduction in the worth of an asset.

1. In appraisal, a loss of value in property due to all causes, including physical deterioration, functional obsolescence, and economic obsolescence.
2. In real estate investment, an expense deduction for tax purposes taken over the period of ownership of the income property.

Depreciation Methods Accounting technique of allocating the cost of an asset over its useful life.

Depreciation Recapture When real property is sold at a gain and accelerated depreciation had been claimed, the owner may be required to pay a tax at ordinary rates to the extent of the excess accelerated depreciation. Excess depreciation on residential real estate after 1980 is recaptured; all depreciation on commercial property after 1980 is recaptured when an accelerated method had been used, under section 1250 of the internal revenue code.

Depression Economic conditions causing severe decline in business activity, reflecting high unemployment, excess supply, and public fear.

Depth Tables A set of percentages indicating the proportion of site value attributable to each additional amount of depth in the lot.

Depth The distance between the curb and the rear property boundary *(lot depth)* or between the front and rear walls of a building.

Derivative Securities Securities that are created artificially, for example, derived from other financial instruments. In the context of CMBS, the most common derivative security is the interest-only strip.

Descent When an owner of real estate dies intestate, the owner's property descends, by operation of law, to the owner's distributees.

Description Formal depiction of the dimensions and location of a property almost always included in Deeds, and Mortgage contracts for Real Property. May be included in Leases and Sales Contracts.

Descriptive Memorandum A term used to describe an offering of property or securities when a prospectus is not required. Typically takes the form of a short circular style page or pages.

Design/Build A system in which a single entity is responsible for both the design and construction.

Designed Agency An agency relationship where a client designates a broker to appoint an office agent to singularly represent his or her interest to the exclusion of all of the other agents in that broker's office.

Detached Housing Residential Buildings in which each dwelling unit is surrounded by freestanding walls and is generally sited on a separate lot. Single family Dwelling. Contrast with duplex, row house, town house.

Determinable Fee Estate A fee-simple estate in which the property automatically reverts to the grantor on the occurrence of a specified event or condition.

Developer One who transforms raw land to improved property by use of labor, capital, and entrepreneurial efforts.

Development Loan See Construction Loan.

Development The process of adding improvements on or to a parcel of land. Such improvements may include drainage, utilities, subdividing, access, buildings, and any combination of these elements. Also the project where such improvements are being made. See Highest and Best Use.

Devise A transfer of real estate by will or last testament. The donor is the devisor and the recipient is the devisee.

Devisee One who receives a bequest of real estate made by will.

Devisor One who bequeaths real estate by will.

Diminishing Returns The principle that applies when a given parcel of land reaches its maximum percentage return on investment, and further expenditures for improving the property yield a decreasing return.

Direct Capitalization Dividing the Net Operating Income by an overall Capitalization Rate to estimate value.

Direct Costs Direct costs are costs that are readily identified in the construction of real estate, such as labor, materials, contractor's overhead, and profit.

Direct Reduction Mortgage A loan that requires both interest and principal with each payment such that the level payment will be adequate for amortization over the loan's term.

Direct Sales Comparison Approach See Market Comparison Approach.

Directional Growth The location or direction toward which a city is growing.

Discharge In Bankruptcy The release of a bankrupt party from the obligation to repay debts that were, or might have been, proved in a bankruptcy proceeding.

Disclaimer
1. A statement whereby responsibility is rejected.
2. Renunciation of ownership of property.

Disclosure and Informed Consent a disclosure provided by an agent or broker. Informed consent is an agreement by a party to a contract or an element of the contract made AFTER the party has been advised of all material facts.

Disclosure Statement A statement required by law, in which sellers of particular kinds of property, or under certain circumstances, must reveal specified information to potential buyers.

Disconnect An electrical ON/OFF switch; typically 20 Amp.

Discount Broker A licensed broker who provides brokerage services for a lower commission than that typical in the market. The services provided may be less extensive than those of a full service broker or may be unbundled, so that a client may contract for specific services. Many discount brokers charge a flat fee rather than a percentage of the selling price.

Discount Points Discount points are also known as mortgage points. They're fees homebuyers pay directly to the lender at the time of closing in exchange for reduced interest rates which can lower monthly mortgage payments.

An added loan free charged by a lender to make the yield on a lower-than-market-value loan competitive with higher-interest loans. See Points.

Discount Rate The rate of interest a commercial bank must pay when it borrows from its federal reserve bank.

Discount The difference between the face amount of an obligation and the amount advanced or received.

Discounted Cash Flow A method of investment analysis in which anticipated future cash income from the investment is estimated and converted into a rate of return on initial investment based on the time value of money. In addition, when a required rate of return is specified, a net present value of the investment can be estimated.

Discounted Loan One that is offered or traded for less than its face value.

Discounted Present Value See Discounted Cash Flow, Net Present Value

Discounting The process of estimating the present value of an income stream by reducing expected Cash Flow to reflect the Time Value Of Money.

Discretion The level of authority granted to an adviser or manager over the investment and management of a client's capital. A fully discretionary account typically is defined as one in which the adviser or manager has total ability to invest and manage a client's capital without prior approval of the client.

Discrimination Applying special treatment in a generally unfavorable way to an individual solely on the basis of the person's race, religion, sex, or sexual orientation.

Disintermediation Situation when deposits are removed from a financial intermediary, such as a Savings And Loan Association, and invested in other assets, generally for the purpose of obtaining higher yields.

Displacement Involuntary movement of population by conversion of their homes to other uses. See Eminent Domain.

Dispossess Proceedings Summary process by a landlord to oust a tenant and regain possession of the premises for nonpayment of rent or other breach of conditions of the lease or occupancy.

Dispossess To oust from land by legal process.

Distinguished Real Estate Instructor (DREI) A real estate teacher, typically of licensing preparation courses, who has been designated by the Real Estate Educators Association.

Distraint The act of seizing personal property of a tenant in default based on the right and interest a landlord has in the property.

Distraint The legal right of a landlord to seize a tenant's personal property to satisfy payment of back rent.

Distress Sale A sale where the seller is under compulsion to sell. Usually a court ordered sale.

Distressed Property Real estate that is under foreclosure or impending foreclosure because of insufficient income production.

Distribution Box A septic system that channel septic tank flow evenly to the absorption field.

Diversification The process of consummating individual investments in a manner that insulates a portfolio against the risk of reduced yield or capital loss, accomplished by allocating individual investments among a variety of asset types, each with different characteristics.

Dividend Cash or stock distribution paid to holders of common stock. REITs must pay at least 90 percent of their taxable income in the form of dividends.

Dividend Yield The annual dividend rate for a security expressed as a percent of its market price (annual dividend/price = yield).

Dividend-Ex Date The first date on which a person purchasing the stock is no longer eligible to receive the most recently announced dividend.

Documentary Evidence Evidence in the form of written or printed papers.

Dodge, F. W. A service that provides cost estimates of buildings for those interested in building, insuring, or appraising. Also collects and reports construction statistics. Data are available both in print and online. F. W. Dodge is part of The McGraw-Hill Companies' Construction Information Group.

Dollar Stop An agreed dollar amount of taxes and operating expense each tenant will pay on a prorated basis.

Domicile The place in which one makes his or her principal residence.

Dominant Tenement A property that includes in its ownership the appurtenant right to use an easement over another's property for a specific purpose.

Donee A recipient, as of a gift.

Donor One who gives.

Door Jamb An area of the door frame onto which it is secured.

Door Operator An automatic garage for opening of door.

Door Stop A wood that the door slab rest on when it is closed.

Doorjamb Interior The surrounding case into which and out of which a door closes and opens.

Dormer A sloping roof opening, the framing that projects out forming a vertical wall for windows or other openings.

Double Declining Balance A method of depreciation for tax purposes whereby twice the straight-line rate is applied to the remaining depreciable balance of an asset. See Declining Balance Depreciation.

Double Glass Window or door made with two panes of glasses.

Double Hung Window A window that has two vertically sliding sashes, whereby both window move up and down.

Double Taxation The taxation of the same income at two levels.

Dower The legal right or interest recognized in some states that a spouse acquires in the property a persons' spouse held or acquired during their marriage. During the lifetime of the now deceased spouse, the right is only a possibility of an interest; on his death it can become an interest in land.

Down Payment The down payment is the amount of cash a homebuyer pays at the time of closing. Conventional home loans require a 20% down payment. Some conforming loans will accept a 5% down payment, and FHA loans will accept a 3.5% down payment.

DOWNREIT An organizational structure that makes it possible for REITs to buy properties using partnership units. The effect is an UPREIT, however, the DOWNREIT is subordinate to the REIT itself, hence the name.

Downspout A pipe made from metal used for carrying rainwater down from the roof's horizontal gutters.

Downzoning The act of rezoning a tract of land for a less intensive use than the existing use or permitted use.

Drag-Along Rights The right that enables a majority shareholder to force a minority shareholder to join in the sale of a company. The majority owner doing the dragging must give the minority shareholder the same price, terms, and conditions as any other seller.

Dragnet Clause A provision in a mortgage that pledges several properties as collateral. A default on one mortgage constitutes a default on the one with the dragnet.

Drain Tile A pipe that is laid at the bottom of the foundation wall, functioning for draining-off excess water from the foundation.

Draw A periodic advance of funds from a construction lender to a developer. Construction loans generally provide for a schedule of draws, either at regular intervals during construction or pending construction of specific segments of the structures.

DREI See Distinguished Real Estate Instructor.

Drip Cap A metal flashing that is on a door's exterior topside or window frame that allows water to drip beyond the outside of the frame.

Drip A member of a cornice or other horizontal exterior finish course with a projection beyond the other parts to be able to throw off water.

Drive-By Appraisal A value estimate prepared without the benefit of an interior inspection. May not conform to USPAP standard.

Dry Ice Carbon dioxide in a solid form. In construction, dry Ice is sometimes used for cleaning bricks.

Dry In Installation of the black roofing felt on the roof.

Dry Mortgage See Nonrecourse Mortgage.

Drywall Also called gypsum board, a paper-coated, gypsum-filled paneling used for interior walls. Sheetrock® is one brand.

DSCR See Debt Service Coverage Ratio.

Dual Agency Representing both principals , *(the seller and the buyer)* in a transaction.

Dual Agent A broker or salesperson that stand in place of both the buyer and seller in one same transaction.

Dual Contract The illegal or unethical practice of providing two different contracts for the same transaction.

Ducts, Ductwork Metal tubing used to distribute heated or cooled air from the HVAC central system throughout a house or building. Can be cylindrical *(typically 6" to 36" in diameter in a home)*, or have a rectangular cross-section.

Due Care The standard of conduct required of an ordinary, prudent, and reasonable person.

Due Diligence
1. Activities carried out by a prospective purchaser or mortgager of real property to confirm that the property is as represented by the seller and is not subject to environmental or other problems.
2. In the case of an IPO registration statement, due diligence is a reasonable investigation by the parties involved to confirm that all the statements within the document are true and that no material facts are omitted.

Due On Sale The concept of accelerating the maturity of a loan if the mortgagor or borrower sells or conveys an interest in mortgaged property prior to the contractually agreed maturity date of the loan.

Due Process The concept of fair treatment through the normal judicial system, especially as a citizen's entitlement. The Fifth Amendment to the U.S. Constitution states: *"No person shall…be deprived of life, liberty, or property, without due process of law."*

Due-On-Sale Clause A due-on-sale clause protects lenders against below-market interest rates. It's a contract provision requiring the seller of the property to repay the mortgage in full when the property is next sold. It is also called an acceleration clause.

Dummy An individual or entity that stands in the place of the Principal to a transaction.

Duplex Two dwelling units under one roof.

Duplex Apartment Two story apartment that has separate entrances for two households.

Dura Board A concrete panel and fiberglass normally used as a ceramic tile backing material. Commonly used on bathtub decks. Also known as Wonder board

Duress Unlawful constraint exercised upon a person whereby the person is forced to do some act against the person's will.

Dutch Auction A bidding process in which the asking price is lowered gradually until someone places a qualifying bid.

Dutch Colonial An early-American-style, moderate-sized, 2- to 2 1/2-story house with a gambrel roof and eaves that flare outward.

DVA Loan Also called a VA Loan. A mortgage loan on approved property made to a qualified veteran by an authorized lender and guaranteed by the Department of Veterans Affairs to limit possible loss by the lender.

Dwang Used to give firmness to frames, normally used between wall studs or floor joists

DWV (Drain Waste Vent) Plumbing system area carrying water and sewer gases away from the home.

DYNA Software provider of software for real estate investment analysis, specializing in institutional real estate. Acquired by Argus Financial Software in June 1999.

E

Earnest Money Deposit Earnest money is a deposit made by a homebuyer at the time they enter into a contract with a seller. Though there is no rule or regulation, it is usually 1-2% of the home's total purchase price. Earnest money demonstrates the buyer's interest in the property and is generally deducted from the total down payment and closing costs at the time of closing. In the event that the buyer, for no valid or legal reason, backs out of the transaction, earnest money is sometimes used as liquidated damages.

Earnest Money See Earnest Money Deposit.

Earthquake Strap Used to stop a water heater from falling over when an earthquake happens.

Early Georgian An English-style house built in America throughout the early 1700s. This style has simple exterior lines and generally fewer of the decorative devices characteristic of the later Georgian houses. Most are 2 or 3-story rectangular houses with two large chimneys rising high above the roof at each end.

Easement A right to use the land of another for a specific purpose, such as for a right-of-way or utilities; an incorporeal interest in land. An easement appurtenant passes with the land when conveyed. An easement grants someone else the legal right to use another person's land or property while leaving the title in the owner's name.

Easement Appurtenant Easement that still applies to an asset even after the owners change.

Easement By Necessity An easement allowed by law as necessary for the full enjoyment of a parcel of real estate.

Easement By Prescription An easement acquired by continuous, open, uninterrupted, exclusive, and adverse of the property for the period of time prescribed by state law.

Easement In Gross An easement that is not created for the benefit of any land owned by the owner of the easement but that attaches personally to the easement owner.

Eastlake House A nineteenth-century-style house with three-dimensional ornamentation made with a chisel, gouge, and lathe rather than the scroll saw. Many of the parts of the ornamentation resemble furniture legs and knobs. This distinctive type of ornamentation is the major characteristic of this style and separates the Eastlake-style house from the Queen Anne or Carpenter Gothic style.

Eastern Townhouse See Brownstone.

Eaves The part of a roof that overhangs the exterior walls of a house.

EBITDA A commonly used accounting term which refers to a formula for analyzing cash flow of a property as *"Earnings Before Interest, Taxes, Depreciation And Amortization"*.

Economic Base The industry within a geographic market area that provides employment opportunities that are essential to support the community.

Economic Depreciation An asset's physical deterioration.

Economic Feasibility The feasibility of a building or project in terms of costs and revenue, with excess revenue establishing the degree of viability.

Economic Life The period of time over which an improved property will earn an income adequate to justify its continued existence.

Economic Obsolescence The impairment of, desirability of, or end of useful life, arising from factors external to the property, such as economic forces or environmental changes, that affect supply-demand relationships in the market. Loss in the use and value of a property arising from the factors of economic obsolescence is to be distinguished from loss in value from physical deterioration and functional obsolescence, both of which are inherent to any property.

Economic Rent The market rental value of a property at a given point in time.

Effective Age The age of a property based on the amount of wear and tear it has sustained.

Effective Date The date on which a registration statement becomes effective and the sale of securities can commence.

Effective Gross Income (EGI) The total income from a property generated by rents and other sources, less a vacancy factor estimated to be appropriate for the property. EGI is expressed as collected income before expenses and debt service.

Effective Gross Rent (EGR) The net rent generated, after adjusting for tenant improvements and other capital costs, lease commissions and other sales expenses.

Effective Interest Rate The rate of interest that is paid on a loan.

Effective Rate The actual rate of return considering all relevant financing expenses.

Effective Rent The actual rental rate to be achieved by the landlord after deducting the value of concessions from the base rental rate paid by a tenant, usually expressed as an average rate over the term of the lease.

Efficiency Ratio The proportion of a building's area that is leasable space.

Efficiency Unit, Efficiency Apartment A small dwelling unit, often consisting of a single room, within a multifamily structure. In most cases, kitchen and bath facilities are minimal and not complete.

EGI See Effective Gross Income.

EGR See Effective Gross Rent.

Egress Access from a land parcel to a public road or other means of exit. In order for a bedroom to be considered a bedroom in most areas of the US it must have a closet and two forms of egress, typically the door to the bedroom and one window.

EIFS (Exterior Insulating And Finish Systems) A synthetic alternative to natural stucco, a cement-based material used for finishing the exterior of houses and other buildings.

Ejectment A form of action to regain possession of real property, with damages for the unlawful retention; used when there is no relationship of landlord and tenant.

Ekistics The science of how people settle land areas, including urban development and city growth, planning, and design. *(The root is Greek: oikos, "house," from which economy and ecology are also derived.)*

Elbow An electrical or plumbing installation used for changing directions in runs of pipe or conduit.

Electric Lateral The location of the electrical service line.

Electric Resistance Coils Wires made of metal that is heated whenever electric current passes through them, mostly used in baseboard heaters, electric water heaters and other appliances.

Electrical Entrance Package The point of entrance of electrical power.

Electrical Permit A separate authorization needed for most electrical work.

Electrical Rough Some work performed by the Electrical Contractor prior to insulation.

Electrical Trim Work carried out by the electrical contractor to prepare the house for and pass the municipal electrical final inspection.

Electronic Authentication Any of several methods used to provide proof that a particular document received electronically is genuine, has arrived unaltered and came from the source indicated.

Elemental Cost Planning Cost planning system allowing the cost of a scheme to be monitored during design development.

Elevation (Drawing) An orthographic meaning non-perspective, drawing of a property from the front, rear, or side that illustrates how the planned or existing structure is situated topographically.

Elevation Sheet The page on the blueprints that depicts the house or room as if a vertical plane were passed through the structure.

Elevation The two dimensional representation of any side of the house.

Elizabethan Style Home An English-style, 2- or 2 1/2-story house, often with part of the second story overhanging the first. It has less stonework and is less fort-like than the Tudor. Stone and stucco walls with half timbers are most common.

Ellwood Technique In the appraisal of mortgaged income property, a technique used to estimate the present value of the property. The appraiser determines and discounts to a present value the annual cash flow to the equity owner and the expected resale proceeds. Those amounts are added together to derive the equity value, then added to the mortgage balance to offer a property value estimate. L. W. Ellwood provided capitalization rate tables that accelerated this process.

Emblements Growing crops that are produced annually through the tenant's own care and labor and that she or he is entitled to take away after the tenancy is ended. Emblements are regarded as personally property even prior to harvest, so if the landlord terminates the lease, the tenant may still reenter the land and remove such crops. If the tenant terminates the tenancy voluntarily, however, she or he generally is not entitled to the emblements.

Eminent Domain The right of eminent domain gives the government the ability to use private property for public purposes. It's only exercisable when and if the government fairly compensates the owner of the property.

Employee Relocation Council A nonprofit professional membership organization committed to the effective relocation of employees worldwide. Transferred employees and companies who transfer employees can learn about costs and various services provided in a transfer.

Employee Retirement Income Security Act (ERISA) Legislation passed in 1974 and administered by the Department of Labor that controls the investment activities primarily of corporate and union pension plans. More public pension funds are adopting ERISA-like standards.

Empty Nesters A person or more typically a couple whose children have grown to adulthood and established separate households. Empty nesters are an important segment of the housing market, since empty nesters often seek to reduce the amount of housing space they occupy.

Encapsulation A method of containing hazardous materials by covering them.

Encasement The coating that is over all building components, both interior and exterior.

Encroachment When a property owner violates the rights of a neighbor by building or adding on to a structure that extends onto a neighbor's land or property line, that is called encroachment.

Encumber To burden a property, as with a debt or obligation.

Encumbrance A real estate encumbrance is any claim against a property that restricts its use or transfer, including an easement or property tax lien.

End Loan See Permanent Mortgage.

Endorsement The act of writing one's name, either with or without additional words, on a negotiable instrument or on a paper attached to such instrument.

Endowment A fund that is made up of gifts and bequests, which are subject to a requirement that the principal be maintained intact and invested to create a source of income for an organization. Institutions of higher education, for example, have endowments to fund research, scholarships, and other activities.

Energy Efficient As applied to buildings, generally indicating the existence of extra insulation, weatherproofing, and/or special features and equipment designed to reduce the us of and therefore cost of energy for heating, cooling, and hot water.

English Covenants of Title In property law, English covenants refers to a set of six traditional covenants of title made by the seller of a parcel of land to the buyer of that parcel. They are

1. Covenant For Seisin
2. Covenant Of The Right To Convey
3. Covenant Against Encumbrances
4. Covenant For Quiet Enjoyment
5. Covenant Of General Warranty
6. Covenant For Further Assurances.

Entity Investing An investment in an entity, such as a company or partnership, that controls an investment rather than directly in the underlying assets. An investment entity is an entity that does both of the following:

1. Pools funds from an investor or investors and provides the investors with professional investment management services, and
2. commits to its investors that its business purpose and only substantive activities are investing the funds for returns from capital appreciation.

Entity The legal form under which property is owned. See Corporation, Limited Partnership, Partnership.

Entity-Level Direct JV The investor is investing at the entity level meaning investing in the securities of the operating company or taking a non-securitized ownership position in the operation company.

Entity-Level Fund A fund that invests at the entity level meaning it invests in the securities of the operating company or take an ownership position in the operating company.

Entrepreneur An individual who generates business activity. A businessman or businesswoman. Often associated with one who takes business risks.

Environmental Assessment (EA) A study of land to determine any unique environmental attributes, considering everything from endangered species to existing hazardous waste to historical significance. Depending on the findings of an EA, an Environmental Impact Statement *(EIS)* may or may not be needed. See Environmental Site Assessment, Environmental Audit.

Environmental Audit A study of the property and its area to determine whether there are any hazards:

1. Phase I. To identify the presence of hazards *(i.e.: asbestos, radon, PCBs, leaking underground storage tanks)*.
2. Phase II. To estimate the cost of remediation or cleanup.
3. Phase III. To remediate the environmental contamination.

Environmental Indemnity An agreement under which a borrower contracts to indemnify, defend and hold another person harmless from any liability arising out of existing of potential environmental violations to the property which is the security for a loan.

Environmental Obsolescence See Economic Obsolescence.

Environmental Protection Agency (EPA) An agency of the U.S. government established to enforce federal pollution abatement laws and to implement various pollution prevention programs.

Environmental Site Assessment An evaluation of a site, prior to acquisition of title to the property, for the existence of hazardous waste. Under the Comprehensive Environmental Response, Compensation, and Liability Act of 1980 *(CERCLA)*, as amended by the Superfund Amendments and Reauthorization Act of 1986 *(SARA)*, anyone acquiring title to a site is responsible for environmental damages resulting from hazardous wastes on the site.

Environmental Impact Statement (EIS) An analysis of the expected effects of a development or action on the surrounding natural and fabricated environment. Such statements are required for many federally supported developments under the National Environmental Policy Act of 1969.

EOY End Of Year.

EPA See Environmental Protection Agency.

Equal Credit Opportunity Act The Equal Credit Opportunity Act *(ECOA)* was enacted on October 28, 1974 and makes it unlawful for creditors to discriminate against any applicant because of race, color, religion, national origin, sex, marital status, age, or because they receive any type of public assistance.

Equalization Rate A rate calculated by a State Board of Equalization or Assessment to measure a municipality's level of assessment.

Equalization The raising or lowering of assessed values for tax purposes in a particular county or taxing district to make them equal to assessments in other counties or districts.

Equitable Conversion A legal doctrine in some states under which a purchaser of real property becomes the equitable owner of title to the property at the time he or she signs a contract binding him or her to purchase the land at a later date.

Equitable Mortgage A legal document that encumbers the property but is not technically a mortgage because of the existence of some legal error.

Equitable Subordination The concept of granting an otherwise junior lien a superior or prior right over a nominally senior lien, most commonly resulting from serious inequitable conduct by the senior lien holder.

Equitable Title The interest held by a vehicle under a contract for deed or an installment contract; the equitable right to obtain absolute ownership to property when legal title is held in another's name.

Equity Buildup The gradual increase in a Mortgagor's Equity in a property directly caused by amortization of loan principal.

Equity Dividend The annual cash flow that an equity investor receives. See Before-Tax Cash Flow, Cash-On-Cash Return.

Equity The difference between what is owed on a home and what a person or entity is willing to purchase the home for. Equity is NOT the value of the home, but the value minus what is owed on it.

Equity Kicker See Kicker.

Equity Loan Junior loan based on a percentage of the equity.

Equity of Redemption A right of the owner to reclaim property before it is sold through foreclosure proceedings, by the payment of the tax debt, interest, and costs.

Equity Participation See Participation Mortgage.

Equity Yield Rate The Rate Of Return on the equity portion of an investment, considering periodic cash flow and the proceeds from resale. Equity Yield Rate considers the timing and amounts of cash flow after annual debt service, but not the income taxes. See After-Tax Equity Yield.

EREIT A Real Estate Investment Trust, or REIT, that invests almost exclusively in real properties, as opposed to mortgages or construction loans on real property. The term stands for equity real estate investment trust. 90% of all REITs are eREITs.

ERISA See Employee Retirement Income Security Act.

Erosion The gradual wearing away of land by water, wind, and general weather conditions. The diminishing of property caused by the elements.

Errors And Omissions Insurance A type of insurance coverage for real estate agents to protect against claims for innocent and negligent misrepresentations.

Escalation Clause See Escalator Clause.

Escalator Clause A provision in a lease that requires the tenant to pay more rent based on an increase in costs.

Escalator Mortgage See Adjustable-Rate Mortgage *(ARM)*.

Escape Clause An escape Clause is a provision in a contract that allows one or more of the parties to cancel all or part of the contract if certain events or situations do or do not occur.

Escheat The reversion of property to the state in the event that its owner dies without leaving a will and has no heirs to whom the property may pass by lawful descent.

Escrow Account An account that is held by a lender, escrow agent, or neutral third party, for a particular purpose defined in the escrow agreement controlling the account. When the conditions in the escrow agreement are triggered, such as when the tax bill comes due, the funds needed for that purpose are paid out of the escrow account.

Escrow Agent A third party who holds and delivers funds and documents under specific instructions. Often when purchasing a property, the escrow agent acts as a custodian of the earnest money or deposit and ensures that the appropriate funds are paid at the closing. In some states, all of the closing documents are delivered through an escrow agent operating under detailed instructions.

Escrow Agreement A written agreement made between an escrow agent and the parties to a contract setting forth the basic obligations of the parties, describing the money to be deposited in escrow, and instructing the escrow agent concerning the disposition of the monies deposited.

Escrow Analysis A report, usually conducted at the completion of a calendar year, itemizing all expenditures from and contributions to an escrow account. Also included is a projection of the following year's monthly payment amount required to reconcile any excess or deficiency in the account.

Escrow Closing A term meaning closing, especially in states where deeds of trust are used instead of mortgages.

Escrow Disbursements Using of escrow cash for payment of property expenses.

Escrow Escrow is part of the homebuying process. It happens when a third party holds something of value during the transaction. Most often, the value the third party holds onto is the buyer's earnest money check; this is when Escrow begins. When the transaction is complete at closing, the third party will release those funds to the seller; this is when escrow ends.

Escutcheon A plate made with ornamental that fits around a pipe extending through a wall so as to hide the cut out hole.

Estate At Sufferance Continuing to occupy property even when legal authorization has expired. See Squatter, Squatter's Rights.

Estate At Will The occupation of lands and tenements by a tenant for an indefinite period, terminable by one or both parties at will.

Estate For Life An interest in property that terminates upon the death of a specified person. See Life Estate.

Estate For Years An interest for a certain, exact period of time in property leased for a specified consideration.

Estate In Land The degree, quantity, nature, and extent of interest that a persona has in real property.

Estate In Reversion The residue of an estate left for the grantor, to commence in possession after the termination of some particular estate granted by the grantor.

Estate In Severalty An estate owned by one person.

Estate Tax A tax based on the value of property left by the deceased. The market value of an estate is subject to taxation as of the date of death or, if lower, six months later.

Estate The degree, quantity, nature, and extent of interest which a person has in real property.

Estimate Method used for calculating project cost through adding labor, materials, and different other costs to a new project.

Estimating The process used to estimate the cost of a project.

Estoppel Certificate A legal instrument executed by a mortgagor showing the amount of the unpaid balance due on a mortgage and stating that the mortgagor has no defenses or offsets against the mortgagee at the time of execution of the certificate.

Estoppel The concept of being prevented from raising or denying a fact or circumstance, typically used in connection with the issuance of an estoppel certificate

Estovers Legally allowed necessities, such as the right of a tenant to use timber on leased property to help support a minimum need for fuel or repairs.

Et Al Latin, meaning *"and others".*

Et Con An abbreviation of the Latin Et Conjunx. Legal term signifying *"and husband."* See ET UX.

Et Ux / Et Uxor Latin, meaning *"and wife".*

Et Vir Latin, meaning *"and husband".*

Ethical Conduct conforming to specific professional standards.

European Real Estate Society (ERES) An organization established in 1994 to create a structured and permanent network between real estate academics and professionals across Europe. ERES provides an open forum for the exchange of ideas and the dissemination of research relevant to applied decision making in real estate finance, economics, appraisal, investment, and asset management.

Evaluation A study of potential property uses, but not to determine its present value.

Evaporator Coil A section of cooling system that evacuates heat from the air in a structure.

Eviction A legal process to oust a person from possession of real estate.

Eviction Actual The process of removing a tenant from property. This is usually done through a legal process.

Eviction, Constructive Any disturbance of the tenant's possession of the leased premises by the landlord whereby the premises are rendered unfit or unsuitable for the purpose for which they were leased.

Eviction, Partial Exists where the possessor of the property, such as a tenant, is deprived of a portion thereof.

Evidence Of Title A proof of ownership of property, which is commonly a certificate of title, a title insurance policy, an abstract of title with lawyer's opinion, or a Torrens registration certificate.

Examination Of Title A title examination reviews all public records tied to a property. It generally reviews all previous deeds, wills, and trusts to ensure the title has passed cleanly and legally to every new owner. See Title Search.

Examination Of Title Research of the title to a piece of real estate; less thorough than a Title Search, usually concentrates on recent records.

Exception An item not covered by an insurance policy.

Excess Accelerated Depreciation The accumulated difference between Accelerated Depreciation claimed for tax purposes and what Straight-Line Depreciation would have been. Generally, excess accelerated depreciation is recaptured as Ordinary Income upon a sale, instead of receiving more favorable Capital Gains treatment. See Depreciation Recapture.

Excess Rent When the rent of an existing lease exceeds the rental rate on comparable existing space. should the lease expire or the tenant break the lease, the new rate will probably be at market rates.

Exchange Under Section 1031 of the Internal Revenue Code, Like-Kind Property used in a trade or business or held as an investment can be exchanged tax free. See BOOT, Realized Gain, Recognized Gain, Delayed Exchange, Starker, Reverse Exchange.

Exchange Value The amount of proceeds from sale of a Relinquished Property which a Taxpayer must spend on Replacement Property in order to have a fully deferred exchange.

Exclusionary Zoning Exclusionary zoning is the use of zoning ordinances to exclude certain types of land uses from a given community. Exclusionary zoning is done to safeguard the individual's property value and reduce traffic congestion, but also can have the affect of exacerbating social segregation by deterring racial and economic integration.

Exclusive Agency An agreement of employment of a broker to the exclusion of all other brokers; if sale is made by any other broker during term of employment, broker holding exclusive agency is entitled to commissions in addition to the commissions payable to the broker who effected the transaction.

Exclusive Agency Listing A listing contract under which the owner appoints a real estate broker as his or her exclusive agent for a designated period of time to sell the property on the owner's stated terms for a commission. The owner, however, reserves the right to sell without paying anyone a commission by selling to a prospect who has not been introduced or claimed by the broker.

Exclusive Listing An exclusive listing is used to motivate an agent to sell a property quickly, usually within a specified number of months. Most listing agreements are for an exclusive listing.

Exclusive Right-To-Sell Listing A listing contract under which the owner appoints a real estate broker as his or her exclusive agent for a designated period of time to sell the property on the owner's stated terms and agrees to pay the broker a commission when the property is sold, whether by the broker, the owner, or another broker. See Exclusive Listing.

Exclusive Use Zoning Restrictive zoning that only the specified usage may be made of property within the zoned district.

Exculpatory Clause A provision in a mortgage allowing the borrower to surrender the property to the lender without personal liability for the loan.

Execute To sign a contract; sometimes, to perform a contract fully.

Executed Contract A contract in which all parties have fulfilled their promises and thus performed the contract.

Execution The signing and delivery of an instrument. Also, a legal order directing an official to enforce a judgment against the property of a debtor.

Executor The person designated in a will to handle the state of the deceased. The probate court must approve any sale of property by the executor.

Executory Contract A contract under which one or more parties has not yet performed.

Executrix An older term for a woman appointed to perform the same duties as an executor. In today's vernacular, the person named to carry out the instructions of a will is usually called an *executor*, regardless of gender.

Exemption A deduction on property taxes allowed to a taxpayer because of a certain status, such as age, dependents, or service in the armed forces.

Exit Strategy The strategy or strategies available to investors when they desire to liquidate all or part of their investment.

Expansion Joint Fibrous material installed inside and around a concrete slab to allow it to move around along the nonmoving foundation wall.

Expansive Soils Soil that expands and contracts based on the amount of water present.

Expense Ratio A comparison of the Operating Expenses to Potential Gross Income. This ratio can be contrasted over time and with that of other properties to determine the relative operating efficiency of the property considered.

Expense Stop See Stop Clause.

Expenses The short-term costs that are deducted from an investment property's income, such as minor repairs, regular maintenance, and renting costs.

Expire To end, terminate.

Exposed Aggregate Finish A way of finishing concrete that washes the mixture of cement/sand away from the top layer of the aggregate usually gravel.

Exposure (Market) The advertising, whether free or paid, of property that is for sale.

Express Agency A relationship that is made by an agreement *(oral or written)* between a principal and an agent.

Expressed Contract An oral or written contract in which the parties state their terms and express their intentions in words.

Expropriation Seizure of private property for public use by an entity with such legal authority. See Condemnation, Eminent Domain.

Extended Coverage Insurance that covers specific incidences normally excluded from standard insurance policies.

Extension Agreement An agreement that extends the life of a mortgage to a later date.

Extension An agreement between two or more parties to extend the time period specified in a contract.

External Obsolescence See Economic Obsolescence.

Extrajurisdictional Territory (EJT) An area outside of the legal authority of a city or other governmental unit over which that government has limited control. The extent of the territory and the specific controls granted are determined by state law.

Extras Additional work needed from a contractor, that Is not original included in the plan. See change Order.

F

Façade Easement An arrangement, usually in a historic preservation program whereby the owner agrees to retain the original street facing façade of a building in exchange for the right to alter other exterior walls and/or the interior.

FAÇADE The outside street facing front wall of a building.

Face Amount See Face Value.

Face Interest Rate The percentage interest that is shown on the loan document. T

Face Nail Installation of nails into the vertical face of a bearing header or beam.

Face Rental Rate The asking rental rate published by the landlord.

Face Value The dollar amount, shown by words and/or numbers, on a document.

Faced Concrete To finish the front part and all the vertical sides of a concrete porch, step*(s)*, or patio.

Facility Space The floor area in hospitality properties dedicated to operating departments such as restaurants, health clubs and gift shops that service multiple guests or the general public on an interactive basis not directly related to room occupancy.

Facing Brick Exposed brick used on the outside of a wall.

Factory-Built Home A general category of housing that is produced largely in a factory. Included are Manufactured Homes, Modular Homes, and Prefabricated Homes.

FAD Multiple Share price of a REIT divided by its funds available for distribution.

FAD See Funds Available for Distribution

Fair Credit Reporting Act The Fair Credit Reporting Act *(FCRA)* was enacted in 1970 and ensures fairness, accuracy, and privacy of personal information contained in files maintained by credit reporting agencies. The goal of this act is to protect consumers from having misinformation used against them.

Fair Housing Act of 1968 The term for Title VIII of the Civil Rights Act of 1968 as amended, which prohibits discrimination based on race, color, sex, religion, national origin, handicaps, and familial status in the sale and rental of residential property.

Fair Housing Law See Federal Fair Housing Law.

Fair Market Rent the amount that a property would command if it were now available for LEASE.

Fair Market Value A property's fair market value is its accurate valuation in a free and open market under the condition that buyers and sellers are knowledgeable about the asset, acting in their best interests, and free of undue pressure to complete the transaction.

False Advertising The act of describing property in a misleading fashion.

Family Limited Partnership A Limited Partnership whose interests are owned by members of the same family. By this arrangement, gift and estate taxes may be reduced, though owners will not enjoy the freedom of ownership or transferability of other ownership vehicles.

Fannie Mae See Federal National Mortgage Association

FAR See Floor Area Ratio.

Farm Service Agency An agency of the federal government that makes mortgage loans on rural property to farmers and to individuals who provide services to farmers and ranchers.

Farmer Mac See Federal Agricultural Mortgage Corporation.

Farmer's Home Administration (FmHA) An agency, within the U.S. Department of Agriculture, that administers assistance programs for purchasers of homes and farms in small towns and rural areas.

Fascia Area facing the outside of a soffit in house construction. Also called a Fascia Board.

FDIC Federal Deposit Insurance Corporation.

Feasibility Study A determination of the likelihood that a proposed development will fulfill the objectives of a particular investor.

Federal Agricultural Mortgage Corporation **(Farmer Mac)** This organization was formed in 1988 to provide a secondary market for farm mortgages.

Federal Emergency Management Agency (FEMA) See National Flood Insurance Program.

Federal Fair Housing Law A federal law that forbids discrimination on the basis of race, color, sex, religion, handicap, familial status, or national origin in the selling or renting of homes and apartments. See Steering.

Federal Home Loan Bank System A federally created banking system primarily intended to assure liquidity to qualified thrift lenders. The Office of Thrift Supervision was established to replace the Federal Home Loan Bank Board, as part of the financial institutions reform, recovery, and enforcement act of 1989 *(FIRREA)*.

Federal Home Loan Mortgage Corporation (FHLMC) A federally chartered corporation created to provide a secondary mortgage market for conventional loans *(Freddie Mac)*.

Federal Housing Administration (FHA) A federal administrative body created by the National Housing Act in 1934 to encourage improvement in housing standards and conditions, to provide an adequate home-financing system through the insurance of housing mortgages and credit, and to exert a stabilizing influence on the mortgage market.

Federal Income Tax An annual tax based on income, including monies derived from the lease, use, or operation of real estate.

Federal National Mortgage Association (FNMA) "Fannie Mae" is the popular name for this federally chartered corporation, which creates a secondary market for existing mortgages. FNMA does not loan money directly, but rather buys DVA, FHA, and conventional loans.

Federal Register The *Federal Register* a daily bulletin published by the U.S. government that provides a record of federal actions. Typically includes executive orders, new federal regulations, and certain other documents.

Federal Reserve System The central federal banking system that regulates and provides services to member commercial banks. Also has the responsibility for conducting federal monetary policy.

Federal Revenue Stamps Stamps that, when affixed to a transaction document, indicate payment of a federal tax imposed upon the transaction. These have not been required since 1968.

Federal Rule A method for determining the just compensation for property taken in condemnation, applied in federal condemnation cases and in a number of states. Also called "Before And After" Rule.

Federal Tax Lien A debt attached against property for unpaid federal taxes; most often used by the internal revenue service to attach property for payment of owner's unpaid income taxes.

Federal Trade Commission (FTC) The FTC is a federal agency, headquartered in Washington, DC, that regulates advertising and other promotion and sales practices of firms engaged in interstate commerce. The FTC does not regulate interstate land sales *(HUD)*, anticompetitive activities *(JUSTICE)*, or sale of securities *(SEC)*.

Federal Deposit Insurance Corporation (FDIC) The FDIC maintains public confidence and encourage stability in the financial system through the promotion of sound banking practices. As of 2018, the FDIC insures deposits up to $250,000 per depositor as long as the institution is a member firm.

Federally Related Mortgage This term refers to a mortgage loan that is, in some way, subject to federal law because it is guaranteed, insured, or otherwise regulated by a government agency such as the Federal Housing Administration *(FHA)*, Veterans Administration *(VA)*, Federal National Mortgage Association *(FNMA)*, or Federal Home Loan Mortgage Corporation *(FHLMC)*.

Federally Related Transaction Real estate transaction that is overseen by a federal agency, including: Federal Reserve Board; Federal Deposit Insurance Corporation; Office of the Comptroller of Currency; Office of Thrift Supervision; National Credit Union Association; and Resolution Trust Corporation.

Federal-Style House An early-American-style house that is box-shaped and has a flat roof.

Fee Absolute See Fee Simple Absolute.

Fee Mortgage A mortgage granted by the owner of the fee simple estate of real property.

Fee See Fee Simple.

Fee Simple Absolute The inheritable estate in land providing the greatest interest of any form of title.

Fee Simple Defeasible A type of property ownership in which the grant of title or duration of ownership is dependent on a specified condition.

Fee Simple Fee simple refers to the most common type of property ownership. It means the owner's rights to the property are indefinite and can be freely transferred or inherited when the owner chooses. It is most often associated with single-family homes, as condominiums and townhomes are purchased With Covenants, Conditions, And Restrictions.

Fee Simple Interest When an owners owns all the rights in a real estate parcel.

Fee-Simple Estate The maximum possible estate or right of ownership of real property continuing forever. See "Fee Simple".

Felt Tar Paper Heavy kraft paper or fiberglass mat that is impregnated with asphalt and installed under the roof shingles. Year ago, it came in two varieties, 15 pound per square (one square = 100 Square feet) and 30 pound per square. While these varieties no longer weigh these amounts, the names have stuck. There is no tar in tar paper.

Female Any part where another part can be inserted.

Ferrule Tubes that is used to keep roof gutters open.

FF&E See Furniture, Fixtures, And Equipment.

FFO Multiple The share price of a REIT divided by its funds from operations.

FFO See Funds From Operations.

FHA Appraisal An FHA evaluation of a property as a security for a loan. Includes the study of the physical characteristics of the property and the surroundings, and the location of the property.

FHA Insured Loan See FHA mortgage.

FHA Loan A loan insured by the FHA and made by an approved lender in accordance with FHA regulations. See FHA mortgage.

FHA Mortgage The Federal Housing Administration *(FHA)* loans have been around since 1934 and are meant to help first-time homebuyers. The FHA insures the loan, making it easier for lenders to offer the homebuyer a better deal, including a lower down payment *(as low as 3.5% of the purchase price)*, low closing costs, and easier credit qualifying.

FHA See Federal Housing Administration

FHA Strap Metal straps used for repairing a bearing wall cutout, and to join wall corners, splices, and bearing headers.

FHLB Federal Home Loan Bank.

FHLMC Federal Home Loan Mortgage Corporation; aka Freddie Mac.

FHLMC See Federal Home Loan Mortgage Corporation.

FIABCI See International Real Estate Federation.

FICO Score The acronym for Fair Isaac Credit Organization. Fair, Isaac and Company, Inc. is a developer of data management systems used to rate credit risk. Fair Isaac Credit Organization changed their name to FICO in 2009. The term has evolved into a shorthand reference to credit scores created using their system.

Fidelity Bond An assurance, generally purchased by an employer, to cover employees who are entrusted with valuable property or funds.

Fiduciary One who acts, in a legal role, in the best interests of others.

Fiduciary Relationship A relationship of trust and confidence, as between trustee and beneficiary, attorney and client, principal and agent.

Field Measure Used for measurements in the home itself rather than using the blueprints.

Fifteen-Year Mortgage A fixed-rate, level-payment mortgage loan with a maturity of 15 years.

Filtering Down The process whereby, over time, a housing unit or neighborhood is occupied by progressively lower-income residents.

Final Value Estimate In an appraisal of real estate, the appraiser's value conclusion.

Finance Charge The amount paid for the privilege of deferring payment of goods or services purchased.

Financial Feasibility The ability of a proposed land use or change of land use to justify itself from an economic point of view. Financial feasibility is one test of the highest and best use of land, but not the only test. Nor does the financial feasibility of a project make it the most rewarding use of the land.

Financial Institution A company whose *"product"* involves money, such as making loans or investments and obtaining deposits. Typically a Bank or Credit Union.

Financial Institutions Reform, Recovery, And Enforcement Act (FIRREA) A federal law passed in 1989 that restructured the regulatory and deposit insurance apparatus dealing with savings and loan associations and changed the rules under which federally regulated S&Ls operate.

Financial Intermediary A firm, such as a bank or savings and loan association, which performs the function of collecting deposits from individuals and investing them in loans and other securities. Also includes credit unions and mutual savings banks.

Financial Leverage The use of borrowed money to complete an investment purchase. See Leverage.

Financial Statement Whether for business or personal, a document that shows income and expenses for an accounting period, including assets, liabilities, and equity as of a point in time.

Financing The Act of borrowing money to buy property.

Financing Expenses Amounts to pay the costs of acquiring real estate, such as interest o all loans, ground rent for leased land. Loan principal payments reduce the debt, so technically they are not expenses.

Financing Statement The form created in connection with the UCC and designed to be filed in one or more official government offices to perfect a creditor's security interest.

Finder's Fee Money paid to someone other than a broker who locates suitable property a purchaser. Prohibited or limited in most states.

Finger Joint Joining two short pieces of wood to create a longer piece.

Finish Out Allowance A provision in a lease for an office or retail space that provides certain sum or amount per square foot to the tenant to customize the space provided.

Fire Block A short horizontal members sometimes nailed between studs, usually about halfway up a wall.

Fire Brick A type of brick that is made from refractory ceramic material which can resist high temperatures.

Fire Rated Fire rated means that a product has been evaluated to determine relative Flame Spread and Smoke Developed indices. Based on these indices, a rating is developed for the product. Fire-rated laminates typically have a special composition in order to have low flame spread and smoke developed properties when burned. See Fire resistant and Fireproof.

Fire Retardant Chemical A chemical that is used to reduce the flammable ability of a material.

Fire Stop A tight enclosure of a concealed space for the prevention of the spread of fire and smoke through such a space.

Fireplace Chase Flashing Pan A large sheet of metal created to limit the spread of fire and smoke to small areas.

Fireproof Having all exposed surfaces constructed of noncombustible materials or protected by such materials.

Fire-Resistant Able to withstand exposure to flame of a specified intensity or for a specified time.

Firewall

1. A partition of fireproof material intended to contain an outbreak of fire to a limited area.
2. A legal barrier in a financial institution to prevent losses in one department from affecting another department.
3. Software or hardware that protects an individual computer or a network from intrusion.

Firm Commitment An irrevocable agreement that commits one of the parties to perform a certain act; most common in reference to commitments by lenders to provide financing.

FIRREA See Financial Institutions Reform, Recovery And Enforcement Act.

First Mortgage The senior mortgage that, by reason of its position, has priority over all junior encumbrances. The holder has a priority right to payment in the event of default. This is a mortgage that creates a superior voluntary lien on the property mortgaged relative to other charges or encumbrances against the property.

First Refusal Right Lease clause giving a tenant the first opportunity to buy a property or lease additional space in a property at the same price and on the same terms and conditions as those contained in a third-party offer that the owner has expressed a willingness to accept.

First-Generation Space Generally refers to new space that is currently available for lease and has never before been occupied by a tenant.

First-Loss Position The position in a security that will suffer the first economic loss if the underlying assets lose value or are foreclosed on. The first-loss position carries a higher risk and a higher yield.

First-Year Depreciation See Additional First-Year Depreciation.

Fiscal Policy The government's policy in regard to taxation and spending programs. The balance between these two areas determines the amount of money the government will withdraw or feed into the economy in an attempt to counter economic peaks and slumps.

Fiscal Year A continuous 12-month time interval used for financial reporting; the period starts on any date after January 1 and ends one year later.

Fish Tape A long strip of spring steel that is used for fishing cables and also for pulling wires through conduit.

Fishplate Gusset Piece of wood or plywood that is used for tightening the ends of two members together at a butt joint with nails or bolts.

Fixed Assets In a company financial statement, tangible property that is used in the business operations and not for sale.

Fixed Bid An estimated cost, based on plans and specifications, that will also be the actual cost of the job.

Fixed Costs Fixed costs are costs that do not fluctuate in proportion to the level of sales or production.

Fixed Expenses In the operation of real estate, those expenses that remain the same regardless of occupancy.

Fixed Lease An arrangement made where the lessee pays an amount that is fixed for the space.

Fixed Payment Mortgage A loan secured by real property that features a periodic payment of interest and principal that is constant over the term of the loan.

Fixed Price Contract A contract that has it price already set.

Fixed Rate An interest rate that remains constant over the term of the loan.

Fixed-Rate Mortgage A fixed-rate mortgage is one of the most common types of loans. It comes with an interest rate that stays the same for the lifetime of the loan, and provides the borrower with more stability and predictability over the lifetime of their loan.

Fixture An article that was once personal property but has been so affixed to real estate that it has become real property.

Flagstone Flat stones that is used for steps, walks, floors, and vertical veneer in the place of bricks. Also called flagging or flags.

Flakeboard A wood panel made out of 1" 2" wood chips and glue. Mostly used for replacing plywood inside the exterior wall and roof sheathing.

Flame Retention Burner An oil burner that is created for holding the flame close to the surface of the nozzle.

Flashing A metal sheet or other material that is used for roofing and wall construction purpose so as to protect a structure from water.

Flat

1. An apartment, generally on one level.
2. A level payment mortgage or lease requirement.

Flat Fee A fee paid to an adviser or manager for managing a portfolio of real estate assets, typically stated as a flat percentage of gross asset value, net asset value or invested capital.

Flat Fee Broker A licensed broker who charges a fixed fee for the provision of brokerage services instead of a commission based on a percentage of the sales price of the property.

Flat Lease See Straight Lease.

Flat Mold A thin wood strips that is mounted over the butt seam of cabinet skins.

Flat Paint Interior paint containing a large amount of pigment and dries to a lusterless finish.

Flatwork A general word used for concrete floors, driveways, basements, and sidewalks.

Flex Space A building that provides a configuration allowing occupants a flexible amount of office or showroom space in combination with manufacturing, laboratory, warehouse, distribution, etc.

Flexible-Payment Mortgage A mortgage with payments that are allowed to vary but should be sufficient to allow amortization over the mortgage term.

Flip Tax A fee that a co-op corporation charges a seller at the closing.

Flipping When an investor buys a property, and then sells it as quickly as possible at a profit.

Float

1. The interval of time after a deposit or withdrawal is made and before the transaction is credited or deducted.
2. The difference between a variable interest rate and the index to which it is pegged.
3. To incur a debt.
4. The number of freely traded shares in the hands of the public.

Floating Rate A loan interest that varies, known as an Adjustable Rate Mortgage (ARM).

Floating Slab Foundation that is constructed by first pouring the footing and then pouring the slab after the footing has set.

Floating Wall A non-bearing wall on a concrete floor.

Floating The second to final stages in concrete and drywall work. In concrete, it is when you smooth the work and bring water to the surface by using hand float.

Flood Insurance An insurance policy that covers property damage due to natural flooding. Flood insurance is offered by private insurers but is subsidized by the federal government.

Floodplain A level land area subject to periodic flooding Floodplains are delineated by the expected frequency of flooding.

Floor Area Ratio (FAR) The ratio of the gross square footage of a building to the square footage of the land on which it is situated.

Floor Load Capacity The weight that a building's floors can support, generally measured per square foot.

Floor Loan The minimum that a lender is willing to advance. See Gap Loan, Bridge Loan.

Floor Plan The arrangement of rooms in a building, or a one-plane diagram of that arrangement.

Floor-Area Ratio (FAR) The arithmetic relationship of the total square feet of a building to the square footage of the land area. The floor-area ratio is often limited by the zoning code and may have an important influence on the land value.

Flue The chamber in a fireplace that helps direct smoke through the chimney to outside air.

Flue Collar Round metal ring that fits around the heat flue pipe when the pipe passes out of the roof.

Flue Damper An automatic door inside a furnace which closes anytime the burner goes off, so as reduce heat loss.

Flue Lining A fire clay that is used for inner lining of chimneys with the brick work done around the outside.

Fluorescent Lighting A glass tube filled with gas, with the inside coated with phosphorus.

Fly Rafters End rafters of the gable overhang supported by roof sheathing and lookouts.

FmHA See Farmer's Home Administration.

FMRR See Financial Management Rate Of Return.

FMV See Fair Market Value.

FNMA See Federal National Mortgage Association.

Follow On Offering See Secondary Offering.

Footer See Footing.

Footing A concrete base that is below the frost line supporting the foundation of a building.

For Sale By Owner Homes listed as for sales by owner *(FSBO)* are being sold without the help of a real estate agent. The biggest benefit to the seller is they avoid paying commission fees -- but there are few benefits to the buyer.

Forbearance

1. A policy of restraint in taking legal action to remedy a default or other breach of contract, generally in the hope that the default will be cured, given additional time.

2. Forbearance is a temporary postponement of mortgage payments or Student Loan Payments . It is a form of repayment relief granted by the lender or creditor in lieu of forcing a property into foreclosure.

Force Majeure A force that cannot be controlled by the parties to a contract and prevents them from complying with the provisions of the contract. This includes acts of God such as a flood or a hurricane, or acts of man such as a strike, fire, or war.

Forced Air Heating A form of heating that is commonly used in the United States.

Forcible Entry And Detainer A summary proceeding for restoring to possession of land one who is wrongfully kept out or has been wrongfully deprived of the possession.

Foreclosing The Right Of Redemption In Tax Sales, If the owner has failed to pay off the lien and the redemption period has expired, the lien holder may then foreclose on the property.

Foreclosure A legal procedure by which property used as security for a debt is sold to satisfy the debt in the event of default in payment of the mortgage note or default of other terms in the mortgage document. The foreclosure procedure brings the rights of all parties to a conclusion and passes the title in the mortgaged property either to the holder of the mortgage or to a third party who may purchase the realty at the foreclosure sale, free of all encumbrances affecting the property subsequent to the mortgage. If a homeowner doesn't make a mortgage payment *(usually, for more than 90 days)*, foreclosure is a legal process during which the owner forfeits all property rights. If they are unable to pay off outstanding debt on the property or sell it via short sale, the property enters a foreclosure auction. If no sale is made there, the lender takes control of the property.

Foreclosure Sale The public sale of a mortgaged property following foreclosure of the loan secured by that property. Depending on the type of foreclosure proceeding, the sale may be administered by the courts *(Judicial Foreclosure)* or by an appointed trustee *(Statutory Foreclosure)*. Proceeds of the sale are used to satisfy the claims of the mortgagee primarily, with any excess going to the mortgagor.

Foreign Acknowledgment An acknowledgment taken outside of the state in which the land lies.

Forfeiture Loss of money or anything else of value because of failure to perform under the terms of the contract.

Form Appraisal See Uniform Residential Appraisal Report *(URAR)*.

Form A structure that is temporary erected to contain concrete during placing and initial hardening.

Forward Commitments Contractual obligations to perform certain financing activities upon the satisfaction of any stated conditions. Usually used to describe a lender's obligation to fund a mortgage.

Foundation

1. A foundation is a nonprofit organization that raises money and invests it to generate income to fund its charitable efforts or donate funds to support other charitable causes.
2. A supporting structure that is below the first floor construction.

Foundation Ties A metal wires holding the foundation wall panels and rebar in place when concrete is poured.

Foundation Waterproofing A Top quality moisture protection. That is used to seal out moisture and prevent corrosion.

Four Quadrants Of The Real Estate Capital Markets
1. Private Equity: Direct real estate investments acquired privately.
2. Public Equity: REITs and other publicly traded real estate operating companies.
3. Private Debt: Whole loan mortgages.
4. Public Debt: Commercial mortgage-backed securities and other securitized forms of whole loan mortgage interests

Four-Plex A building containing four dwelling units.

Four-Three-Two-One Rule For an area with commercial lots of uniform depth, the idea that 40% of the value lies in the front quarter, 30% in the next quarter, then 20%, and 10%. If part of the property is condemned by eminent domain, this provides some guidance as to the value of the part taken.

FPM Flexible Payment Mortgage.

Fractional Interest Ownership of some but not all of the rights in real estate.

Frame Inspection The process of inspecting the home's structural integrity and verifying its compliance with local municipal codes. Typically completed when home is *"In the Dry"*.

Framer The carpenter contractor that fixes the lumber and erects and installs all beams and any work that is related to wood structure of the property.

Framing Wood that is used for the structural part of a house, like studs, joists, and rafters.

Franchise A private contractual agreement to run a business using a designated trade name and

Fraud A misstatement of a material fact made with intent to deceive or made with reckless disregard of the truth and that actually does deceive.

Freddie Mac See Federal Home Loan Mortgage Corporation.

Free And Clear Title The title to a property without encumbrances. Generally used to refer to a property free of mortgage debt.

Freehold An interest in real estate, not less than an estate for life.

Freehold Estate An estate in land in which ownership is for an indeterminate length of time, in contrast to a leasehold estate.

French Provincial A French-style formal, 1 to 2-story house that is perfectly balanced with a high, steep hip roof and curve-headed upper windows that break through the cornice.

Friable Crumbly, brittle. When asbestos is friable, it crumbles and may release fibers or particles that become airborne dust. In that state it is hazardous because it may enter a person's lungs.

Frieze Board Wooden part fastened under the soffit against a wall.

Frieze A horizontal member that links the top of the siding with the soffit of the cornice.

Front Foot A linear foot of property frontage on a street.

Front Money Cash necessary to start a development project.

Frontage The linear distance of a piece of land along a lake, river, street, or highway.

Frost Lid A typically round metal lid installed on a water meter pit.

Frost Line The depth of frost penetration in soil or depth at which the earth will freeze and swell.

FSBO See For Sale By Owner

FSG See Full Service Gross.

FTC See Federal Trade Commission.

Full Bath A bathroom that has sink, toilet, and a bathtub.

Full Disclosure A requirement to reveal all information pertinent to a transaction.

Full Recourse A loan on which an endorser or guarantor is liable in the event of default by the borrower.

Full Service Gross (FSG) A lease requiring the owner to pay all Operating Expenses, such as cleaning, maintenance and repairs, utilities, insurance, and ad valorem taxes.

Full-Service Rent An all-inclusive rental rate that includes operating expenses and real estate taxes for the first year. The tenant is generally still responsible for any increase in operating expenses over the base year amount.

Fully Amortized Loan One having payments of interest and principal that are sufficient to liquidate the loan over its term. Self-liquidating.

Fully Amortizing Mortgage A Mortgage that comes with a scheduled uniform payment for the loan repayment over the term of the mortgage. See Fully Amortized Loan.

Fully Diluted Shares The number of shares of common stock that would be outstanding if all convertible securities were converted to common shares.

Fully Indexed Rate In conjunction with Adjustable Rate Mortgages, the interest rate indicated by the sum of the current value of the index and margin applied to the loan. This rate is the interest rate that is used to calculate monthly payments in the absence of constraints imposed by the Initial Rate or Caps.

Functional Depreciation See Functional Obsolescence.

Functional Modern House A post-World War II style house with an exterior style that is an integral part of the overall design. Its function is to enclose some living areas with modern materials while integrating the indoor and outdoor space into one unit.

Functional Obsolescence The impairment of functional capacity or efficiency; the inability of a structure to perform adequately the function for which it currently is employed. Functional obsolescence reflects the loss in value brought about by factors that affect the property, such as overcapacity, inadequacy, or changes in the art.

Funding Supplying cash for a loan.

Funding Fee A fee required by the Department of Veterans Affairs for making a VA guaranteed loan. The funding fee is added in with the loan and then forwarded to the VA to guarantee a veteran's loan.

Funds Available For Distribution (FAD) Funds from operations less deductions for cash expenditures for leasing commissions and tenant improvement costs.

Funds From Operations (FFO) A ratio intended to highlight the amount of cash generated by a company's real estate portfolio relative to its total operating cash flow. FFO is equal to net income, excluding gains or losses from debt restructuring and sales of property, plus depreciation and amortization.

Furniture, Fixtures, And Equipment (FF&E) a term frequently found in the ownership of a hotel or motel. This type of property wears out much more rapidly than other components of a hotel or motel, so an owner or prospective buyer needs to establish the condition, cost, and frequency of replacement of FF&E.

Furring Strips Strips of wood, typically about 1 X 2 used in shimming out and providing a level fastening surface for a wall or ceiling.

Fuse A device that is found in homes with old design so as to prevent overloads in electrical lines.

Future Interest A person's present right to an interest in real property that will not result in possession or enjoyment until sometime in the future, such as a reversion or right of reentry.

Future Proposed Space A space in a proposed commercial development that is not yet under construction or where no construction start date has been set. It also may refer to the future phases of a multi-phase project not yet built.

Future Worth Of One Per Period See Compound Amount Of One Per Period.

Future Worth Of One See Compound Amount of One.

FY See Fiscal Year.

G

GAAP See Generally Accepted Accounting Principles.

Gable Roof A roof that consists of two different opposite sloping planes intersecting at a level ridge.

Gable The end and upper triangular area in a house that is beneath the roof.

Gain An increase in money or property value. See Capital Gain, Realized Gain, Recognized Gain.

Gambrel Roof One having two slopes on two sides with a steeper lower slope than the upper, flatter sections.

Gang Nail Plate A plate attached to both sides at each joint of a truss. Also known as gusset. See Fishplate.

Gap A defect in the chain of title of a particular parcel of real estate; a missing document or conveyance that raises doubt as to the present ownership of the land.

Gap Loan One that fills the difference between the Floor Loan and the full amount of the Permanent Loan. See Bridge Loan, Swing Loan.

Garden Apartments A housing complex whereby some or all tenants have access to a lawn area.

Gas Lateral Trench where the gas line service is situated, or the work of fixing the gas service to a home.

Gate Valve A type valve that allows you stop the flow within a pipe.

Gated Community A fenced housing development, typically having a security guard.

Gazebo A small, partially enclosed roofed structure in a park or garden affording shade and rest.

Gazumping A slang term to describe the practice of reneging on an oral commitment to buy or sell a property. Often it means the seller raises the price after he and the buyer agreed verbally on a lower price.

GEM See Growing Equity Mortgage.

General Agent An agent who has the authority to act for a principal's business within certain limitations.

General And Administrative Expenses (G&A) The compensation for management to operate or build a property.

General Contractor A construction specialist who enters into Typically written and at least formal construction contracts with a landowner, master lessee, developer, or other entity in control of a property, to construct a real estate building or project. The general contractor usually contracts with and manages many subcontractors specializing in various aspects of the building process to perform individual jobs.

General Lien A lien on all real and personal property owned by a debtor.

General Partner A member of a partnership who has authority to bind the partnership and shares in the profits and losses of the partnership.

General Warranty Deed A deed that states that the title conveyed therein is good from the sovereignty of the soil to the grantee therein and that no one else can successfully claim the property. This type of deed contains several specific warranties sometimes referred to as the English Covenants of Title.

Generally Accepted Accounting Principles (GAAP) The set of rules considered standard and acceptable by Certified Public Accountants.

Gentrification The displacement of lower-income residents by higher-income residents in a neighborhood. Generally occurs when an older neighborhood is rehabilitated or revitalized.

Geographic Information Systems (GIS) A computer mapping program where land characteristics and/or demographic information are color coded and often overlaid. The purpose is to determine locations of certain activity.

Georgian Style Home A large, English-style, formal 2 or 3-story rectangular house that is characterized by its classic lines and ornamentation.

GFCI Also called GFI & Ground Fault Circuit Interrupter. An ultra-sensitive plug which includes its own circuit breaker, made for switching off all electric current. Mostly used in bathrooms, kitchens, exterior waterproof outlets, garage outlets.

GI Loan See VA Loan.

Gift Deed A deed for which consideration is *"love and affection"* and no material consideration is involved.

Gift Tax The federal tax imposed upon a monetary gift to a relative or friend. Generally, each person may give up to $10,000 per year to each donee without imposition of a federal gift tax. on higher gifts, there may be a gift tax, or the gift may affect the donor's estate tax.

GIM See Gross Income Multiplier.

Ginnie Mae Slang name for Government National Mortgage Association.

Ginnie Mae Pass Through A Pass-Through Certificate secured by a pool of mortgage loans insured by the Government National Mortgage Association, an arm of the federal government.

Girder The main beam of wood or steel that is used in supporting concentrated loads at isolated points along its length.

GIS See Geographic Information Systems.

GLA See Gross Leasable Area.

Glazing The method used in installation of glass, which is usually secured with glazier's points and glazing compound.

Glide Path The formula in the design of a target date fund that defines the asset allocation mix for the fund, based on the number of years to the target date. The glide path defines an asset allocation that becomes more conservative *(more fixed-income assets and fewer equities, for example)* the closer a fund gets to its target date.

Globe Valve A valve used to adjust water flow to any rate between fully on and fully off.

Gloss Enamel Paint material used for finishing that forms hard coating and gives maximum smoothness of surface and dries to a sheen or luster

Glued Laminated Beam A structural beam made from wood laminations or lams.

Glulam Slang term for Glued Laminated Bean.

GNMA See Government National Mortgage Association.

GNP See Gross National Product.

Going Concern Value The entire value of a business, which includes not only its assets if liquidated, but also the premium often commanded by a business for being a unified organization with customers, an existing work force, market share, credit lines, and so on.

Going-In Capitalization Rate The capitalization rate computed by dividing the projected first year's net operating income by the value of the property.

Good And Marketable Title The title to a piece of real estate that can be shown, usually by title search or abstract of title to be vested in the owner of record, and free of any claims or liens that would impair its marketability.

Good And Merchantable Title See Good And Marketable Title.

Good Faith The general concept of honesty in business.

Good Faith Estimate Under the Real Estate Settlement Procedures Act, an estimate of closing costs that must be given by a lender to mortgage applicants *(for residential loans on one to four units)* within three days after loan application is made.

Good Faith Money See Earnest Money.

Good Title See Good And Marketable Title, Clear Title.

Goodwill An asset created by good customer relations.

Government lots Fractional sections in the rectangular survey system *(government survey method)* that are less than one full quarter-section in area.

Government National Mortgage Association (Ginnie Mae or GNMA) A government organization to assist in housing finance. Nicknamed GINNIE MAE, there are two main programs:

1. To guarantee payments to investors in mortgage-backed securities
2. To absorb the write-down of low-interest rate loans that are used to finance low-income housing

Government Rectangular Survey A rectangular system of land survey that divides a district into 24-square mile quadrangles from the meridian *(north-south line)* and the baseline *(east-west line)*; the tracts are divided into 6-mile-square parts called townships, which are in turn divided into 36 tracts, each 1 mile square, called sections. See Public Land Survey System.

Government-Sponsored Enterprise (GSE) A quasi-govern-mental organization that is privately owned but was created by the government and retains certain privileges not afforded to private entities.

GPM Graduated-Payment Mortgage.

Grace Period Additional time allowed to perform an act or make a payment before a default occurs.

Grade Beam A foundation wall poured at a level with or just below the grade of the earth.

Grade Ground level or the elevation at any given point: The work of leveling dirt or the designated quality of a manufactured piece of wood.

Graded Lease See Step Up Lease, Graduated Lease

Gradient the slope or rate of increase or decrease in the elevation of a surface; usually expressed as a percentage:

Grading Permit Approval to change the contour of the land through excavation and dirt work.

Graduated lease A lease that provides for rent increases at set future dates; typically Long term in nature.

Graduated Payment Mortgage A mortgage loan for which the initial payments are low but increase over the life of the loan.

Grain The size, direction, arrangement, appearance, or quality of the light and dark fibers in wood.

Grandfather Clause A clause that allows an activity to continue once considered acceptable or legal but has since had the rules or laws changed.

Grant Deed A type of deed that includes three basic warranties:
1. The owner warrants that she or he has the right to convey the property.
2. The owner warrants that the property is not encumbered other than with those encumbrances listed in the deed.
3. The owner promises to convey any after-acquired title to the property. Grant deeds are popular in states that rely heavily on title insurance

Grant The act of conveying or transferring title to real property.

Grantee A person to whom real estate is conveyed; the buyer.

Grantor A person who conveys real estate by deed; the seller.

Grantor/Grantee Index A reference kept with public records that cross-indexes grantors and grantees with one another and the properties they relate to.

Greenbelt An area of undeveloped land around a residential area, intended to preserve open space and a natural environment. Often enforced by covenant, deed restriction, or city zoning.

GRI A graduate of the Realtors® Institute, which is affiliated with the National Association Of Realtors®.

Grid The completed assembly of main and cross tees in a suspended ceiling system before the ceiling panels is installed.

GRM See Gross Rent Multiplier.

Gross Area The total floor area of a building, usually measured from its outside walls.

Gross Building Area The sum of areas at each floor level, including basements, mezzanines and penthouses included within the principal outside faces of the exterior walls and neglecting architectural setbacks or projections.

Gross Earnings An individual's taxable income before any adjustments such as deductions, depreciation and other calculations are made. See, Gross Income.

Gross Income Multiplier (GIM) See Gross Rent Multiplier.

Gross Income Total income from property before any expenses are deducted. See Gross Earnings.

Gross Investment In Real Estate The total amount of equity and debt invested in real estate investments, including the gross purchase price, all acquisition fees and costs, plus subsequent capital improvements, less proceeds from sales and partial sales.

Gross Leasable Area The portion of total floor area designed for tenants' occupancy and exclusive use, including storage areas. It is the total area that produces rental income.

Gross Lease A lease or property under which a landlord pays all property charges regularly incurred through ownership, such as repairs, taxes, insurance, and operating expenses. Most residential leases are gross leases.

Gross National Product (GNP) The total value of all goods and services produced in the United States *(or other country)* in any given year.

Gross Possible Rent See Gross Potential Income.

Gross Potential Income See Total Scheduled Rental Income.

Gross Profit Ratio In an installment sale, the relationship between the gross profit *(gain)* and the contract price. the resulting fraction is applied to periodic receipts from the buyer to determine the taxable gain from each receipt.

Gross Real Estate Asset Value The market value of the total real estate investments under management in a fund or individual accounts. It typically includes the total value of all equity positions, debt positions and joint venture ownership positions, including the amount of any mortgages or notes payable related to those assets.

Gross Real Estate Investment Value The market value of real estate investments held in a portfolio without regard to debt, equal to the total of real estate investments as shown on a statement of assets and liabilities on a market-value basis.

Gross Rent Multiplier (GRM) A figure used as a multiplier of the gross monthly rental income of a property to produce an estimate of the property's value.

Gross Square Foot Unit of measurement of a building used when measuring from out-side the exterior walls.

Ground Fault Circuit Interrupter An ultra-sensitive device that is installed in outlet plugs made for monitoring and disrupting the flow of electrical current when a hazardous events happens. See GFCI.

Ground Iron Waste lines and plumbing drain installed under the basement floor.

Ground Lease A lease of land only, on which the tenant usually owns a building or is required to builder her or his own building as specified in the lease. Such leases are usually long-term net leases; a tenant's rights and obligations continue until the lease expires or is terminated through default.

Ground Rent Earnings of improved property credited to earning of the ground itself after allowance made for earnings of improvements.

Ground An electrical way of seeking the shortest route to earth.

Groundwater Water from an aquifer or subsurface water source.

Group Boycott An agreement between members of a trade to exclude other members from fair participation in the trade.

Group Home A residence serving the special needs of a group of people. Not considered a household. Most often, group homes allow the physically or mentally disabled or those recovering from some affliction or dependency to live together and access support services from those operating the home.

Group Quarters Types of housing in which unrelated groups of people reside. See Group Home.

Grout A mixture of Portland cement, sand and water that is wet; flowing into masonry or ceramic crevices to seal the cracks between the different pieces.

Growing-Equity Mortgage (GEM) A mortgage loan in which the payment is increased by a specific amount each year, with the additional payment amount applied to principal retirement. As a result of the added principal retirement, the maturity of the loan is significantly shorter than a comparable level-payment mortgage.

Guaranteed Sale Plan An agreement between the broker and the seller that if the seller's real property is not sold before a certain date, the broker will purchase it for a specified price.

Guaranty The agreement of a person or entity to pay amounts due, or otherwise perform the obligations, of another person or entity.

Guardian One who guards or cares for another person's rights and properties. A guardian has legal custody of the affairs of a minor or a person incapable of taking care of his or her own interests, called a ward.

Gusset A flat wood, plywood that is used to provide connection at the intersection of wood members. Commonly used at a joints of wood trusses.

Gutter Shallow channel set below or along the fascia in a house to trap and carry off rainwater from the roof.

Gyp Board A panel design with a core of Gypsum rock, covering interior walls and ceilings. See Drywall.

Gypsum Plaster Gypsum made to be used together with sand and water for basecoat plaster.

H

H Clip A small metal clips with an *"H"* shape that connects at the joints of two plywood sheets to stiffen the joint. Used mostly on plywood or OSB roof decking sheets.

HVAC An abbreviation meaning Heat, Ventilation, and Air Conditioning

Habendum Clause The deed clause beginning *"to have and to hold,"* which defines or limits the extend of ownership in the state granted by the deed.

Half Bath A room in a residence that contains a toilet and wash basin but no bath or shower. Sometimes a bathroom will be called ¾ which generally means it has a shower stall, with a sink and toilet, but no bath.

Handyman's Special In real estate classified advertising, generally refers to a house that requires extensive repair and remodeling, selling at a relatively low price. Used most often by those who refer to themselves as wholesalers.

Hangout The remaining balance of a loan when the term of the loan is beyond the term of a lease.

Hard Cost The cost of actually constructing property improvements.

Hard Money Loans Used by investors who may have a risky credit background. The basis for these loans is solely the *"quick sale"* value of the property.

Hard Money See Hard Money Loans.

Hardware This is a term used to denote all the metal fittings used in the home.

Haunch An extension, that is knee-like in extension of the foundation wall that a concrete porch or patio used for support.

Hazard Insurance Protection from damage caused by fire, windstorms, or other common hazards. Many lenders require borrowers to carry it in an amount at least equal to the mortgage.

Hazardous Substance Any of a broad variety of contaminants regulated under CERCLA.

Hazardous Waste A type of solid waste that poses a significant threat to human health.

Header
1.   A beam that is placed perpendicular to joists to which joists can be nailed in framing for a chimney, stairway, or other opening.
2.   A lintel made from wood
3.   The horizontal structural member over an opening.

Hearing A formal procedure, with issues of fact or law to be tried, in which parties have a right to be heard. Similar to a trial and may result in a final order.

Hearth The inside and outside flooring of a fireplace. Made from of stone, tile, or brick.

Heat Meter An electrical municipal inspection of the electric meter breaker panel box.

Heat Pump A device that uses the system of compression and decompression of gas for heating or cooling in the house.

Heat Rough Work carried out by the Heating Contractor after the stairs and interior walls are built.

Heat Trim The finish work carried out by the Heating and Air Contractor to get the home ready for the municipal Final Heat Inspection.

Heating Load Amount of heat that is needed to keep a building at a specific temperature during the winter, regardless of outside temperature. Usually Measured in BTUs.

Hectare A metric land measurement equal to about 2.471 acres or about 107,637 square feet.

Heel Cut A notch cut that is made in the end of a rafter to make it to fit flat on a wall and on the top, doubled, exterior wall plate.

Heir One who might inherit or succeed to an interest in land under the state law of descent when the owner dies without leaving a valid will.

Heirs And Assigns A term often found in deeds and wills to grant a fee simple estate.

HELOC See Home Equity Line of Credit

Hereditaments Every kind of inheritable property, including person, real, corporeal, and incorporeal.

Hidden Defect A title defect that is not apparent from examination of the public record. See Latent Defect.

Hidden Fees Fees put in the contract without being disclosed to the borrower.

High Interest Loans A loan that is 8% above the yield on a comparable treasury on a first mortgage according to Home Ownership and Equity Protection Act of 1994 *(HOEPA)* guidelines, or a loan that is 10% above the yield on a comparable treasury on a second mortgage.

High Loan-To-Value Loan Aa loan covering more than 100% of the market value of the home. Typical coverage is 125% of value. Such loans are used exclusively as a refinancing tool, which essentially makes them a Home Equity Loan. Loans of this type are inherently high-risk and generally are reserved for the lowest-risk borrowers. Lenders also are gambling on the borrower's aversion to foreclosure, since a portion of the loan is unsecured, based on the equity of the property.

High Victorian A nineteenth-century-style house with three different kinds of window arches, the primary distinguishing characteristic of this style. The arches are straight-sided, flat-topped, and rectangular.

Highest And Best Use The reasonably probable and legal use of vacant land or an improved property that is physically possible, appropriately supported, financially feasible and that results in the highest value.

Highlights A light spot, area, or streak on a painted surface.

High-Rise In the central business district, this could mean a building higher than 25 stories above ground level, but in suburban markets, it generally refers to buildings higher than seven or eight stories.

Hip Roof One formed by four walls sloped in different directions with the two longer sides forming a ridge at the top.

Historic District A geographically definable area that possesses a significant concentration of buildings that are united architecturally, historically, or aesthetically.

Historic Structure A building that is officially recognized for its historic significance and therefore has special income tax status. This encourages rehabilitation and discourages demolition or substantial alteration of the structure. Qualified rehabilitation expenses to Certified Historic Structures can be eligible for up to a 20% tax credit.

HOA See Homeowner's Association

Hold Harmless Clause In a contract, a clause whereby one party agrees to protect another party from claims.

Holdbacks A portion of a loan commitment that is not funded until an additional requirement is met, such as completion of construction.

Holder In Due Course One who acquires a bearer instrument in good faith and is eligible to keep it even though it may have been stolen.

Holding Company One that owns or controls another company or companies.

Holding Costs See Carrying Costs.

Holding Period The length of time an investor expects to own a property from purchase to sale.

Holdout A landowner in the path of an assemblage who attempts to realize the highest possible price by refusing to sell in the early stages of assemblage.

Holdover Tenancy A tenancy by which a lessee retains possession of a leased property after her or his lease has expired and the landlord, by continuing to accept rent from the tenant, agrees to the tenant's continued occupancy as defined by state law.

Hold-Over Tenant A tenant retaining possession of the leased premises after the expiration of a lease.

Holographic Will A will that is written, dated, and signed in the handwriting of the maker.

Home A structure or space considered by its occupants to be their primary residence. A House. A Dwelling.

Home Equity Conversion Mortgage The Home Equity Conversion Mortgage (HECM) is an FHA reverse mortgage program enabling homeowners to withdraw equity on their home through either a fixed monthly payment, a line of credit, or a combination of the two.

Home Equity Line of Credit Often called HELOC, is a loan in which the lender agrees to lend a maximum amount within an agreed period called a term, where the collateral is the borrower's equity in his/her house. Typically it is seen as a second mortgage. Usually it is a revolving account. Because a home often is a consumer's most valuable asset, many homeowners use home equity credit lines only for major items, such as education, home improvements, or medical bills, and choose not to use them for day-to-day expenses.

Home Equity Loan A loan secured by a second mortgage on one's principal residence, generally to be used for some non-housing expenditure. Generally two types are available. A Line-Of-Credit home equity loan establishes a credit line that can be drawn upon as needed. A traditional Second Mortgage provides lump-sum proceeds at the time the loan is closed.

Home Equity Loan See Home Equity Line of Credit.

Home Improvement Loan A loan, usually secured by a mortgage on the home, used to pay for major remodeling, reconstruction, or additions to the home.

Home Inspection A home inspection is carried out by an objective third party to establish the condition of a property during a real estate transaction. An inspector will report on such things as a home's heating system, the stability of the foundation, and the condition of the roof. The inspection is meant to identify major issues that might affect the value of the home and the stability of your and your lender's investment and return.

Home Inspector A professional who evaluates the structural and mechanical condition of a home prior to its being sold. Some states require home inspectors to be bonded or licensed.

Home Loan See Mortgage.

Home Office A portion of one's home used for business purposes.

Home Run The electrical cable that carries power from the main circuit breaker panel to the first electrical box, plug, or switch in the circuit.

Home Sale Tax See Section 121.

Homeowner Warranty Insurance See Homeowners' Warranty Program.

Homeowner's Association A homeowner's association *(HOA)* is usually found when you purchase a condominium, townhome, or other planned development property. To purchase the home, you must also join the HOA and pay monthly or yearly HOA fees. These fees can cover common area maintenance, repairs, and general upkeep. The more amenities your building or development offers, the higher the HOA fees typically are.

Homeowner's Insurance Policy A standardized package insurance policy that covers a residential real estate owner against financial loss from fire, theft, public liability, and other common risks. See Homeowner's insurance.

Homeowner's Insurance When you purchase a home, it's also necessary to purchase homeowner's insurance to cover any losses or damages you might incur, such as natural disaster, theft, or damage. It also protects the homeowner from liability against any accidents in the home or on the property. Insurance payments are usually included in your monthly mortgage payments.

Homeowner's Warranty Program (HOW) An insurance program offered to buyers by some brokerages, warranting the property against certain defects for a specified period of time.

Homeowners Protection Act Of 1997   Requires private mortgage companies to inform borrowers of their right to cancel mortgage insurance when the loan amount is no more than 80 percent of the value of the home. When the loan is no more than 78 percent of value, insurance is automatically cancelled. Covers mortgage loans originated after July 31, 1999. Automatic cancellation under the law is based on the value of the home when the loan was originated or may be based on a market-value appraisal paid for by the borrower. Lenders may retain insurance coverage on loans where there has been a recent history of delinquent payments.

Homeownership Rate   The percentage ratio of owner-occupied dwelling units to total occupied dwelling units in an area.

Homeownership   The state of living in a structure that one owns. Contrasted with being a renter or tenant in one's home.

Homer Hoyt Institute (HHI)   An independent, nonprofit research and educational foundation established in 1968 that contributes to improving the quality of public and private real estate decisions.

Homestead Estate   Property protected as a homestead.

Homestead Exemption   In some jurisdictions, a reduction in the assessed value allowed for one's principal residence.

Homestead Provision   The land and the improvements thereon designated by the owner as his or her homestead and, therefore, protected by state law, either in whole or in part, from forced sale by certain creditors of the owner.

Homestead   The primary residence of a property owner. Many states provide property tax exemptions for the primary residence.

Homogeneous   Uniform or of like characteristics or quality. Opposite of heterogeneous . The values of an area tend to be maximized when properties are homogeneous, because low-valued or unusual properties are likely to reduce the value of other nearby properties of higher cost.

Honeycombs   The appearance concrete makes when rocks in the concrete are visible and where there are void areas in the foundation wall, especially around concrete foundation windows.

Horizontal Property Laws   State statutes that enable condominium ownership of property. Whereas property laws generally recognize ownership rights to all space from the center of the earth to some distance in the air, condominium laws allow individual ownership to be split on a horizontal plane that generally limits the unit owner's interest to the inside dimensions of the unit. See Common Elements.

Hose Bib   Sill cock or an exterior wall faucet.

Hose Wire   A type of wire used to transfer electrical current to other receiving device, usually a black wire.

House   In real estate usage, a residential structure containing a single Dwelling Unit.

House Rules   A document that spells out all of the community and lifestyle rules that co-op tenant shareholders must obey on a daily basis.

Household   One or more persons inhabiting a housing unit as their Principal Residence. Group Quarters residents are not considered households.

Housing Affordability Index   A statistical indicator of the ability of households in an area to purchase housing at prevailing prices with currently available financing. Most commonly used indexes contrast the amount of income of the typical household in an area to the required monthly payment of the typical house in the area.

Housing And Urban Development Department (HUD)   A U.S. Government agency established to implement certain federal housing and community development programs. This federal agency attempts to assure decent, safe, and sanitary housing for all Americans, and investigates complaints of discrimination in housing.

Housing Code   A local government ordinance that sets minimum standards of safety and sanitation for existing residential buildings. Not the Building Code, which pertain to new construction.

Housing Permit   Authorization issued by a municipality allowing a builder to construct a house or apartment; See Building Permit.

Housing Starts   An estimate of the number of dwelling units on which construction has begun during a stated period.

Housing Stock   The total number of Dwelling Units in an area.

Housing   Structures intended for residential use.

HOW   Homeowners' Warranty Program.

HUD   The Department of Housing and Urban Development; regulates FHA and GNMA.

HUD-1 Form   See Uniform Settlement Statement.

Hud-Code Home   Another term for a Manufactured Home.

Humidifier   An appliance normally attached to the furnace, or portable unit device designed to increase the humidity within a room or a house by means of the discharge of water vapor.

Hundred Percent Location   See One-Hundred Percent Location.

Hurricane Clip   Also known as Teco clip, they refer to nailed metal straps meant to secure trusses & roof rafters towards horizontal wall plate's top.

HVAC   The acronym for heating, ventilating and air conditioning.

Hybrid debt   A mortgage position with equity-like participation features in both cash flow and the appreciation of the property at the time of sale or refinance.

Hypothecate   To pledge a thing as security without having to give up possession of it.

Hypothecation   The pledge of property as security of a loan in which the borrower maintains possession of the property while it is pledged as security.

I

IAAO See International Association Of Assessing Officers.

I Beam An *"H"* shaped steel beam in cross section. In structural Steel, it is known as a "W-Section". When the roof & wall loads bear down over opening, it's used on wide wall openings *(double garage door)* or basement beams for longer spans.

iBuyer *iBuyer* is a company that uses technology to make an offer on your home quickly or "instantly" as the term implies. iBuyers represent a dramatic shift in the way people are buying and selling homes, offering in many cases, a simpler, more convenient alternative to a traditional home sale.

ICF See Insulating Concrete Forms.

I Joist Manufactured structural building component shaped like letter *"I"*. It is used as floor joists and rafters.

Illiquidity Inadequate cash to meet obligations. Real estate is considered an illiquid investment because of the time and effort required to convert to cash.

Immobility and Tangibility The two criteria that sets real estate apart from other goods and services. Real Estate cannot be moved from place to place and is a physical item which can be touched.

Impact Fee An expense charged against private developers by the city as a condition for granting permission to develop a specific project. Most often, impact fees are applied to residential projects. The purpose of the fee is to defray the cost to the city of expanding and extending public services to the development.

Implied Agency Occurs when the words and actions of the parties indicate that there is an agency relationship.

Implied Cap Rate Net operating income divided by the sum of a REIT's equity market capitalization and its total outstanding debt.

Implied Contract A contract under which the agreement of the parties is demonstrated by their acts and conduct.

Implied Easement See Easement By Prescription.

Implied Grant A method of creating an easement. One party may be using another's property for the benefit of both parties.

Implied Warranty One that is not written but exists under the law. Contrast with *"expressed."*

Impound Account See Escrow Account.

Impound To hold or take by court order.

Improved Land Land that has improvements. Land that has been partially or fully developed for use. See Highest and Best Use.

Improvement
1. Improvements on land: any structure, usually privately owned, erected on a site to enhance the value of the property;
2. Improvements to land: usually a publicly owned structure.

3.   In the context of leasing, the term typically refers to the improvements made to or inside a building but may include any permanent structure or other development, such as a street, sidewalk, utilities, etc.

Improvement Ratio The relative value of improvements to the value of unimproved property.

Imputed Interest In a mortgage that states an insufficient interest rate, the law will impute that the rate is higher, and the principal is less. See Implied interest.

In Rem A proceeding against the realty directly; as distinguished from a proceeding against a person. Most often used by governments in taking land for nonpayment of taxes.

Incandescent Lamp A lamp employing an electrically charged metal filament that glows at white heat.

Incentive Fee Applies to fee structures where the amount of the fee that is charged is determined by the performance of the real estate assets under management.

Inchoate Right Incomplete right, such as a wife's dower interest in her husband's property during his life.

Inchoate The lien buyer's interest in the property is known as an inchoate interest. It is an interest in real estate which is not a present interest, but which may ripen into a vested estate, if not barred, extinguished, or divested. In general, you have a right to the real estate as long as the following occurs:

1.   The redemption period expires, and the lien has not been paid back, plus interest.
2.   You comply with any State specific rules the statute requires, including providing notice to those who have An Interest In The Property.
3.   Filing Certain Documents With The Court.

Income Approach The process of estimating the value of an income-producing property by capitalization of the annual net income expected to be produced by the property during its remaining useful life.

Income Capitalization Value The indication of value derived for an income-producing property by converting its anticipated benefits into property value through direct capitalization of expected income or by discounting the annual cash flows for the holding period at a specified yield rate.

Income Earnings or other benefit coming from the use of property, skill, investment, or business.

Income Limits Maximum that a family can earn and still be eligible for various government housing assistance programs. Limits vary by family size and geographic area.

Income Multiplier The relationship of price to income. See Gross Rent Multiplier.

Income Participation See Participation Mortgage.

Income Property Real estate that is owned or operated to produce revenue.

Income Return The percentage of the total return that is generated by the income from operations of a property, fund, or account.

Income Statement A historical financial report that indicates sources and amounts of revenues, amounts of expense accounts, and profit or loss. Generally prepared on either an accrual or a cash basis.

Income Stream A regular flow of money generated by a business or investment.

Income/Expense Ratio See Expense Ratio.

Incompetent A person who is unable to manage his/her own affairs by reason of insanity, imbecility, or feeblemindedness.

Incorporate
1. To form a corporation under state regulations provided by the Secretary of State.
2. To provide a geographic area the legal status of a political subdivision of the state.

Incorporeal Right A nonpossessory right in real estate, such as an easement.

Increasing Returns The principle that applies when increased expenditures for improvements to a given parcel of land yield an increasing percentage return on investment.

Incumbrance See Encumbrance.

Incurable Depreciation A defect that cannot easily be cured, or that is not financially practical to cure; a defect in the *"bone structure"* of a building.

Indemnification One party's agreement to compensate someone else for loss or damage.

Indemnify
1. To protect another person against loss or damage.
2. To compensate a party for loss or damage.

Indenture A written agreement made between 2 or more persons having different interests.

Independent Appraisal A value estimate provided by someone who does not participate in the income or value of the property.

Independent Contractor One who is retained to perform a certain act but who is subject to the control and direction of another only as to the end result, and not as to how he or she performs the act. Unlike an employee, an independent contractor pays all of his or her expenses, pays his or her income and Social Security taxes, and receives no employee benefits. Many real estate salespeople are independent contractors.

Independent Fee Appraiser One who estimates the value of property, has no interest in the property, and is not associated with a lending association or other investor.

Index
1. A statistic that indicates some current economic or financial condition. Indexes are often used to adjust wage rates, rental rates, loan interest rates, and pension benefits set by long-term contracts.
2. To adjust contract terms according to an index. See Indexed Loan.

Index Lease A lease that allows the rent to be increased or decreased periodically, based on changes in a selected economic index, such as the Consumer Price Index.

Indexed Loan A long-term loan in which the term, payment, interest rate, or principal amount may be adjusted periodically according to a specific index. The index and the manner of adjustment are generally stated in the loan contract.

Indirect Costs Development costs other than direct material and labor costs that are directly related to the construction of improvements, including administrative and office expenses, commissions, architectural, engineering and financing costs.

Individual Account Management Accounts established for individual plan sponsors or other investors for investment in real estate, where a firm acts as an adviser in acquiring and/or managing a direct real estate portfolio.

Industrial Development Research Council (IDRC) Provides helpful real estate information for the nation's largest corporations; Fortune 500.

Industrial Park An area set aside, designed, and zoned for manufacturing, production, and/or other associated activities.

Industrial Property All land and buildings used or suited for use in the production, storage, or distribution of tangible goods.

Industrial Real Estate Land or property intended to be used for manufacture or warehouse purposes. See Industrial Property.

Infiltration The passage of air or moisture from indoors to outdoors and vice versa; term is usually associated with drafts from cracks, seams, or holes in buildings.

Inflation The annual rate at which consumer prices increase.

Inflation A loss in the purchasing power of money; an increase in the general price level. Generally measured by the Consumer Price Index, published by the Bureau of Labor Statistics.

Inflation Hedge An investment that tends to increase in value at a rate greater than inflation and helps contribute to the preservation of the purchasing power of a portfolio.

Information Reporting Reports provided to the Internal Revenue Service *(IRS)*, such as commissions earned by real estate sales agents and real estate transactions of home sellers, reported by the broker

Infrastructure The basic features or structure needed for the functioning of a municipality such as roads, bridges, buildings, etc.

Ingress And Egress Right or ability to enter and exit through land owned by another. See Egress, Ingress.

Ingress The right or ability to enter a parcel of land that is used as ingress and egress, or both entering and leaving.

Inheritance Tax A tax, based on property value, imposed in some states on those who acquire property from a decedent.

Initial Interest Rate The beginning rate applied to an Adjustable-Rate Mortgage.

Initial Public Offering (IPO) The first time a private company offers securities for sale to the public.

Injunction An order issued under the seal of a court to restrain one or more parties to a legal proceeding, from performing an act deemed inequitable to another party or parties in the proceeding.

Inner City Generally, the older and more urbanized area of a large city surrounding the Central Business District. The term often refers to densely populated blighted areas characterized by low-income residents and a high proportion of minority racial and/or ethnic groups.

Innocent Purchaser A party not responsible for cleanup of contaminated property. Under SARA, anyone who is in the chain of title becomes responsible for such cleanup, even those with no responsibility for the pollution. One exception is a purchaser who knew nothing about the contamination and had an investigation done *(Phase I)* prior to the purchase. See Brownfields, Superfund

Inside Corner The point at which two walls forms an internal angle, as in the corner of a room.

Inside Lot In a Subdivision, a lot surrounded on each side by other lots, as opposed to a corner lot, which has road frontage on at least 2 sides.

Insider Rights The rights given to tenants occupying a part of a building in the process of converting to a coop or condominium, giving them the exclusive right to buy their apartments for a limited period of time and normally at a discounted price.

Inspection A physical scrutinizing review of property or of documents.

Inspection Report Written record of a property's condition, including the foundation, interior, roof, kitchen & baths, foundation, heating & A/C.

Inspector Someone that checks the property and makes evaluation based on damages, mechanical, electrical or any sort of issue which may call for repairs after purchase of property.

Installment Contract See Land Contract.

Installment Sale A method of reporting gain received from the sale of real estate when the sale price is paid in two or more installments over two or more years. If the sale meets certain requirements, a taxpayer can spread recognition of the reportable gain over more than one year, which may result in tax savings.

Installment To Amortize One Dollar A mathematically computed factor derived from compound interest functions that offers the level periodic payment required to retire a $1.00 loan within a certain time frame. The periodic installment must exceed the periodic interest rate. See Amortization, Amortization Schedule.

Installments Parts of the same debt, payable at successive periods as agreed; payments made to reduce a mortgage.

Institute For Professionals In Taxation An organization founded in 1976 dedicated to uniform and equitable administration of ad valorem and sales and use taxes, and to minimizing the cost of tax administration and compliance. The organization maintains a strict Code of Ethics and Standards of Professional Conduct for its members.

Institute Of Real Estate Management (IREM) A professional organization of property managers. Affiliated with the National Association Of Realtors®. Publishes the *Journal of Property Management*.

Institutional Lender Financial intermediaries who invest in loans and other securities on behalf of their depositors or customers; lending and investment activities are regulated by laws to limit risk.

Institutional-Grade Property Various types of real estate properties generally owned or financed by institutional investors. Core investments typically include office, retail, industrial and apartments. Specialty investments include hotels, healthcare facilities, senior housing, student housing, self-storage facilities, and mixed-use properties.

Instrument A written legal document; created to affect the rights of the parties.

Insulating Concrete Forms (ICFS) Hollow foam blocks or panels that crews stack into the shape of the exterior walls of a building. They then pour reinforced concrete inside, creating a foam-concrete sandwich. The forms are left in place to provide insulation. Over 40 brands of ICFs are sold in North America, in the form of panels, planks, and blocks of various kinds. Some of these materials contain up to 85% post-consumer recycled polystyrene.

Insulating Glass A door or window where a couple of glass panes are used with a sealed air space between them. Also known as double glass.

Insulation Board, Rigid A structural building board made of coarse wood or cane fiber in ½. and 25/32 inch thickness. It can be obtained in various size sheets and densities.

Insulation Any material high in resistance to heat transmission that, when placed in the walls, ceiling, or floors of a structure, and will reduce the rate of heat flow.

Insurable Interest Insurable interest is the amount of property qualifying for insurance.

Insurable Title A title to land that a title company will insure.

Insurable Value The cost of total replacement of destructible improvements to a property.

Insurance (Mortgage) A service, generally purchased by a borrower, that will indemnify the lender in case of foreclosure of the loan. Indemnification is generally limited to losses suffered by the lender in the foreclosure process. See FHA Mortgage Loan, Private Mortgage Insurance.

Insurance Company Separate Account A real estate investment vehicle that may only be offered by life insurance companies. This ownership arrangement enables an ERISA-governed fund to avoid the creation of unrelated taxable income for certain types of property investments and investment structures.

Insurance The indemnification against loss from a specific hazard or peril through a contract *(called a policy)* and for a consideration *(called a premium)*.

Insured Value The insured value is the amount that a structure is insured and should include the cost of replacing the structure if completely destroyed.

Intangible Value The value that cannot be Seen or touched.

Intelligent Building A building with computer and electrical systems that sense the areas to heat and cool for maximum efficiency and then transfer air with the appropriate temperature from one place to another.

Inter Vivos Latin for *"during one's life"*.

Inter Vivos Trust A trust set up during one's lifetime.

Intercreditor Agreement The agreement between two or more creditors of the same borrower, governing joint or unilateral action, and the manner in which common collateral will be held and foreclosed

Interest
1. A charge made by a lender for the use of money.
2. The price paid for the use of capital.

Interest Rate The interest rate is the cost of borrowing money from a lender. Rates will vary and will change over time.

Interest-Only Loan A loan in which interest is payable at regular intervals until loan maturity, when the full loan balance is due. Does not require Amortization.

Interest-Only Strip A derivative security consisting of all or part of the interest portion of the underlying loan or security.

Interest Rate Spread The difference between the retail interest rate charged to a borrower and the wholesale rate accepted by the financial industry when acquiring home mortgage loans.

Interim Financing A short-term loan usually made during the construction phase of a building project, often referred to as a construction loan.

Interim Interest The interest owed by the borrower to the lender on the mortgage loan from the day of the closing top the date covered by the first payment.

Interior Finish Material that is used for covering the interior framed areas of walls and ceilings.

Intermediation The normal flow of funds into Financial Intermediaries such as S&Ls, which lend out the money.

Internal Rate Of Return (IRR) A discounted cash-flow analysis calculation used to determine the potential total return of a real estate asset during an anticipated holding period.

Internal Revenue Code (IRC) The law, passed by Congress, that specifies how and what income is to be taxed, and what may be deducted from taxable income.

Internal Revenue Service (IRS) An agency of the federal government that is responsible for the administration and collection of federal income taxes. The IRS prints and distributes tax forms and audits tax returns.

International Architecture An early-twentieth-century-style house whose design is very simple with no ornamentation. The windows appear to be continuous rather than appearing to be holes in the walls.

International Association Of Assessing Officers (IAAO) A professional organization of property tax assessors. Awards the designation of Certified Assessment Evaluator *(CAE)*. Publishes the quarterly *Assessors Journal*.

International Code Council (ICC) Established in 1994 as a nonprofit organization dedicated to developing a single set of comprehensive and coordinated national building codes.

International Council Of Shopping Centers (ICSC) A nonprofit association that provides information to its members about shopping centers, including financial, leasing, and legal matters.

International Facility Management Association (IFMA) An organization whose members are concerned with the practice of coordinating the physical workplace with the people and work of the organization, integrating the principles of business administration, architecture, and the behavioral and engineering sciences.

International Real Estate Federation An organization with worldwide membership that is devoted to encouraging private rights to real estate. The international abbreviation is FIABCI; its American chapter is an affiliate of the National Association Of Realtors®.

International Real Estate Society (IRES) A federation of regional real estate societies. Each affiliated society maintains control over its own activities while participating in the federation to get the benefits of global cooperation. Members are The American Real Estate Society *(ARES)*, European Real Estate Society *(ERES)*, Pacific Rim Real Estate Society *(PRRS)*, Asian Real Estate Society *(AsRES)*, African Real Estate Society *(AfRES)*, and Latin American Real Estate Society *(LARES)*.

International Right Of Way Association (IR/WA) An individual membership association *(no corporate membership)* that offers courses covering various phases of right-of-way work. Educational curriculum includes law, engineering, appraisal. Offers a designation, SR/WA, and a bimonthly magazine.

Interstate Land Sales Act A federal law, administered by the Department of Housing And Urban Development *(HUD)*, which requires certain disclosures and advertising procedures when selling land to purchasers in other states.

Interval Ownership See Time-Sharing.

Intestate The condition of a property owner who dies without leaving a will. Title to such property passes to his or her heirs as provided in the state law of descent.

Intrinsic Value The inherent value of tangible property.

Invalid Having no force or effect.

Invalidate To render null and void.

Inventory All space within a certain proscribed market without regard to its availability or condition.

Inventory Property held for sale or to be used in the manufacture of goods held for sale. Does not qualify for capital gains tax treatment.

Inverse Condemnation A legal procedure to obtain compensation when a property interest has been taken or diminished in value by a government activity.

Investment Analysis A study of the likely return from a proposed real estate investment with the objective of evaluating the amount an investor may pay for it, the investment's suitability to that investor, or the feasibility of a proposed real estate development. Appraised value is based on a synthesis of people in the market whereas investment analysis is based on the value to a specific investor.

Investment Bank Investment banks do not accept deposits; they are intermediaries only. Investment banks sell products or assist companies with raising capital, typically by underwriting and/or acting as the firm's agent in the issuance of securities. They also act as a *"market maker"* by facilitating the trading of securities.

Investment Banker One who brings new securities *(e.g., stocks or bonds)* to the market.

Investment Committee The governing body overseeing corporate pension investments. Also, the subcommittee of a board of trustees charged with developing investment policy for board approval.

Investment Life Cycle The time span from acquisition of an investment to final disposition.

Investment Manager Any company or individual that assumes discretion over a specified amount of real estate capital, invests that capital in assets via a separate account, co-investment program or commingled fund, and provides asset management.

Investment Money directed toward the purchase, improvement, and development of an asset in expectation of income or profits. A good financial investment has the following characteristics: safety, regularity of yield, marketability, acceptable denominations, valuable collateral, acceptable duration, required attention, and potential appreciation.

Investment Policy A document that formalizes an institution's guidelines for investment and asset management. An investment policy typically will contain goals and objectives; core and specialty investment criteria and methodology; and guidelines for asset management, investment advisory contracting, fees and utilization of consultants and other outside professionals.

Investment Property A property that brings income or is to be used for investment purposes rather than as a primary residence.

Investment Strategy The investment parameters used by the manager in structuring the portfolio and selecting the real estate assets for a fund or account. This includes a description of the types, locations, and sizes of properties to be considered, the ownership positions that will be used, and the stages of the investment lifecycle.

Investment Structures Unleveraged acquisitions, leveraged acquisitions, traditional debt, participating debt, convertible debt, triple-net leases, and joint ventures.

Investment Tax Credit A reduction in income tax generally based on the cost and life of certain assets purchased.

Investment Value The value to an individual in meeting their personal investment objectives, not those of the general marketplace.

Investment-Grade CMBS Commercial mortgage-backed securities with ratings of *"AAA," "AA," "A"* or *"BBB"*.

Investor Status In reporting to clients and consultants, all investors are divided into two categories: taxable and tax-exempt. The tax-exempt category includes all qualified pension and retirement accounts. The taxable category includes all other accounts under management, including offshore capital.

Involuntary Alienation The transfer of title to property due to lien foreclosure sale, adverse possession, filing a petition in bankruptcy, condemnation under power of eminent domain, or, upon the death of the titleholder, to the state if there aren't any heirs.

Involuntary Conversion Condemnation or sudden destruction due to act of God.

Involuntary Lien A lien imposed against property without consent of the owner, e.g., taxes, special assessments.

Inwood Annuity Factor A number that, when multiplied by the periodic payment from a Level Payment Income Stream, indicates the present value of the income stream, based on a specific interest rate.

Inwood Tables A set of Annuity Factors for various Interest Rates and Maturities. See Inwood Annuity Factor.

IPO See Initial Public Offering.

IR/WA See International Right Of Way Association.

IREM Institute Of Real Estate Management.

IRR See Internal Rate of Return

Irrevocable Incapable of being recalled or revoked; unchangeable; unalterable.

Irrigation A lawn or other sprinkler system.

IRS See Internal Revenue Service.

Italian Villa A Latin-style, massive 2 or 3-story house of masonry with large overhanging eaves.

J

J Channel Metal or vinyl edging which h is the most common piece of siding trim. Besides being used for inside corners, it's used for trimming around windows and doors. It is also used where siding meets a soffit or roof at an angle.

Jack Post A metal column that is adjustable normally used in changing older supporting post in a building.

Jack Rafter A rafter that extend the distance from the wall plate to a hip or from a valley to a ridge.

Jamb The side and head lining of a doorway, window, or other opening.

Jeopardy Risk. A possibility or danger of loss, harm or failure.

Joint And Several Liability A creditor can demand full repayment from any and all of those who have borrowed. Each borrower is liable for the full debt, not just the prorated share.

Joint Cement See Joint Compound.

Joint Compound A powder that is usually mixed with water and used for joint treatment in gypsum wallboard finish. Also known as spackle and/or drywall mud.

Joint Ownership Property ownership by two or more people.

Joint Tenancy The ownership of real estate by two or more parties who have been named in one conveyance as joint tenants. On the death of a joint tenant, her or his interest passes to the surviving joint tenant or tenants by the right of survivorship.

Joint Trench When the electric company and telephone company dig one trench and *"drop"* both of their service lines in.

Joint Venture The joining of two or more people to conduct a specific business enterprise. A joint venture is similar to a partnership in that it must be created by agreement between the parties to share in the losses and profits of the venture. It is unlike a partnership in that the venture is for one specific project only, rather than for a continuing business relationship.

Joint The area that is between the touching surfaces of two members or components held together by nails, glue, cement, mortar.

Joist Hanger A metal *"U"* shaped item used to support the end of a floor joist and attached with hardened nails to another bearing joist or beam.

Joist a relatively larger piece of dimensional lumber that runs parallel to one other and support a floor or ceiling, and supported in turn by larger beams, girders, or bearing walls.

Judgment Clause A provision that may be included in notes, leases, and contracts by which the debtor, lessee, or obligor authorizes any attorney to go into court to confess a judgment against him or her for a default in payment. Also called a cognovit.

Judgment Creditor One who has received a court decree or judgment for money due from the judgment debtor.

Judgment Debtor One against whom a judgment has been issued by a court for money owed, and that remains unsatisfied.

Judgment Lien The claim upon the property of a debtor resulting from a judgment.

Judgment The official and authentic decision of a court on the respective rights and claims of the parties to an action or suit. When a judgment is entered and recorded with the county recorder, it usually becomes a general lien on the property of the defendant for a ten-year period.

Judicial Deed The Judicial Deed is the deed the court transfers to the lien buyer after an auction. This is a readily transferable deed since it is free from claims from outside owners and is free of risk from litigation of defect.

Judicial Foreclosure Judicial foreclosures are mandatory in some but not all states. They require all foreclosures go through the court system to confirm the debt is in default before putting the property up for auction. The goal of judicial foreclosures is to protect property owners from corrupt lenders.

Jumbo Loan Conforming loan limits cap the dollar value that can be backed by government-sponsored programs. A jumbo mortgage exceeds these conforming loan limits, which are tied to local median home values. Qualifications for these loans are more stringent and the loans themselves are manually underwritten to mitigate risk to the lender. Generally, a mortgage loan for $250,000 or more.

Jumbo Mortgage See Jumbo Loan.

Jumpers Water pipe that is mounted in a water meter pit, or an electric wire that is installed in the electric house panel meter socket before the meter is installed.

Junior Financing A loan relationship which is junior or lower in priority to a first or more senior loan.

Junior Lien A lien which is subordinate to or lower in priority to another *(senior)* lien.

Junior Mortgage A mortgage whose claim against the property will be satisfied only after prior mortgages have been repaid. See First Mortgage, Second Mortgage.

Junk Fees Charges assessed at the closing of a mortgage that go to the lender like settlement fees, signup fees, underwriting fees, funding fees, translation fees and messenger fees.

Jurisdiction Geographic or topical area of authority for a specific government entity.

Just Compensation The amount paid to the owner of a property when it is acquired under Eminent Domain. See Condemnation.

Just Title See Clear Title.

K

Keeper The metal latch plate in a door frame into which a doorknob plunger latches.

Key Money The money paid to a building owner or landlord by a tenant so as to secure a desired tenancy.

Keyless A plastic fixture that operates by a pull string. Located in the basement, crawl space , and attic areas.

Keyway A slot formed and poured on a footer or in a foundation wall when another wall will be installed at the slot location. This gives additional strength to the joint/meeting point.

Kicker Added cost that has to be paid on a mortgage in order to get a loan approved. An example would be an equity stake in receipts of a retail or rental property.

Kick-Out Clause A provision in a sales contract that allows the seller to void the agreement if a better offer is received before the sale is closed.

Kick Plate A metal plate installed at the base of a door or panel to protect it from damage or wear.

Kilowatt (kW) One thousand watts. A measure of the power consumption of a building, or other closed system.

King Stud The vertical frame lumber *(left and right)* of a window or door opening and runs continuously from the bottom sole plate to the top plate.

Kiosk An independent stand from which merchandise is sold, often placed in the common area of a regional Shopping Center.

Knee Wall A short wall that is used as a support to the rafters in timber roof building.

Knot A term used in lumber, this is the portion of a branch or limb of a tree that appears on the edge or face of the piece.

L

"Location, Location, Location" A term coined by real estate agents and brokers; the *"three most important things about real estate"*. A popular statement, typically by realtors and brokers, which emphasizes the relative importance of location with respect to the value of urban and suburban real estate.

L/V See Loan-To-Value Ratio.

Laches An equitable doctrine used by the courts to bar a legal claim or prevent the assertion of a right because of undue delay, negligence, or failure to assert the claim or right.

Lambda Alpha International (LAI) An organization whose purpose is the exchange of information and ideas relating to land economics.

Laminated Shingles These are shingles with extra dimensionality due to extra layers or tabs, producing a shake-like appearance. Also known as architectural shingles

Laminating A way of joining together two or more layers of materials.

Land Acquisition Costs The price paid for actual land and making payment for broker fees and permits.

Land Banking The activity of purchasing land that is not presently needed for use.

Land Contract A real estate installment selling arrangement whereby the buyer may use, occupy, and enjoy land, but no deed is given by the seller until all or a specified part of the sale price has been paid. See Contract for Deed and Installment Land Contract.

Land Economics The branch of economics that concentrates upon the economic attributes of land and the economics of agriculture.

Land Lease Community A housing development in which homeowners lease the land under their homes from a landowner who often provides community infrastructure and amenities as well. The most common such communities are the modern equivalent of the mobile home park, in which owners of manufactured homes lease their sites.

Land Lease A situation whereby a building and other land improvement are rented for a term of years. See Ground Lease.

Land Residual Technique In appraisal, a method of estimating the value of land when given the Net Operating Income *(NOI)* and value of improvements. Used for feasibility analysis and Highest And Best Use. See Income Approach.

Land Sale-Leaseback The sale of land and simultaneous leasing of it by the seller, who becomes the tenant.

Land The measurable area of the earth's surface extending downward to the center of the earth and upward infinitely into space.

Land Use Intensity A measure of the extent to which a land parcel is developed in conformity with zoning ordinances.

Land Use Planning An activity, generally conducted by a local government, that provides public and private land use recommendations consistent with community policies. Generally used to guide decisions on zoning.

Land Use Regulation Government ordinances, codes, and permit requirements intended to make the private use of land and natural resources conform to policy standards. See Zoning.

Land Use Succession A change in the predominant use of a neighborhood or area over time. See Neighborhood Life Cycle.

Land, Tenements, And Hereditaments A phrase used in early English law to express all sorts of real estate.

Land/Building Ratio A ratio of relative values of the land to improvements.

Landing A platform that is between flights of stairs or at the termination of a flight of stairs.

Landlocked The condition of a lot that has no access to a public thoroughfare except through an adjacent lot. See Egress.

Landlord One who rents property to another.

Landlord's Warrant A warrant from a landlord to levy upon a tenant's personal property and to sell this property at a public sale to compel payment of the rent or the observance of some other stipulation in the lease.

Landmark An item or structure that is at least 30 years old and has notable physical features, historical or cultural significance.

Landmarks Commission A city governmental agency assigned responsibility for recommending properties and neighborhoods to be landmarked and that ensures that landmarks are preserved properly.

Lands Available See Lands for Sale.

Lands for Sale Lands for Sale is the over-the-counter liens *(OTC)* that you can purchase from a taxing authority. They are usually properties that were not bid on in the auction and can be purchased through the mail. They are easier to purchase because you don't have to go through the bidding process, however, they were passed up at the auction typically because they were less desirable properties.

Landscape Architect A professional who designs building sites, subdivisions, and other projects that require work on drainage, grading, vegetation, installation of utilities, and site improvements.

Lap To cover the surface of one shingle or roll with another.

Latch A beveled metal tongue that is operated through a spring loaded knob or lever.

Late Charge A penalty for payments made after the due date plus a grace period.

Late Fee See Late Charge.

Latent Defects Flaws that are hidden but are likely to surface later.

Lateral The underground trench and related services that will be buried within the trench.

Lath A building material made of narrow wood, metal, gypsum, or insulating board that is fastened to the frame of a building to act as a base for plaster, shingles, or tiles.

Lattice An open framework of crisscrossed wood or metal strips that form regular, patterned spaces.

Lead A metal once common in plumbing pipes and paint but now considered a Hazardous Substance. Home sellers must disclose any knowledge they have of the presence of Lead-Based Paint.

Lead Manager The investment banking firm that handles the principal responsibilities for coordinating the new issuance of securities.

Lead-Based Paint A substance considered a hazardous material. According to the Federal Government, it is potentially poisonous and its existence in property is to be disclosed to a buyer. Its presence is often difficult to determine because applications of lead-based paint may have been covered by more recent paint applications that are free of lead.

Lease A contract between a landlord *(the lessor)* and a tenant *(the lessee)* transferring the right to exclusive possession and use of the landlord's real property to the lessee for a specified period of time and for a stated consideration *(rent)*. By state law, leases for longer than a certain period of time *(generally one year)* must be in writing to be enforceable.

Lease Agreement The formal legal document entered into between a landlord and a tenant to reflect the terms of the negotiations between them.

Lease Commencement Date The date usually constitutes the commencement of the term of the lease, whether or not the tenant has actually taken possession, so long as beneficial occupancy is possible.

Lease Escalation Clause Increase in expenses for items such as utilities, tax escalations, increases based on cost of living, or maintenance of the premises often are included in the terms of the lease.

Lease Expiration Exposure Schedule A listing of the total square footage of all current leases that expire in each of the next five years, without regard to renewal options.

Lease Option A lease option is like rent-to-own for real estate. It gives the lessee the ability to lease property with the option to buy. It includes a legal agreement with a monthly rental amount due, while also including an option to buy the property for a predetermined price at any time during the length of the agreement.

Lease Proposal An offering made to a prospective tenant that includes highlights of lease terms.

Lease With Option To Purchase A lease that gives the lessee *(tenant)* the right to purchase the property at an agreed-upon price under certain conditions. See Lease Option.

Leased Fee The landlord's ownership interest of a property that is under lease.

Leasehold Estate

1. A tenant's right to occupy real estate during the term of a lease, generally considered to be a personal property interest.
2. An interest in real estate granted by a lease, typically limited to a specified term of years, and which estate terminates at the end of the lease.

Leasehold Improvements Fixtures attached to real estate that are generally acquired or installed by the tenant. Upon expiration of the lease, the tenant can generally remove them, provided such action does not damage the property nor conflict with the lease.

Leasehold Interest The right to hold or use property for a fixed period of time at a given price, without transfer of ownership.

Leasehold Mortgage A mortgage and security interest in a leasehold estate.

Leasehold The interest or estate which a lessee of real estate has therein by virtue of the lessee's lease.

Leasehold Value The value of a tenant's interest in a lease, especially when the rent is below market and the lease has a long remaining term.

Ledger In a Structural Floor, the wooden perimeter frame lumber member that bolts onto the face of a foundation wall and supports the wood structural floor.

Ledger Strip A strip of lumber nailed along the bottom of the side of a girder on which joists rest.

Leech Field An approach used to treat or dispose sewage in rural areas with a municipal sewer system.

Legacy A disposition of money or personal property by will.

Legal Age The official standard of maturity upon which one is held legally responsible for one's acts. Contracts for the sale or lease of real estate by a minor are voidable by the minor. See Minor, Major.

Legal Description
1. A description of a specific parcel of real estate sufficient for an independent surveyor to locate and identify it. The most common forms of legal description are rectangular survey, metes and bounds, and subdivision lot and block known as a plat.
2. A geographical description identifying a parcel by government survey, metes and bounds, or lot numbers of a recorded plat including a description of any portion that is subject to an easement or reservation.

Legal Notice Notification of others using the method required by law. See Constructive Notice, Notice.

Legal Owner The legal owner has title to the property, although the title may actually carry no rights to the property other than as a lien.

Legal Residence Generally, one's permanent home.

Legal Title A collection of rights of ownership that are defined or recognized by law or that could be successfully defended in a court of law.

Legality Of Object An element that must be present in a valid contract. If a contract has for its object an act that violates the laws of the United States or the laws of a state to which the parties are subject, it is illegal, invalid, and not recognized by the courts.

Legatee One who receives property by a will. See Devisee.

Legislative Body A Legislative body sets policies, approves budgets and passes ordinances regarding land use, zoning, cluster zoning and other important items.

Lender In real estate, the lender refers to the individual, financial institution, or private group lending money to a buyer to purchase property with the expectation the loan will be repaid with interest, in agreed upon increments, by a certain date.

Lender Liability
1. The responsibility of a lender for damage to a business, when the lender fails to fund a loan commitment.
2. The possible responsibility of a lender who forecloses on and operates a business that is the site of environmental contamination for cleanup of the property. Under Fleet Factors and the EPA's April 29, 1992, rule, lenders who foreclose just to protect security interest may not be liable for the cleanup.

Lender Participation See Participation Mortgage.

Lender Rebate A payment made by the lender to the mortgage broker.

Lending Regulations Regulations and rules issued periodically by federal *(US)* or state governmental agencies such as the Federal Reserve Bank, the Federal Deposit Insurance Corporation or the Office of Thrift Supervision which govern the lending and other business practices of banking and thrift/savings institutions.

Less Than Freehold Estate An estate in land that has a predetermined time span; most commonly a leasehold.

Lessee The tenant who leases a property.

Lessor One who leases property to a tenant

Let-In Brace Nominal boards used into notched studs diagonally.

Letter Of Attornment See Attornment.

Letter Of Commitment Official notification to a borrower of the lender's intent to grant a loan. Generally specifies the terms of the loan and sets a date for the closing.

Letter Of Credit A commitment by a bank or other person that the issuer will honor drafts or other demands for payment upon full compliance with the conditions specified in the letter of credit. Letters of credit are often used in place of cash deposited with the landlord in satisfying the security deposit provisions of a lease.

Letter Of Intent A preliminary agreement stating the proposed terms for a final contract.

Level Of Assessment A rate determined by the assessing unit and applied to the market value of properties, to determine assessed value. The level of assessment is also known as *"uniform percentage of value"*.

Level Payment Mortgage A loan with identical monthly payments over the life of the loan.

Level True Horizontal A tool used to determine level.

Level Annuity See Annuity.

Level-Payment Income Stream See Annuity.

Leverage The use of credit to finance a portion of the costs of purchasing or developing a real estate investment. Positive leverage occurs when the interest rate is lower than the capitalization rate or projected internal rate of return. Negative leverage occurs when the current return on equity is diminished by the employment of debt.

Levy To assess, seize, or collect. To levy a tax is to assess a property and set the rate of taxation. To levy an execution is to seize officially the property of a person to satisfy an obligation.

Liability
1. A debt or financial obligation.
2. A potential loss.

Liability Insurance A type of insurance that protects against an alleged claim that the insured person was responsible for bodily injury or property damage of another due to negligence or some inappropriate action.

Liable To be legally responsible or obligated.

LIBOR (London Interbank Offered Rate) The interest rate offered on Eurodollar deposits traded between banks, also called swaps.

License
1. A privilege or right granted to a person by a state to operate as a real estate broker or salesperson.
2. The revocable permission for a temporary use of land – a personal right that cannot be sold.

License Laws Laws that govern the activities of real estate salespersons.

Licensed Appraiser Generally an Appraiser who meets certain state requirements but lacks the experience or expertise of a certified appraiser. See Certified General Appraiser, Certified Residential Appraiser.

Licensee One who holds a real estate license; a licensed salesperson or broker. See Licensing Examination.

Licensing Examination A written test given to a prospective real estate broker or salesperson to determine ability to represent the public in a real estate transaction. Most states offer examinations on at least 5 dates each year.

Lien
1. A property lien is unpaid debt on a piece of property. It's a legal notice and denotes legal action taken by a lender to recover the debt they are owed. It can come from unpaid taxes, a court judgement, or unpaid bills and can slow down the homebuying process when unattended.
2. A right given by law to certain creditors to have their debt paid out of the property of a defaulting debtor, usually by means of a court sale.

3. An interest in property granted by the owner of that property, to another party *(the lienholder)*, until the property owner fulfills a legal duty to the lienholder, such as the repayment of a loan or the payment of lawful charges for work done on the property.

Lien Foreclosure Sale A lien foreclosure sale is the sale of property without consent of the owner, as ordered by a court or authorized by state law due to a debt resulting in a lien.

Lien Waiver Waiver of a mechanic's lien rights that is often required before the general contractor can receive a draw under the payment provisions of a construction contract. It may also be required before the owner can receive a draw on a construction loan. See Waiver.

Lien, Junior See Junior Mortgage, Subordination.

Lienholder One who holds, or benefits from, a lien.

Lien-Theory States States whose laws give a lien on property to secure debt. contrasted With Title Theory States in which the lender becomes the title owner. in either case the borrower has the right to use and enjoy the property in the absence of default; in the event of default, lenders may foreclose.

Life Cap A life cap refers to the maximum amount an interest rate on an adjustable rate loan can increase over the lifetime of the loan. A life cap is also known as an absolute interest rate or interest rate ceiling and keeps interest rates from ballooning too high over the term of the loan.

Life Estate An interest in real or personal property that is limited in duration to the lifetime of its owner or some other designated person.

Life Of Loan Cap A contractual limitation on the maximum interest rate that can be applied to an adjustable rate mortgage during the term of the loan. See Adjustable Rate Mortgage.

Life Tenant A person in possession of a life estate.

Lifecycle The various developmental stages of a property: pre-development, development, leasing, operating and redevelopment *(or rehab)*.

Life-Support System A building's security systems, such as camera surveillance, fire protection, communications system, backup lighting system, and the like.

Light Generally , any space in a window sash set for a single pane of glass.

Like Kind Exchange An exchange of property that is similar, as defined in the Internal Revenue Code that can be performed without recognition of taxable gain at the time of transfer.

Like-Kind Property A term used in an exchange of property held for productive use in a trade or business or for investment. Unless cash is received, the tax consequences of the exchange are postponed pursuant to Section 1031 of the Internal Revenue Code.

Limit Switch A safety control that automatically shuts off a furnace if it gets too hot. Can also control blower cycles.

Limited Appraisal An appraisal of real estate under and resulting from invoking the Departure Provision Of USPAP.

Limited Liability Company An LLC. It is a business structure that combines the pass-through taxation of a partnership or sole proprietorship with the limited liability of a corporation. Can mean Limited Liability Company, and/or Limited Liability Corporation, depending on the laws of the given state.

Limited Liability The restriction of one's potential losses to the amount invested. The absence of personal liability.

Limited Partnership A type of partnership comprised of one or more general partners who manage the business and are personally liable for partnership debts, and one or more limited partners who contribute capital and share in profits but who take no part in running the business and incur no liability above the amount contributed.

Lincoln Graduate Center An organization that offers real estate education, especially appraisal courses. See National Association Of Master Appraisers.

Line Of Credit An agreement whereby a financial institution promises to lend up to a certain amount without the need to file another application. See Home Equity Loan.

Lineal Foot A measure of one foot, in a straight line, along the ground. Sometimes, A unit of measure for lumber equal to 1 inch thick by 12 inches wide by 12 inches long. See Linear Foot.

Link A measure of distance used by Surveyors.

Lintel A horizontal structural member supporting the load over an opening like a door or window.

Liquidate To dissolve a business or personal property or to retire debts.

Liquidated Damages Liquidated damages occur when, by contractual agreement, defaulted earnest money becomes the personal property of the seller.

Liquidation Value The amount a property would bring under an immediate sale, minus transaction costs.

Liquidity Ease of converting assets to cash.

Liquidity Fund A prominent private firm that buys interests in Real Estate Investment Trusts and Real Estate Limited Partnerships.

Liquidity The ability to sell an asset and convert it into cash at a price close to its true value.

Lis Pendens A public notice that a lawsuit affecting title to or possession, use, and enjoyment of a parcel of real estate has been filed in either a state or federal court. Literally means "Lawsuit Pending".

List To obtain a real estate listing.

Listing Agreement A contract between a landowner *(as principal)* and a licensed real estate broker *(as agent)* by which the broker is employed as agent to list and sell real estate on the owner's terms within a given time, for which service the landowner agrees to pay a commission.

Listing An employment contract between principal and agent, authorizing the agent to perform services for the principal involving the latter's property. See Listing Agreement.

Listing Broker The broker in a multiple-listing situation from whose office a listing agreement is initiated, as opposed to the selling broker, from whose office negotiations leading to a sale are initiated. The listing broker and the selling broker may, of course, by the same person.

Litigation The act of carrying on a lawsuit.

Littoral Rights
1. A landowner's claim to use water in large lakes and oceans adjacent to her or his property.
2. The ownership rights to land bordering these bodies of water up to the high-water mark.

Load Bearing Wall All exterior walls and any interior wall aligned above a support beam or girder.

Loan Application A document required by a lender prior to issuing a Loan Commitment. The application generally includes the following information:
1. Name of the borrower
2. Amount and terms of the loan
3. Description of the subject property to be mortgaged
4. Borrower's financial and employment data
5. Borrower's Social Security Number.

Loan Application Fee A charge required by a loan originator to be paid by the borrower to cover the credit report, property appraisal, and other incidental expenses associated with underwriting the loan. The fee is generally not refundable.

Loan Approval Decision by a lender to extend credit in a specified amount. May also include a Loan Commitment for specified loan terms. See Preapproval.

Loan Closing See Closing.

Loan Commitment An agreement to lend money, generally of a specified amount, at specified terms at some time in the future.

Loan Constant See Mortgage Constant.

Loan Correspondent See Mortgage Correspondent.

Loan Coverage Ratio See Debt Coverage Ratio.

Loan Officer Residential loan officers, or mortgage loan officers, *(MLO)*, assist the homebuyer with purchasing or refinancing a home. Loan officers are often employed by larger financial institutions and help borrowers choose the right type of loan, compile their loan application, and communicate with appraisers. Loan Officers are Licensed under NMLS.

Loan Origination Fee The fee charged by a lender for processing a loan application, typically calculated as a percentage of the mortgage amount. See Origination Fees.

Loan origination Loan origination is the process during which a borrower submits a loan application and a financial institution or lender processes that application. There is usually an origination fee associated with this process.

Loan Package The collection of documents associated with a specific loan application.

Loan Points See Discount Points, Points.

Loan Proceeds The net amount of money that a lender disburses for a loan.

Loan Processing The steps a lender takes in the loan approval process, from application for a home mortgage through to closing.

Loan Servicing Loan servicing is a term for the administrative aspects of maintaining your loan, from the dispersal of the loan to the time it's paid in full. Loan servicing includes sending the borrower monthly statements, maintaining payment and balance records, and paying taxes and insurance. Servicing is usually carried out by the lender of the loan, typically a bank or financial institution.

Loan Terms The major requirements of a loan, which determine how it is repaid.

Loan The money to be borrowed.

Loan To Cost Ratio Ratio that is used in commercial property construction for comparing the amount of the loan used to finance a project to the cost to build the project.

Loan-To-Value Ratio (LTV) See Loan-To-Value.

Loan-To-Value The loan-to-value *(LTV)* ratio is the mortgage loan balance divided by the home's value. It shows how much you're borrowing from a lender as a percentage of your home's appraised value. The higher your LTV, the riskier you'll appear during the loan underwriting process because a low down payment denotes less equity or ownership in your property making you more likely to default on your loan.

Lock-Box Structure A structure whereby the rental or debt-service payments are sent directly from the tenant or mortgagor to the trustee.

Locked-In Interest Rate The rate promised by a lender at the time of loan application. The promise is a legal commitment of the lender, though there may be qualifications or contingencies that allow the lender to charge a higher rate.

Lock-In Period The period of time in which a borrower cannot repay their loan in full without incurring a penalty fine by the lender.

Lock-In/Rate Lock Agreement An agreement by the lender guaranteeing the applicant a particular interest rate on the mortgage loan provided the loan closes within a set period of time.

Lockout The period during which a loan may not be prepaid.

Loft An open living space that was converted from commercial space to residential space. It contains very high ceilings, large windows, and open space.

Log Cabin An early-American-style house which uses unfinished logs for at least the other shell.

Long-Term Capital Gain For income tax purposes, the gain on a Capital Asset held long enough to qualify for special tax considerations. Typically Held more that 12 months.

Long-Term Financing See Permanent Mortgage.

Long-Term Lease In most markets, this refers to a lease whose term is at least three years from initial signing to the date of expiration or renewal.

Lookout A short wood bracket or cantilever that supports an overhang portion of a roof.

Loss Severity The percentage of principal lost when a loan is foreclosed.

Lot Generally one of several contiguous parcels of land making up a fractional part or subdivision of a block, the boundaries of which are shown on recorded maps and plats.

Lot And Block Description A description of real property that identifies a parcel of land by reference to lot and block numbers within a subdivision, as identified on a subdivided plat duly recorded in the county recorder's office.

Lot Line A line bounding a lot as described in a property survey.

Lottery Sales Lottery Sales is a type of biding where buyers are selected at random. The winner of the lottery may then decide if they would like to purchase the lien.

Louver An opening into the house with so many horizontal slats and arranged to permit ventilation but to exclude rain, snow, light, insects, or other living creatures.

Low-Ball Offer An offer from a prospective property buyer that is much lower than the listing price. Such an offer may indicate the buyer's belief that the property will not attract many good offers and that the asking price is unrealistic. Also, it probably means the buyer is interested in the property only if it can be purchased at a bargain price.

Low-Income Housing Housing that is eligible for special tax credits of up to 9% of their cost *(4% in certain situations)* under the 1986 tax act. Strict rules must be followed concerning tenant qualification, certification, and project financing.

Low-Income Housing Limited Partnerships A Limited Partnership interest in housing that is rented to qualified low-income tenants. These investments generally return a small annual cash distribution, with most of the return coming from tax deductions for interest and depreciation and/or tax credits.

Low-rise A building with fewer than four stories above ground level.

LTV Loan-To-Value Ratio.

Lumens Term used for measuring the total light output. This is the amount of light that fall on a surface of one square foot.

Lump-Sum Contract A type of construction contract requiring the general contractor to complete a building or project for a fixed cost normally established by competitive bidding. The contractor absorbs any loss or retains any profit.

M

MACRS See Modified Accelerated Cost Recovery System.

Magic Page Included in the offering prospectus, the magic page is a projected growth story, describing how a new REIT will accomplish its future expectations for funds from operations or funds available for distribution.

MAI A professional appraisal designation conferred by the Appraisal Institute. To acquire the designation MAI, an Appraiser must pass several written proficiency examinations, perform acceptable appraisal work for a specific period of time, and prepare a demonstration narrative appraisal report.

Maintenance A monthly fee that shareholders pay the co-op corporation. This money is divided among a number of obligations, including upkeep of the common areas and all budgeted recurring expenses, payments for the building's underlying mortgage, insurance, and a reserve fund for repairs and renovations.

Maintenance Fee An assessment used by a Homeowners' Association or a Condominium Owners' Association, to pay costs of operating the Common Elements.

Majority
1. The age at which one is no longer a Minor and is fully able to conduct one's own affairs. Majority is 18 to 21 years, depending on the state.
2. More than half.

Maker One who creates or executes a promissory note and promises to pay the note when it becomes due.

Male Any Part Made To Fit Into Another Female Part.

Mall A public area connecting individual stores in a shopping center; generally enclosed. Also, an Enclosed Shopping Center.

Mall Stores Retail stores in a shopping mall other than the Anchor Tenant.

Management Agreement A contract between the owner of property and someone who agrees to manage it. See Property Management.

Management Fee The cost of professional Property Management. The fee is typically set at a fixed percentage of total rental income generated by the property managed.

Management Proposal A proposal or plan detailing the commitments of a property manager regarding a property, should they be hired. The proposal includes a description of the property to be managed, a list of all maintenance required, maintenance records and accounting procedures the manager will use, an operating budget and a proposed management fee.

Managing Agent Used for the building operations.

Mandate A mandate is an authorization or directive to carry out a policy or course of action. For example, an investment manager could receive a mandate from an investor to use an allocation of funds for a specific purpose or strategy.

Mandatory Requiring strict conformity or obedience.

Mansard Roof One having two slopes on all four sides, with the lower slope steeper than the upper, flatter sections.

Mansion Tax A State tax of some percentage, typically 1% levied on a seller from the selling price levied on the buyer of any residence costing in excess of $1,000,000.

Mantel The shelf that is above a fireplace opening.

Manufactured Home See Mobile Home, Mobile Home Park.

Manufactured Housing A term used to describe a factory-built house transported to a lot. In contrast to structures referred to as Mobile Homes, modern units must pass a federal inspection at the factory. Also includes Modular Housing.

Manufactured Housing Institute (MHI) A national trade organization representing all segments of the manufactured housing industry. MHI serves its membership by providing research, promotion, education, and government relations programs, and by building consensus within the industry.

Manufactured Wood Lumber like truss, beam, gluelam, or microlam that is designed out of smaller wood pieces and glued or mechanically fastened to form a larger piece.

Manufacturer's Specifications A written manual guide or maintenance instructions that comes with a product.

MAO Maximum Allowable Offer.

Margin A constant amount added to the value of the index for the purpose of adjusting the interest rate on an Adjustable Rate Mortgage.

Marginal Lease A lease agreement that barely covers the costs of operation for the property.

Marginal Property Property that is barely profitable to use.

Marginal Real Estate Land that barely covers the costs of operation.

Marginal Tax Bracket T he amounts of income tax that an investor would pay on the next dollar of income. Generally, the marginal rate is higher than the average rate because of the progressive tax rate structure.

Marital Deduction The tax-free amount one transfers by will to one's spouse. Current tax law allows an unlimited amount to be transferred without federal estate tax.

Mark to Market The process of increasing or decreasing the original investment cost or value of a property asset or portfolio to a level estimated to be the current market value.

Market
1. Place where buyers and sellers congregate; process by which things of value are exchanged for money.
2. Conditions under which a commodity or product is sold.

Market Allocation An agreement between members of a trade to refrain from competition in specific market areas.

Market Analysis A study of the supply and demand conditions in a specific area for a specific type of property or service. A market analysis report is generally prepared by someone with experience in real estate, economics, or marketing. It serves to help decide what type of project to develop and is also helpful in arranging permanent and construction financing for a proposed development.

Market Approach See Market Comparison Approach.

Market Area A geographic region from which one can expect the primary demand for a specific product or service provided at a fixed location.

Market Capitalization One measure of the value of a company; it is calculated by multiplying the current share price by the current number of shares outstanding.

Market Capture See Capture Rate.

Market Comparison Approach One of three Appraisal Approaches. Value is estimated by analyzing sales prices of similar properties called comps recently sold.

Market Data Approach See Market Comparison Approach.

Market Delineation The process of defining the geographic extent of the demand for a specific property.

Market Indicators Statistical data that indicate construction, sales, and leasing activity. This data is used to consider economic trends.

Market Penetration See Capture Rate.

Market Price The actual selling price of a property.

Market Rent The rent that a comparable unit would command if offered in the competitive market.

Market Rental Rates The rental income that a property most likely would command in the open market, indicated by the current rents asked and paid for comparable space.

Market Research Gathering, analyzing, and interpreting data concerning market conditions. See Feasibility Study.

Market Segmentation The process of defining the socio-economic characteristics of the demand for a specific property or properties.

Market Study See Market Analysis.

Market Survey A collection of primary information on other properties that sell or lease in the same market. At a minimum, the characteristics or classification of each building, its rent levels, and tenant occupancy will be included. See Market Analysis.

Market Value The most profitable price a property will bring in a competitive and open market under all conditions requisite to a fair sale. The price at which a buyer would buy, and a seller would sell, each acting prudently and knowledgeably, and assuming the price is not affected by undue stimulus.

Market/Data Approach A method of appraising or evaluating real property based on the proposition that an informed purchaser would pay no more for a property than the cost to him or her of acquiring an existing property with the same utility. This approach is applicable when an active market provides sufficient quantities of reliable data that can be verified from authoritative sources. The approach is relatively unreliable in an inactive market or in estimating the value of properties for which no real comparable sales data are available. It also is questionable when sales data cannot be verified with principals to the transaction. Also referred to as the market comparison or direct sales comparison approach.

Marketability Study An analysis, for a specific client, of the likely sales of a specific type of real estate product.

Marketability The speed or ease with which a property can be sold at or near its market value; its expected market appeal.

Marketable Title A title free from encumbrances that could be readily marketed to a willing purchaser.

Marshall& Swift A publisher of materials that provide information about construction costs for various types of buildings, quality levels, and geographic areas. It incorporates the building cost data of F. W. Dodge.

Masonry Stone, brick, concrete, hollow tile, concrete block, or other similar building units for bonded together with mortar to form a wall.

Mass Appraising Typically used by tax assessors, an effort to determine salient characteristics of properties in a given submarket, to allow an approximation of value for each. Sophisticated statistical techniques are used frequently in Mass Appraising.

Master Deed Used by a condominium developer or converter for recording a condominium development. It divides a single property into individually owned units, includes restrictions on their use and provides for ownership of common areas.

Master Lease A primary lease that controls subsequent leases and may cover more property than subsequent leases.

Master Limited Partnership (MLP) A type of limited partnership that is publicly traded. There are two types of partners in this type of partnership: The limited partner is the person or group that provides the capital to the MLP and receives periodic income distributions from the MLP's cash flow, whereas the general partner is the party responsible for managing the MLP's affairs and receives compensation that is linked to the performance of the venture.

Master Mortgage Loan The mortgage debt existing on a building used for cooperative housing. While each co-op tenant-shareholder is obligated for a portion of the loan, this debt is separate from the loans that may have been used to purchase the individual coop shares.

Master Plan A long term plan created by the Planning Board to guide the physical development of the community.

Master Servicer An institution that acts on behalf of a trustee for the benefit of security holders in collecting funds from a borrower, advancing funds in the event of delinquencies and, in the event of default, taking a property through foreclosure.

Mastic Pasty material that is used as cement or a coating

Material Fact A fact that is germane to a particular situation; one that participants in the situation such as a trial, may reasonably be expected to consider.

Material Participation A tax term introduced by the 1986 tax act, defined as year round active involvement in the operations of a business activity on a regular, continuous, and substantial basis. Three main factors to consider in determining the presence of material participation are:

1. Is the activity the taxpayer's principal trade or business?
2. How close is the taxpayer to the business?
3. Does the taxpayer have knowledge and experience in the enterprise?

Materialman A person who supplies materials used in the construction or repair of a building or other property.

Maturity

1. The due date of a loan.
2. The end of the period covered by a contract.

Maturity Date The date when the total principal balance comes due.

Maximum Allowable Offer (MAO) In real estate investing, the maximum allowable offer based on the After Repair Value *(ARV)* minus Holding costs, improvement costs, and expected profit.

Maximum Contamination Level (MCL) Under the Safe Drinking Water Act, the maximum allowable concentration of some contaminants in surface or groundwater to be used in the drinking water supply.

MBA

1. Mortgage Bankers Association Of America.
2. Master of Business Administration degree.

Mechanic's Lien A statutory lien created in favor of contractors, laborers, and materialmen or material suppliers who have performed work or furnished materials in improving real property.

Meeting Of The Minds When all parties to a contract agree to the substance and terms thereof.

Meeting Space In hotels, space made available to the public to rent for meeting, conference or banquet uses.

Megan's Law Federal law requiring states to develop programs to notify communities when convicted sex offenders are released into their neighborhood. In most cases, a public register is maintained to indicate the presence of an offender. Formally, the Child Protection Act of 1996.

Merchantable Title See Marketable Title.

Merger The fusion of 2 or more interests, such as businesses or investments.

Meridian A longitudinal reference line that traverses the earth in a north-south direction; all meridians circle the earth through the equator and converge at the north and south poles. It is used by surveyors in describing property under the Government Rectangular Survey Method.

Metal Lath Sheets of metal that are slit to form openings within the lath. Used as a plaster base for walls and ceilings and as reinforcing over other forms of plaster base.

Metes and Bounds See Metes-and-Bounds description.

Metes-and-Bounds Description A legal description of a parcel of land that begins at a well-marked point and follows the boundaries, using direction and distances around the tract, back to the point of beginning. The term *"metes"* refers to a boundary defined by the measurement of a straight run, specified by a distance between two points, and an orientation or direction. The term *"bounds"* refers to a more general boundary description, such as along a certain road, or the centerline of a river.

Metropolitan Statistical Area (MSA) One or more counties having a population of at least 50,000. A Consolidated Metropolitan Statistical Area *(CMSA)* is an area with two or more Primary Metropolitan Statistical Areas *(PMSA)* A CMSA must also include at least 1 million people.

Mezzanine Financing See Mezzanine Loan.

Mezzanine Loan A loan usually secured not by a lien on property but secured by the ownership of equity interests of a borrower.

MGIC Mortgage Guaranty Insurance Corporation.

Microlam A manufactured structural wood beam. It is constructed of pressure and adhesive bonded wood strands of wood.

Mid-rise A building with four to eight stories above ground level. In a central business district this might extend to buildings up to 25 stories.

Milar Also called Mylar. A plastic, transparent copy of a blueprint.

Milking A Project See Bleeding A Project.

Mill A tax rate used by municipalities to compute property tax. See Millage Rate.

Millage Rate A tax rate applied to property. Each mill represents $1 of tax assessment per $1,000 of assessed property value.

Millwork All building materials that is made of finished wood and developed in millwork plants such as doors, window and door frames, blinds, mantels, etc.

Mineral Lease An agreement that provides the lessee the right to excavate and sell minerals on the property of the lessor or to remove and sell petroleum and natural gas from the pool underlying the property of the lessor. In return, the lessor typically receives a royalty payment based on the value of the minerals removed.

Mineral Rights The privilege of usage and removal of oil, gas, and other valuable resources found on land. See Mineral Lease.

Minimum Bid Starting bid price. Minimum amount of money a county or other governmental entity will sell property for at an auction. Value is set at a discounted market value established by an Office of Real Property, Commissioner of Finance, county assessor or other official but is not less than amount of back taxes.

Minimum Lot Area The smallest building lot area allowed in a subdivision for purposes of building, generally specified by a Zoning Ordinance.

Minimum Rent See Base Rent.

Mini-Warehouse   A building separated into relatively small lockable individual units, typically with a garage-door-styled opening, that provide storage. Units are typically rented month to month.

Mini-Storage   See Mini-Warehouse.

Minor   A person under an age specified by law; usually under 18 years of age.

Minority Discount   A reduction from the market value of an asset because the minority interest owner cannot direct the business operations. See Family Limited Partnership.

Minority Interest   Ownership of less than 50% of an entity. See Minority Discount.

MIP   See Mortgage Insurance Premium.

Misrepresentation   To represent falsely; to give an untrue idea of a property. May be accomplished by omission or concealment of a material fact.

Mission House   A nineteenth-century-style house that looks like the old mission churches and houses of Southern California. The doors and windows are arch-shaped.

Mistake   An unintentional error made in preparing a contract. May be corrected by mutual consent of all parties without voiding contract.

Miter Joint   The joint of two pieces at an angle that bisects the joining angle.

Mixed-Use   A building or project that provides more than one use, such as office/retail or retail/residential.

MLP   See Master Limited Partnership.

MLS   See Multiple Listing Service.

Mobile Home   A dwelling unit manufactured in a factory and designed to be transported to a site and semi-permanently attached.

Mobile Home Park   A subdivision of plots designed for siting of mobile homes. Plots are generally leased to mobile homeowners and include utilities, parking space, and access to utility roads. Many parks also include such amenities as swimming pools and clubhouses.

Model Unit   A representative home, apartment, or office space used as part of a sales campaign to demonstrate the design, structure, and appearance of units in a development.

Modern Portfolio Theory (MPT)   An approach to quantifying risk and return in a portfolio of assets. Developed in 1959 by Harry Markowitz, MPT is the foundation for present-day principles of investment diversification. It emphasizes the portfolio rather than individual assets, and how assets perform in relation to each other based on the assumption that investors can benefit from diversification when asset class returns do not move in lock step with one another. See Modern Investment Theory.

Modernize   To alter a property by installing up-to-date equipment, making contemporary cosmetic improvements, and deleting obsolete facilities.

Modified Accelerated Cost Recovery System (MACRS) A system of depreciation for income tax purposes. Specifies annual depreciation tax deductions.

Modular Housing A factory-built home that complies with local building codes.

Moisture Barrier A layer of foil, plastic, or paper used in the construction of exterior walls, ceilings, and foundations to prevent moisture penetration into wooden members or insulation.

Molding Wood strip with an engraved or decorative surface. Often Spelled *"Moulding"*.

Monetary Institution Deregulation Act See Depository Institutions Deregulation And Monetary Control Act.

Monetary Policy The government regulation of the amount of money in circulation through such Institutions As The Federal Reserve Board.

Money Judgment A court judgment ordering payment of money rather than specific performance of a certain action.

Money Market Those institutions, such as banks, savings-and-loan associations, and life insurance companies, who supply money and credit to borrowers.

Monolithic Slab A monolithic slab is a type of foundation in which the footing and slab are poured at the same time.

Monopost A metal column that is adjustable used for supporting a beam or bearing point.

Monterey Architecture A nineteenth-century-style, 2-story house with a balcony across the front at the second-floor level.

Month-to-Month tenancy A periodic tenancy. The tenant rents for one period at a time. In the absence of a rental agreement, whether oral or written, a tenancy generally is considered to be from month to month.

Monument Fixed natural or artificial objects, used in metes-and-bounds description, to establish the boundaries; located at the corners.

Moratorium A time period during which a certain activity is not allowed.

Mortar A mixture of cement, sand and water used in masonry work.

Mortgage
1. A mortgage is the agreement between a borrower and a lender giving the lender the right to the borrower's property if the borrower is unable to make loan payments *(with interest)* within an agreed upon timeline.
2. A conditional transfer or pledge of real estate as security for a loan. Also, the document creating a mortgage lien.

Mortgage (Loan) Pre-Approval A process whereby a specific mortgage lender certifies that a prospective borrower is financially qualified and creditworthy for a specific type of loan with specified terms for an amount up to a specified maximum. Actual advancement of the loan will depend on the suitability and value of the collateral property, which is unspecified at the time of pre-approval.

Mortgage (Loan) Pre-Qualification A simple exercise through which prospective borrowers can get an estimate of how large a loan they may be able to obtain based on their current financial situation. The lender doing the analysis considers the borrowers' income and indebtedness but does not access the borrowers' Credit Report or examine the collateral for the loan. Therefore, there is no promise of a loan approval involved in the process. Also called *"Pre-Qual",* Pre Approval, or Pre-Qualification

Mortgage Assumption See Assumption Of Mortgage.

Mortgage Banker A mortgage banker works directly with a lending institution to provide mortgage funds to a borrower. They can only obtain funds from a specific institution and are responsible for each part of the mortgage process, including property evaluation, financial due diligence, and overseeing the application process.

Mortgage Bankers Association Of America (MBA) An organization that provides educational programs and other services for mortgage bankers. Offers the Certified Mortgage Banker *(CMB)* designation. Publishes *Mortgage Banker* magazine.

Mortgage Bonds Tax-exempt securities sold by municipal and state authorities for the purpose of providing low-interest rate mortgage loans to qualified individuals. For most programs, mortgage borrowers must be first-time home buyers with moderate income.

Mortgage Broker A mortgage broker shops several lenders, acting as a middleman between lending institutions and the borrower. A broker can Contrast mortgages from several different institutions, giving the borrower a better deal.

Mortgage Broker Dual Agency Disclosure Form Discloses to the borrower when a real estate broker is also acting as a mortgage broker in the same transaction.

Mortgage Burning Party See Satisfaction.

Mortgage Commitment A formal indication by a lending institution that it will grant a mortgage loan on property in a certain specified amount and on certain specified terms.

Mortgage Company A firm that borrows money from a bank and gives it to consumers as a loan to purchase homes, then sells the loans to investors.

Mortgage Constant The percentage ratio between the annual debt service and the loan principal.

Mortgage Correspondent One who services loans for a fee.

Mortgage Credit Certificate (MCC) A certificate allowing a borrower to claim a portion of mortgage interest as a credit against federal income tax. Each state or local government may issue a limited number of these to qualified residents, who must be first-time homebuyers and comply with maximum income limits.

Mortgage Deed A Legal document establishing a loan on property.

Mortgage Discount An amount of principal that lenders deduct at the beginning of the loan. See Discount Points.

Mortgage Guarantee Insurance Company (MGIC) A private company that insures, to lenders, loan repayment in the event of default and/or foreclosure.

Mortgage Insurance If a homebuyer makes a down payment of less than 20% of the purchase price of a home or is the recipient of an FHA or USDA loan, they'll usually be required to pay mortgage insurance. It lowers the risk of a lender giving you a loan, but it also increases the cost of the loan.

Mortgage Insurance Premium (MIP) A charge paid by the borrower, which is usually as part of the closing costs, to obtain financing, especially when making a down payment of less than 20 percent of the purchase price, for example on an FHA-insured loan.

Mortgage Lien A lien or charge on a mortgagor's property that secures the underlying debt obligations.

Mortgage Life Insurance See Mortgage Insurance.

Mortgage Loan See Mortgage.

Mortgage Note A document signed at closing that has the borrower's promise to repay the money borrowed.

Mortgage Origination Fee A charge for work involved in preparing and servicing a mortgage application

Mortgage Origination See Loan Origination.

Mortgage Out To obtain financing in excess of the cost to construct a project. In the mid 1980s developers could mortgage out by obtaining a permanent loan commitment based on a high percentage of the completed project's value. This enabled the developer to borrow more than the cost of developing the project. Since then, opportunities to mortgage out have been virtually eliminated by lower loan-to-value ratios, higher capitalization rates and higher construction costs.

Mortgage Pool A collection of loans of similar nature that are sold as a unit in the secondary market or used to back a security that is then sold in the capital markets.

Mortgage Reduction Certificate An instrument executed by the mortgagee, setting forth the present status and the balance due on the mortgage as of the date of the execution of the instrument.

Mortgage Relief Acquired freedom from mortgage debt, generally through Assumption Of Mortgage by another party or debt retirement. In a tax-free exchange, mortgage relief is considered boot received. In many foreclosures, where the property is the sole collateral for the loan, or the borrower fails to pay anything in addition to the real estate, the transaction is treated for tax purposes as a sale for the mortgage debt. If the taxpayer's basis is less than the mortgage relief, the difference is a taxable gain.

Mortgage Satisfaction The full payment of a mortgage loan.

Mortgage Servicing A Mortgage Banking activity that consists of collecting monthly interest and principal payments, taxes, and insurance from borrowers, as well as assuring that taxes and insurance are paid to the assessor and insurer and that interest earned and principal are paid to the investor.

Mortgage-Backed Bonds   See Collateralized Mortgage Obligation, Mortgage-Backed Security.

Mortgage-Backed Security A bond or other financial obligation secured by a pool of mortgage loans. See Collateralized Mortgage Obligations, REMICs.

Mortgagee In Possession Situation in which a lender takes possession and control of a mortgaged property upon foreclosure of the loan secured by the mortgage. The lender possesses the property, collecting any income produced, until it is sold at the fore-closure sale.

Mortgagee The party who lends money and takes a mortgage to secure the payment thereof.

Mortgage-Equity Technique See Ellwood Technique.

Mortgagor One who, having all or part of title to property, pledges that property as security for a debt; the borrower.

Mortise A slot cut into a board, plank, or timber, normally edgewise to receive the tenon of another board, plank, or timber to form a joint.

Most Probable Selling Price The property's most likely selling price when not all the conditions required for a Market Value estimate are relevant.

Motivated Seller One who urgently needs to dispose of property.

Mother-In-Law Quarters See Accessory Apartment.

MPT See Modern Portfolio Theory.

Mudsill Bottom horizontal member of an exterior wall frame which rests on top a foundation, sometimes called sill plate.

Mull Bar See Mullion

Mullion A vertical divider in the frame between windows, doors, or other openings.

Multifamily Housing A type of residential structure with more than one dwelling unit in the same building.

Multiple-Asset Exchange An exchange that includes both real property and personal property. Farm, hotels, and motels are prime examples of properties that would be involved in such an exchange, because there is a combination of buildings, land, and necessary business equipment involved.

Multiple Dwelling A structure that has two or more residential units. See Multi-Family Housing.

Multiple Listing See Multiple Listing Service. An exclusive listing with the additional authority and obligation on the part of the listing broker to distribute the listing to other brokers in the multiple-listing organization.

Multiple Listing Service (MLS) An MLS is a suite of around 700 regional databases containing their own listings. Each database has its own listings, requires agents to pay dues for access, and allows agents to share listings across regions, without paying dues to each one. It is widely considered the most comprehensive listing service available.

Multiplier A factor, used as a guide, applied by multiplication to derive or estimate an important value.

Municipal Ordinances The laws, regulations, and codes enacted by the governing body of a municipality.

Municipality A town, village, city, or county with its own local government.

Municipality Utility District (MUD) A utility that serves a limited geographic area, formed as a municipality rather than a private corporation to take advantage of lower interest rates available to municipal bonds. Allows development in an area that might otherwise not have utility services.

Muniments Of Title The documents, such as deeds or contracts, one uses to indicate ownership.

Muntin A small member which divides the glass or openings of sash or doors.

Muriatic Acid A Chemical used for cleaning bricks after the completion of masonry work.

Mushroom An occurrence that is unacceptable when the top of a caisson concrete pier spreads out and hardens to become wider than the foundation wall thickness.

Mutual Rescission The act of putting an end to a contract by mutual agreement of the parties.

Mutual Savings Banks Located mostly in the northeastern U.S., these state-chartered banks are owned by the depositors and operated for their benefit. Most of these banks hold a large portion of their assets in home mortgage loans.

Mylar See Milar.

N

NACORE See National Association Of Corporate Real Estate Executives.

NAEBA See National Association Of Exclusive Buyer Agents.

NAEP See National Association Of Environmental Professionals.

NAHB See National Association Of Home Builders.

NAHRO See National Association Of Housing And Redevelopment Officials.

NAIFA See National Association Of Independent Fee Appraisers.

Nail Inspection A check carried out by a municipal building inspector after the drywall material is hung with nails and screws.

Nailer A wooden strip attached to a concrete, masonry, or steel deck to allow roofing materials to be mechanically fastened.

NAIOP See National Association Of Industrial And Office Properties.

NAMA See National Association Of Master Appraisers.

NAMB See National Association Of Mortgage Brokers An association representing the interests of mortgage brokers in the United State.

NAR See National Association Of Realtors®.

NARA/MU See National Association Of Review Appraisers And Mortgage Underwriters.

NAREA See National Association Of Real Estate Appraisers.

NAREB See National Association Of Real Estate Brokers.

NAREE See National Association Of Real Estate Editors.

NaREIA See National Real Estate Investors Association.

NAREIT See National Association of Real Estate Investment Trusts The national, not-for-profit trade organization that represents the real estate investment trust industry.

National Association Of Real Estate Investment Trusts See NAREIT.

NARELLO See National Association Of Real Estate License Law Officials.

National Apartment Association (NAA) An organization of apartment owners, with local chapters in metropolitan areas, that provides information and services for members concerning apartment rentals, lease forms, occupancy rates, and other matters.

National Association Of Corporate Real Estate Executives (NACORE) Their membership includes those active with purchasing, selling, and managing real estate held by corporations.

National Association Of Environmental Professionals (NAEP) A multidisciplinary association dedicated to the advancement of the environmental professions in the United States and abroad; a forum for state-of-the-art information on environmental planning, research, and management; a network of professional contacts and exchange of information among colleagues in industry, government, academe, and the private sector; and a resource for structured career development from student membership to certification as an environmental professional.

National Association Of Home Builders (NAHB) An organization of home builders, providing educational, political information, and research services. Publishes a monthly magazine, *Builder.*

National Association Of Housing And Redevelopment Officials (NAHRO) Housing and community development advocate for the provision of adequate and affordable housing and strong, viable communities for all Americans particularly those with low and moderate incomes.

National Association Of Independent Fee Appraisers (NAIFA) An organization of real estate appraisers that offers these professional designations:

1. IFA: Member
2. FAS: Senior Member
3. IFAC: Appraiser/Counselor

National Association Of Industrial And Office Properties (NAIOP) A trade association, founded in 1967, with over 7,000 members who are developers, owners, investors, and related professionals in industrial and office real estate in 47 chapters across the United States and Canada.

National Association Of Master Appraisers (NAMA) An association that offers the Master Senior Appraiser *(MSA)* designation.

National Association Of Real Estate Appraisers (NAREA) A professional organization, founded in 1966, making estate appraisers available to those requiring professional appraisal reports. Offers the following membership classes or designations: CREA *(Certified Real Estate Appraiser)*, CCRA *(Certified Commercial Real Estate Appraiser)*, and RPM *(Registered Professional Member).*

National Association Of Real Estate Brokers (NAREB) An organization mostly of minority real estate salespersons and brokers who are called realtists.

National Association Of Real Estate Editors (NAREE) A professional association, founded in 1929, for writers, editors, columnists, authors, and communication professionals covering residential and commercial real estate.

National Association Of Real Estate Investment Trusts (NAREIT) A trade association that serves REITs. It collects data on the performance of REITs, and prepares definitions to be used for the industry, including FFO and CAD.

National Association Of Real Estate License Law Officials (NARELLO) Their membership is composed of commissioners from state real estate licensing agencies.

National Association Of Realtors ® (NAR) An organization of Realtors®, devoted to encouraging professionalism in real estate activities. There are over 600,000 members of NAR, 50 state associations, and several affiliates. Members are required to abide by the code of ethics of the NAR.

National Association Of Review Appraisers And Mortgage Underwriters (NARA/MU*)* An organization that awards the Certified Review Appraiser *(CRA)* designation.

National Council Of Real Estate Investment Fiduciaries (NCREIF) Organization that collects historical data on various institutional-grade property types, sorted by geographic areas. Publishes data on income and value changes. Index, called *Russell-NCREIF Real Estate Performance Report,* is often cited as the benchmark for institutional real estate performance.

National Multi Housing Council An organization that provides leadership for the apartment industry on legislative and regulatory matters, advances research and the exchange of strategic business information, and promotes the desirability of apartment living.

National Network Of Commercial Real Estate Women (NNCREW) An organization of attorneys, brokers, lenders, developers, property managers, appraisers, and designers dedicated to furthering the success of its members by providing opportunities that foster productive and supportive relationships and enhance personal and professional growth.

National Real Estate Index The data provider for many types of property in more than 50 cities.

National Real Estate Investors Association (NaREIA) An organization that works with local investor groups to share resources and exchange information.

National Realty Committee A group whose membership is primarily composed of large, high-profile owners and developers. Their paramount concern is the legislative arena, especially the government's policy toward real estate finance, taxation, and investment.

National Retail Merchants Association This Organization publishes the *Department Store Lease Study,* which includes data on rental rates for retail property.

National Society Of Real Estate Appraisers An affiliate of the National Association of Real Estate Brokers that offers the professional designations RA, CRA, MREA.

National Tenant Lessee with a presence in most of the United States. These are better known and typically have better credit than local tenants.

National Association Of Exclusive Buyer Agents An organization devoted to real estate agents who represent buyers only.

Nationwide Multistate Licensing System (NMLS) NMLS stands for the Nationwide Mortgage Licensing System and Registry. NMLS is a web based platform for regulatory agencies to administer initial license applications and ongoing compliance requirements.

National Flood Insurance Program See Flood Insurance.

Natural Finish A transparent finish that does not change the original color or grain of the natural wood.

Natural Gas Meter A mechanical measuring and recording device of the volume of natural gas passing a given point.

Natural Vacancy Rate The average vacancy rate for a rental property market that would result if supply and demand were in balance. The level to which vacancy rates adjust over the long term. A benchmark by which current vacancy rates in the market are considered high or low.

NAV See Net Asset Value

NCREIF National Council of Real Estate Investment Fiduciaries. An association of real estate professionals who serve on working committees, sponsor research articles, seminars, and symposiums, and produce the NCREIF Property Index.

National Council Of Real Estate Investment Fiduciaries. See NCREIF.

NCREIF Property Index (NPI) The index reports quarterly and annual returns consisting of income and appreciation components. The index is based on data collected from the voting members of NCREIF. Specific property-type sub-indices include apartment, office, retail, industrial and hotel; regional sub-indices include West, East, South and Midwest.

NEC National Electrical Code. A set of rules governing safe wiring methods.

Needle Beam A steel/wood beam threaded through a hole in a bearing wall, which is used to support the wall and its superimposed loads during underpinning of its foundation.

Negative Amortization Amortization refers to the process of paying off a loan with regular payments, so the amount owed on the loan gradually decreases. Negative amortization happens when the amount owed continues to rise, regardless of regular payments, because the mortgager is not paying enough to cover the interest each month. The Idea is to get into a property for a lower payment now, and refinance later when equity and ability to pay have increased. These loans were popular in areas with very high appreciation such as California prior to the Financial Crisis of 2008.

Negative Cash Flow Situation in which a property owner must make an outlay of funds to operate a property.

Negative Leverage See Reverse Leverage.

Negative Pledge When the condominium places restrictions on the unit deed and trust agreement restricting the right of an owner to finance a condominium unit for more than a specified amount.

Negligence Carelessness and inattentiveness resulting in violation of trust. Failure to do what is required.

Negotiable Instrument A promise to pay money, transferable from one person to another.

Negotiation The process of bargaining that precedes an agreement. Successful negotiation generally results in a contract between the parties.

Neighborhood A district or locality characterized by similar or compatible land uses. *Neighborhoods* are often identified by a place name and have boundaries composed of major streets, barriers, or abrupt changes in land use.

Neighborhood Association A voluntary membership organization that deals with social, political, zoning, and other issues which typically affect the members' properties and usually does not maintain commonly owned property.

Neighborhood Life Cycle A generalized pattern that describes the physical and social changes that residential areas experience over time. See Abandonment, Filtering Down, Urban Renewal, Land Use Succession.

Neighborhood Shopping Center See Shopping Center.

Net Asset Value (NAV) The value of an individual asset or portfolio of real estate properties net of leveraging or joint venture interests.

Net Asset Value Per Share The current value of a REIT's assets divided by shares outstanding.

Net Assets Total assets less total liabilities on a market-value basis.

Net Cash Flow Generally determined by net income plus depreciation less principal payments on long-term mortgages.

Net Effective Income The income figure after totaling gross income, minus the vacancy/credit loss, plus miscellaneous income.

Net Income

1. In accounting, the amount remaining after all expenses have been met.
2. In appraisal See Net Operating Income.

Net Income Multiplier A factor that, when applied by multiplication to a property's Net Operating Income, results in a property value estimate.

Net Investment In Real Estate Gross investment in real estate less the outstanding debt balance.

Net Investment Income The income or loss of a portfolio or entity resulting after deducting all expenses, including portfolio and asset management fees, but before realized and unrealized gains and losses on investments.

Net Leasable Area In a building or project, floor space that may be rented to tenants. The area upon which rental payments are based. Generally excludes common areas and space devoted to the heating, cooling, and other equipment of a building.

Net Lease A lease requiring the tenant to pay not only rent but also costs incurred in maintaining the property, including taxes, insurance, utilities, repairs. If the tenant pays for everything, it is referred to as a triple net lease.

Net Listing A price below which an owner will not sell the property, and at which price a broker will not receive a commission; the broker receives the excess over and above the net listing as the broker's commission. Illegal in New York.

Net Operating Income (NOI) A before-tax computation of gross revenue less operating expenses and an allowance for anticipated vacancy. It is a key indicator of financial strength.

Net Present Value (NPV) Net present value usually is employed to evaluate the relative merits of two or more investment alternatives. It is calculated as the sum of the total present value of incremental future cash flows plus the present value of estimated proceeds from sale. Whenever the net present value is greater than zero, an investment opportunity generally is considered to have merit.

Net Purchase Price Gross purchase price less associated debt financing.

Net Real Estate Investment Value The market value of all real estate less property-level debt.

Net Realizable Value (NRV) The amount a property is expected to bring after deductions for time on the market, selling expenses, and holding costs. Often applied to distressed properties, properties in depressed markets, or foreclosed properties owned by lending institutions.

Net Rentable Area See Net Leasable Area.

Net Returns Returns to investors net of fees to advisers or managers.

Net Sales Proceeds Proceeds from the sale of an asset or part of an asset less brokerage commissions, closing costs and market expenses.

Net Spendable Income See After-Tax Cash Flow.

Net Square Footage The space required for a function or staff position

Net Worth The excess of assets over liabilities. The amount of equity.

Net Yield The return on an investment after subtracting all expenses. See Current Yield, Yield To Maturity.

Neutral Wire The neutral wire carries electricity from an outlet back to the service panel.

New England Colonial An early-American-style, 2 1/2-story boxlike house that is generally symmetrical, square, or rectangular with side or rear wings. The traditional material is narrow clapboard siding. The roof is usually the gable type covered with shingles.

New England Farmhouse An early-American-style house that is simple and box-shaped. The traditional material for the exterior siding is white clapboard. A steep pitched roof is used to shed heavy snow.

New Town A large mixed-use development designed to provide residences, general shopping, services, and employment. The basic concept of a new town is to construct a community in a previously undeveloped area under a central plan, to avoid unplanned development. Some European and South American countries use new towns to attract population into less developed regions.

Newel Post The large starting post to which the end of a stair guard railing or balustrade is fastened.

NLA Net Leasable Area.

NNCREW National Network Of Commercial Real Estate Women.

NMLS See Nationwide Multistate Licensing System.

No Bid A decision by the Veterans Administration, when a loan it has guaranteed goes into default, to pay the guarantee amount to the lender instead of acquiring the property in foreclosure. The result is that often the lender obtains the property at the sale. The VA guarantees 60% of the loan amount or a fixed amount, whichever is lower.

No Cash-Out Refinance A no cash-out refinance is a type of loan used to improve the rate the borrower pays on the loan but does not receive any cash at closing. It might also shorten the lifetime of a loan to benefit the borrower. In a no cash-out refinance, the borrower refinances an existing mortgage for equal to or less than the outstanding loan balance. the goal is to lower interest rates on the loan or change certain terms of the mortgage.

No Money Down General term referring to real estate acquisition strategies based on seller-provided financing and/or existing loan assumption and minimal use of cash down payments. It is a method of achieving maximum profits from real estate investments.

No Money Down Loan This is a mortgage loan where the borrower receives a loan amount equivalent to the total value of the property to be purchased.

No-Cost Mortgage A no-cost mortgage is a type of refinancing in which the lender pays the borrower's loan settlement costs and extends a new loan typically in exchange for the borrower paying higher interest rates. The mortgage lender then sells the mortgage to a secondary mortgage market for a higher price because of the high interest rate.

NOI See Net Operating Income

Nominal Loan Rate See Face Interest Rate.

Nominal Yield The yield to investors before adjustments for fees, inflation, or risk.

Nominee One who, in a limited sense, acts for or represents another.

Non-bearing Wall A wall supporting no load other than its own weight.

Non-Compete Clause A clause that can be inserted into a lease specifying that the business of the tenant is exclusive in the property and that no other tenant operating the same or similar type of business can occupy space in the building. This clause benefits service-oriented businesses desiring exclusive access to the building's population.

Nonconforming Loan A loan that does not meet the standards of, or is too large to be purchased by, FNMA or FHLMC. The interest rate is at least half a percentage point higher than for a conforming loan.

Nonconforming Use A use of property that is permitted to continue after a zoning ordinance prohibiting it has been established for the area.

Non-discretionary Funds Funds allocated to an investment manager requiring the investor's approval on each transaction.

Non-disturbance Clause
1. An agreement in mortgage contracts on income-producing property that provides for the continuation of leases in the event of loan foreclosure.
2. An agreement in a sales contract, when the seller retains mineral rights, that provides that exploration of minerals will not interfere with surface development.

Non-disturbance The concept of consenting to *"not disturbing"* the rights of another, used typically in the context of a lender agreeing to permit a tenant to remain in its leasehold when the tenant's landlord *(who would be the lender's borrower)* defaults under its loan to the lender. See Non-disturbance Clause.

Non-exclusive Listing See Open Listing.

Non-Homestead Any real property which is not the primary residence of a property owner.

Non-homogeneity A lack of uniformity; dissimilarity. Because no two parcels of land are geographically alike, real estate is said to be nonhomogeneous, or heterogeneous.

Non-investment-grade CMBS Securities rated *"BB"* or *"B,"* also referred to as high-yield CMBS.

Non-performing Loan A loan that is unable to meet its contractual principal and interest payments.

Non-Recourse Borrower not personally liable, however, lender will require some protection in the event of a bankruptcy or other default of terms of the loan

Non-Recourse Carve-Outs Exceptions to non-recourse provisions of a loan, identifying circumstances and events for which a lender could Seek recovery from a borrower's assets other than the specific pledged collateral.

Non-Recourse Debt A loan that, in the event of a default by the borrower, limits the lender's remedies to a foreclosure of the mortgage, realization on its assignment of leases and rents, and acquisition of the real estate.

Non-Recourse Note A type of note where the borrower does not have personal liability for payment.

Non-Recourse The concept of a lender not having recourse against any assets of a borrower other than those assets specifically given as collateral.

Non-Residential
1.   Refers to property other than housing, such as office buildings, shopping centers, industrial parks, churches, or hotels.
2.   In taxation, when less than 80% of rent is from dwelling units, the owners cannot claim depreciation rates and lives used for residential property.

Non-solicitation Order A rule adopted by the Secretary of State which prohibits any or all types of solicitation directed towards homeowners within a defined geographic area. Such rule may be adopted after a public hearing and upon the Secretary's determination that homeowners within the subject area have been subject to intense and repeated solicitations by real estate brokers or salespersons and that such solicitations have caused owners to reasonably believe that property values may decrease because persons of different race, ethnic, religious or social backgrounds are moving or about to move into such area. See Block Busting, Steering.

Normal Wear And Tear Physical depreciation arising from age and ordinary use of the property.

Nosing The projecting edge of a molding or drip or the front edge of a stair tread.

Notarize To certify or attest to a document, as by a notary public.

Notary Colloquial term for Notary Public.

Notary Public A public officer who is authorized to take acknowledgments to certain classes of documents, such as deeds, contracts, mortgages, and before whom affidavits may be sworn.

Notch A crosswise groove at the end of a board.

Note An instrument of credit given to attest a debt.

Note Rate The note rate is the interest rate stated on a mortgage note. It is also commonly referred to as the nominal rate or face interest rate.

Notice Of Completion Legal notice filed after completion of construction. An unpaid contractor has a set amount of time after completion to file a mechanic's lien.

Notice Of Default A notice given to the public from a court stating that a mortgage borrower is behind in payments.

Notice Of Lis Pendens A public record used to warn all concerned parties that title to a property is the subject of a lawsuit and any lien resulting from the suit will be attached to the title. See Lis Pendens.

Notice Official communication of a legal action or one's intent to take an action. See Public Offering, Public Sale.

Notice To Quit A written notice, given to a tenant by a landlord, stating that the landlord intends to regain possession of the leased premises, and instructing the tenant to vacate the rented property.

Notorious Possession Generally acknowledged possession of real estate. One of the requirements to gain ownership of real estate through Adverse Possession.

Novation Acceptance by parties to an agreement to replace an old debtor with a new one. A novation releases liability.

Nozzle A portion of a heating system that sprays the fuel or fuel-air mixture to the combustion chamber.

NPV See Net Present Value

Nuisance
1. A land use whose associated activities are incompatible with surrounding land uses.
2. Activities that produce noxious fumes or air pollution in residential areas

Null And Void An Expression which means *"that which cannot be legally enforced"*, as with a contract provision that is not in conformance with the law.

O

O.C. On Center. T he measurement of spacing for studs, rafters, and joists in a building from the center of one member to the center of the next.

Oakum Loosely wound hemp rope or twine that's impregnated with tar or pitch and used to caulk large seams or for packing plumbing pipe joints.

OAR Overall rate of capitalization. Same as Overall Rate Of Return.

Oatmeal Paper Wallpaper that is made through sprinkling sawdust on top of adhesive surface.

Obligee The person in whose favor an obligation is entered into.

Obligor The person who binds himself/herself to another; one who has engaged to perform some obligation; one who makes a bond.

Obsolescence Loss in value due to reduced desirability and usefulness of a structure because its design and construction become obsolete; loss because of becoming old fashioned, and not in keeping with modern means, with consequent loss of income.

Occupancy A building code term referring to the permitted use of a building.

Occupancy Agreement, Limited One that allows a prospective buyer to obtain possession under a temporary arrangement, usually prior to closing.

Occupancy Report A summary of a building's occupancy. See also rent roll.

Occupancy Rate Or Level Percentage of currently rented units in a building, city, neighborhood, or complex.

Offer Term used to describe a stated price or spread to sell whole loans or securities.

Offer And Acceptance See Offer And Notification Of Acceptance.

Offer And Notification Of Acceptance The two components of a valid contract; a *"Meeting Of The Minds."*

Offeree One who receives an offer. Generally a buyer offers a purchase contract to an owner, which makes the owner the offeree. When the seller offers a contract to a buyer, the buyer is the offeree.

Offering Plan A document submitted to the attorney general by the sponsor of a co-op or condominium that fully describes the plans, pricing, and rules for a community. Potential buyers are given a copy of this report to read before buying into the co-op or condominium community.

Offeror One who extends an offer to another.

Office Building A structure primarily used for the conduct of business, such as administration, clerical services, and consultation with clients and associates. Such buildings can be large or small and may house one or more business concerns. See Building Owners And Managers Association, Black's Guide, Real Estate Information Systems.

Office Of Interstate Land Sales Registration (OILSR) A division of the U.S. Department of Housing And Urban Development that regulates offerings of land for sale across state lines. See Interstate Land Sales Act.

Office Of Real Property Services (ORPS) The agency that oversees assessing units in New York State. Their mission is to support local governments in their pursuit of real property tax equity.

Office Of Thrift Supervision (OTS) The federal agency created by FIRREA to regulate and supervise federally chartered Savings And Loan Associations. The OTS takes over the thrift regulatory duties exercised by the Federal Home Loan Bank Board prior to passage of the Act. The agency is part of the Treasury Department.

Office Park A planned development specially designed for office buildings and supportive facilities, such as restaurants. Some office parks, such as a research park or a medical services park, are designed to attract specific tenants.

Officer's Deed A deed by sheriffs, trustees, guardians, etc.

Offset Hinge. A hinge with a 90 degree offset in one or both legs, designed to shift the center of rotation of the door.

Offsite Construction A property built at various locations than the location of use.

Off-Site Costs Expenditures related to construction that are spent away from the place of construction.

Off-Site Improvements The portions of a subdivision or development that are not directly on the lots to be sold.

Oil And Gas Lease An agreement that gives the right to explore for oil, gas, and sometimes other minerals and to extract them from the ground. Provisions include the granting of subsurface and surface rights, lease duration, extension terms, royalties, surface damages, assignments, and warranties. See Mineral Rights.

OILSR Office Of Interstate Land Sales Registration.

One Hundred Percent Commission Plan A salesperson compensation plan by which the salesperson pays his or her broker a monthly service charge to cover the costs of office expenses and receives 100% of the commissions from the sales that he or she negotiates.

One Way Concrete Joist System A reinforced concrete framing system where closely spaced concrete joists span in between the parallel beams.

One-Hundred-Percent Location The particular spot in an urban area where land value and rents are the highest; the *"best"* location.

Open Hole Inspection An inspection done by an engineer on the open excavation and examines the earth to ascertain the type of foundation that should be installed in the hole.

Open House A time period where a house or other dwelling is created to be opened to buyers for viewing.

Open Housing A condition under which housing units may be purchased or leased without regard for racial, ethnic, color, or religious characteristics of the buyers or tenants.

Open Listing A listing contract under which the broker's commission is contingent on the broker producing a *"Ready, Willing, And Able"* buyer before the property is sold by the seller or another broker; the principal, That is the owner reserves the right to list the property with other brokers.

Open Mortgage A mortgage that has matured or is overdue and is therefore open to foreclosure at any time.

Open Space An area of land or water dedicated for public or private use or enjoyment.

Open-End Fund A commingled fund that does not have a finite life, continually accepts new investor capital, and makes new property investments.

Open-End Mortgage A mortgage loan expandable by increments up to maximum dollar amount, all of which is secured by the same original mortgage.

Open-Ended Listing Contract A contract that is between a seller and a real estate broker without a termination date.

Operating Budget A detailed projection of all estimated income and expenses during a given period of time.

Operating Capital Money used to finance everyday activities of the business.

Operating Cost Escalation Although there are many variations of escalation clauses, all are intended to adjust rents by reference to external standards such as published indexes, negotiated wage levels, or expenses related to the ownership and operation of a building.

Operating Expense The actual costs associated with operating a property, including maintenance, repairs, management, utilities, taxes, and insurance.

Operating Expense Ratio The mathematical relationship derived by dividing Operating Expenses by Potential Gross Income.

Operating Income See Net Operating Income.

Operating Lease A lease between the lessee and the sublessee who actually occupies and uses the property. See Sublease.

Operating Leverage Automatic increases in the Net Operating Income or Cash Flow of income-producing real estate when income and expenses increase at the same rate; further enhanced when expenses are fixed.

Opinion Of Title A certificate, generally from an attorney, as to the validity of title to property being sold. See Title Abstract.

Opportunistic A phrase generally used by advisers and managers to describe investments in underperforming and/or undermanaged assets that hold the expectation of near-term increases in cash flow and value through "turnaround" strategies. These investments typically imply the assumption of more risk in exchange for a higher return. Total return objectives for opportunistic strategies tend to be 18 percent or higher. Opportunistic investments often include development-oriented or repositioning/redevelopment strategies and typically involve a high degree of leverage Typically 60 percent to 100 percent on an asset basis and 60 percent to 80 percent on a portfolio basis.

Opportunity Cost A term used in economics; when taking a particular action, the loss of the value of the next-best action.

Option The right to purchase property within a definite time at a specified price. No obligation to purchase exists, but the seller is obligated to sell if the option holder exercises the right to purchase.

Option To Purchase A contract that gives one the right but not the obligation to buy a property, within a certain time, for a specified amount, and subject to specified conditions.

Option To Renew An option to renew is a provision in a lease that states the method and terms of a lease renewal.

Optionee One who receives or purchases an option.

Optionor The party that grants or gives an option.

Oral Contract An unwritten agreement. With few exceptions, unwritten agreements for the sale or use of real estate are unenforceable. In most states, contracts for the sale or rental of real estate are, unless they are in writing, unenforceable under the Statute Of Frauds. Oral leases for a year or less are often acceptable.

Ordinance A statute, law or rule enacted by the government of a municipality.

Ordinary Annuity A series of equal payments, each payment occurring at the end of each equally spaced period.

Ordinary Income Defined by the Internal Revenue Code to include salaries, fees, commissions, interests, dividends, and many other items. Taxed at regular tax rates.

Ordinary Loss For income tax purposes a loss that is deductible against Ordinary Income. Usually more beneficial to a taxpayer than a Capital Loss, which has limitations on deductibility.

Ordinary And Necessary Business Expenses A tax term that allows a current deduction for business expenses.

ORE, OREO Other real estate, other real estate owned. Generally, foreclosed property held by lending institutions. An account at banks or savings and loan associations that includes property other than real estate used for bank operations. See REO.

Orientation The position of a structure on a site relative to sunlight angles and prevailing winds.

Oriented Strand Board (OSB) A manufactured wood panel made out wood chips and glue, usually sold in 4' x 8' sheets.

Original Equity The amount of cash initially invested by the underlying Real Estate owner. Distinguished from Sweat Equity, Capital Calls.

Original Principal Balance The original principal balance is the amount owed on a mortgage before the first payment has been made.

Originate Issue a loan; See loan origination.

Origination Fee The fee a borrower pays a lender to cover the costs of processing their loan application.

Origination Fees Charges to a borrower to cover the costs of issuing the loan, such as credit checks, appraisal, and title expenses.

Origination Process The process by which a loan is funded, including the due diligence process, financial structure, and lender committee approvals.

Origination See loan origination.

Origination The first step in the mortgage loan process that consist of the completion of the application.

Originator A company that sources and underwrites commercial and/or multifamily mortgage loans.

ORPS See Office of Real Property Services.

OSB See Oriented Strand Board.

OTC Over The Counter.

OTC Deed Deeds that were not bid on at a tax sale and still have option for purchase. You can then purchase these deeds through the mail, or at the county offices. Typically, the deeds left over from a sale were not purchased because there was something negative about the property.

OTC Lien These are liens that were not bid on at a tax sale and still have option for purchase. You can then purchase these liens through the mail or at the county offices. Typically, the liens left over from a sale were not purchased because there was something negative about the property or they were not worth it.

Other People's Money A colloquial term meaning borrowed funds invested in a moneymaking venture. This term implies that debt can be used to maximize investment profits or minimize risk of personal loss.

Out-Parcel Individual retail sites in a shopping center.

Outrigger An extension of a rafter beyond the wall line. Usually a smaller member nailed to a larger rafter to form a cornice or roof overhang.

Outside Corner The point where two walls form an external angle, one you usually can walk around.

Outstanding Balance The amount currently owed on a debt.

Over Improvement A land use considered too intense for the land.

Overage In leases for retail stores, amounts to be paid, based on gross sales, over the base rent. See Percentage Lease.

Overall Capitalization Rate See Overall Rate Of Return.

Overall Rate Of Return (OAR) The percentage relationship of Net Operating Income divided by the purchase price of property. See Capitalization Rate.

Overallotment A practice through which underwriters offer and sell more shares than they have agreed to buy from the issuer.

Overhang Outward projecting eaves and soffit area of a roof; the part of the roof that hangs out beyond the exterior walls.

Override The fee paid to someone higher in the organization, or above a certain amount. An estate carved out of a working interest in an Oil And Gas Lease.

Owner Financing Owner financing takes place when a borrower finances the purchase of a home through the seller, bypassing conventional mortgage lenders and financial institutions. See Seller Financing.

Owner Occupant A tenant of a residence who also owns the property.

Owner Of Record The person, persons, or entity who, according to the Public Records, are the owners of a particular property.

Ownership Form Methods of owning real estate, which affect income tax, estate tax, continuity, liability, survivorship, transferability, disposition at death and at bankruptcy.

Ownership In Severalty The title to a property held in the name of one person only.

Ownership The exclusive right to hold, possess or control, and dispose of a tangible or intangible thing. A person, corporation, or governmental entity may hold ownerships.

P

P Trap A curved *"U"* section of drainpipe holding a water seal that stop sewer gasses from entering the home through a fixtures water drain.

P & I Principal And Interest.

P3 See Public-Private Partnership

Pacific Rim Real Estate Society (PRRES) An organization established in 1993 to provide a formal focus for property researchers, educators, and practitioners in the Pacific Rim region. An affiliate, along with ARES and ERES of the International Real Estate Society *(IRES)*.

Pack Out See Pad Out.

Package Mortgage A method of financing in which the purchase of the land also finances the purchase of certain personal property items.

Package Policy An insurance policy that combines coverage from two or more types of insurance *(liability and property for example)* into a single policy.

Pad Out To shim out or add strips of wood to a wall or ceiling in order that the finished ceiling/wall will appear correct.

Pad Site An individual freestanding site for a retailer, often adjacent to a larger Shopping Center.

Padding A material that is installed under carpet to add foot comfort, isolate sound, and to elongate carpet life.

Paint A combination of pigments with suitable thinners or oils to provide decorative and protective coatings. Can be oil based, acrylic based, or latex based.

Paired Shares Shares of stock in a company issued in two different forms, one of which is designed to get most of the dividend, the other most of the appreciation. Also called stapled stock. Tax law prevents this for future issues.

Pallets Wooden platforms used for storing and shipping material. Forklifts and hand trucks are used to move these wooden platforms around.

Panel A flat piece of wood, plywood, or any other material that is framed by stiles and rails as in a door or fitted into grooves of thicker material with molded edges for decorative wall treatment.

Paper Credit Credit which is given or evidenced by a written obligation that is backed by property.

Paper Profit An increase in value above original cost or basis that would be realized if the property were sold; however, the property is not offered for sale.

Paper, Building A term that is used for papers, felts, and other sheet that are similar used in buildings without reference to their properties or uses.

Parapet A wall placed at the edge of a roof to prevent people from falling off.

Parcel A parcel is a specific portion of land such as a lot.

Parking ratio Dividing the total rentable square footage of a building by the building's total number of parking spaces provides the amount of rentable square feet per each individual parking space.

Parol Evidence Oral evidence, rather than that contained in documents. The parol evidence rule states that when parties put their agreement in writing, all previous oral agreements merge into the written agreement. Oral testimony cannot contradict the written agreement, unless there was a mistake or fraud

Parol Evidence Rule A law that states that no prior or contemporary oral or extraneously written agreement can change the terms of a contract.

Partial Eviction A case in which the landlord's negligence deprives the tenant of the use of all or part of the premises.

Partial Interest
1. Ownership of a part of the ownership rights to a parcel of real estate.
2. Infrequently used to describe an undivided interest in property shared with several other owners.

Partial Release A provision in a mortgage that allows some of the property pledged to be freed from serving as collateral.

Partial Sales The sale of an interest in real estate that is less than the whole property. This may include a sale of easement rights, parcel of land or retail pad, or a single building of a multi-building investment.

Partial Taking The taking of part of an owner's property under the laws of eminent domain.

Partially Amortized Loan One that requires some payments toward principal but does not fully retire the debt, thereby requiring a balloon payment.

Participating Debt In addition to collecting a contract interest rate, participating debt allows the lender to have participatory equity rights through a share of increases in income and/or increases in residual value over the loan balance or original value at the time of loan funding.

Participating Mortgage See Participating Loan.

Participation Agreement The document providing for an allocation and ordering of rights and obligations of two or more lenders who are jointly funding a loan, or to whom a piece of a loan is sold after the loan closing.

Participation Financing A mortgage in which the lender participates in the income of the mortgaged venture beyond a fixed return or receives a yield on the loan in addition to the straight interest rate.

Participation Loan A loan funded by two or more lenders, or a loan funded by one lender who then sells off pieces of the loan to another lender or lenders.

Participation The sharing of ownership in a loan by two or more investors.

Particle Board Plywood replacement created from course sawdust mixed with resin and pressed into sheets.

Parting Stop Small wood piece that is used on the side and head jambs of double hung windows to separate the upper sash from the lower sash.

Parting Strip See Parting Stop.

Partition
1. The division of cotenants' interests in real property when the parties do not all voluntarily agree to terminate the co-ownership; takes place through court procedures.

2. A wall used for dividing spaces within any story of a building.

Partnership An association of two or more individuals who carry on a continuing business for profit as co-owners. Under the law, a partnership is regarded as a group of individuals rather than as a single entity. A general partnership is a typical form of joint venture in which each general partner shares in the administration, profits, and losses of the operation. A limited partnership is a business arrangement by which the operation is administered by one or more general partners and funded by limited partners, also called silent partners, who are by law responsible for losses only to the extent of their investment.

Party In Interest Under ERISA's 2002 Modernization Act, Parties in Interest include employers, unions and, in certain circumstances, fiduciaries. It excludes service providers and their affiliates. Fiduciaries would only be parties in interest where they act on behalf of a plan sponsor in entering into a transaction. An affiliate of a party in interest does not include remote affiliates of employers, unions, and fiduciaries, as well as employees of such remote affiliates.

Party Wall A wall built along the line separating two properties, partly on each, which wall either owner, the owner's heirs and assigns has the right to use; such right constituting an easement over so much of the adjoining owner's land as is covered by the wall.

Party Wall Easement The easement which incorporates a wall that is located on or at a boundary line between two adjoining parcels for the use of the owners of both properties. See Party Wall.

Passive Activity Income An activity that results in a profit, but the taxpayer does not physically participate. Examples would include rental property, limited partnerships, or other types of investments.

Passive Income
1. Generally, income from rents, royalties, dividends, interest, and gains from the sale of securities.
2. A meaning created by the Tax Reform Act of 1986 distinguishes passive income or loss from active income and portfolio income. See Passive Activity Income.

Passive Income Generator (PIG) A business or investment that produces Passive Income that can be used to offset passive losses.

Passive Investor One who invests money but does not manage the business or property. See Passive Income, Portfolio Income.

Passive Loss A loss made by investment real estate when real estate is not the taxpayer's primary business.

Passive Solar Heating A system of features incorporated into a building's design to use and maximize the effects of the sun's natural heating capability. See Active Solar Heating.

Pass-Through Certificate Payments of principal and interest from the underlying pool of mortgages are passed through to the holders of the certificates.

Paver A man-made stones that are laid down to make a firm surface.

Payback Period The amount of time required for cumulative estimated future income from an investment to equal the amount initially invested. It is used to

Payee The party that receives payment.

Payment Cap A contractual limit on the percentage amount of adjustment allowed in the monthly payment for an adjustable rate mortgage at any one adjustment period. Generally it does not affect the interest rate charged. If the allowable payment does not cover interest due on the principal at the adjusted rate of interest, Negative Amortization will occur.

Payment Schedule A pre-agreed upon schedule of payments to a contractor usually based upon the amount of work completed.

Payor The party that makes payment to another.

Payout Ratio The percentage of the primary earnings per share, excluding extraordinary items, paid to common stockholders in the form of cash dividends during the trailing 12 months.

Pedestal A metal box installed at various locations along utility easements that contain electrical, telephone, or cable television switches and connections.

Penalty Clause A provision in a contract that provides for a reduction in the amount otherwise payable under a contract to a contractor as a penalty for failure to meet deadlines or for failure of the project to meet contract specifications.

Penalty Money one will pay for breaking a law or violating part or all of the terms of a contract.

Pending A sales is considered pending if all contingencies have been met and the buyer and seller are moving toward closing. At this point, it's unlikely the sale will fall through, and the buyer or seller risk losing the earnest money if they walk out on the deal at this point.

Penny As applied to nails, it originally indicated the price per hundred.

Pension Fund A fund established by an employer to facilitate and organize the investment of employees' retirement funds contributed by the employer and employees. The pension fund is a common asset pool meant to generate stable growth over the long term, and provide pensions for employees when they commence retirement

Pension Liability The total amount of capital required to fund vested pension fund benefits.

Pension Real Estate Association (PREA) A nonprofit organization devoted to enhancing real estate investment by pension funds.

Penthouse Apartment on the highest floor, typically a luxury or executive level dwelling.

Per Diem Per diem or per day fees are charged if a loan isn't approved by the date the loan was scheduled to be completed. These charges are payable to the lender during closing.

Per Stirpes A legal method of distributing an estate to include the descendants of a deceased legatee, whose share is apportioned among linear descendants.

Percentage Lease A lease commonly used for retail property in which the rental is based on the tenant's gross sales at the premises; often stipulates a base monthly rental plus a percentage of any gross sales above a certain amount.

Percentage Lease A lease that has a rental amount that is a combination of a fixed amount plus a percentage of the lessee's gross sales.

Percentage Rent Rent payable under a lease that is equal to a percentage of gross sales or gross revenues received by the tenant. It is commonly used in retail center leases.

Percolation Test Determines if the soil is sufficiently porous for the installation of a septic tank.

Percolation Percolation is the movement of water through soil.

Perfecting a Loan A loan is issued against a personal property, recorded in the county clerk's office against the name of the borrower.

Perfecting Title The act of removing A cloud or claim against a title to real estate.

Perfection The concept of confirming the granting of a security interest. It is governed by the UCC with respect to personal property.

Performance The quarterly changes in fund or account values attributable to investment income, realized or unrealized appreciation, and the total gross return to the investors both before and after investment management fees. Formulas for calculating performance information are varied, making comparisons difficult.

Performance Bond A binding agreement, often accompanied by surety and usually posted by one who is to perform work for another, that assures that project or undertaking will be completed as per the agreement or contract.

Performance Measurement The process of measuring an investor's real estate performance in terms of individual assets, advisers/managers, and portfolios. The scope of performance measurement reports varies among managers, consultants, and plan sponsors.

Performance-Based Fees Fees paid to advisers or managers based on returns to investors, often packaged with a modest acquisition and asset-management fee structure.

Performing Loan Generally, one on which payments are less than 90 days past due.

Perimeter Drain 3 inches or 4 inches perforated plastic pipe that goes around the perimeter, either inside or outside of a foundation wall before backfilling and collects and diverts ground water away from the foundation.

Period Of Redemption See Redemption Period.

Periodic Estate A lease from month to month or year to year. Also known as periodic tenancy.

Periodic Tenancy See Periodic Estate.

Permanent Lender One who makes Permanent Loans.

Permanent Loan The long-term mortgage on a property.

Permanent Mortgage A mortgage for a long period of time typically more than 10 years.

Permanent Reference Marker (PRM) Referred to as a PRM, it is a fixed object that leads the surveyor to the point of beginning *(POB)*. In most surveys, two different PRMs are used to locate the POB.

Permeability A measure of the ease with which water penetrates a material.

Permit (Demolition) An approval to tear down and remove an existing structure.

Permit (Electrical) A separate permit required for most electrical work.

Permit (Grading) Authorization to change the contour of the land.

Permit (Plumbing) A separate permit required for new plumbing and larger modifications of existing plumbing systems.

Permit (Septic) A health department authorization to build or modify a septic system.

Permit (Zoning\Use Permit) Approval to make use of a property for a particular use like a garage, a single family residence etc.

Permit A document, issued by a government regulatory authority, that allows the bearer to take some specific action.

Perpetuity The condition of being never ending. Most states attempt to outlaw perpetuities because of potential problems. A perpetual income stream may cause bankruptcy. A deed that keeps property in a family in perpetuity can cause financial hardship.

Person In Law, An entity having legal responsibility. Legally, a natural person is a human being who has reached majority. An artificial person may be a corporation; in some instances partnerships, governments, and certain other bodies are considered persons.

Personal Assistant A n individual working for a broker or salesperson who handles non-sales-related aspects of real estate transactions. However, if the personal assistant is licensed, then he or she can also handle the sales-related aspects of the transaction.

Personal Liability An individual's responsibility for a debt. Most mortgage loans on real estate are recourse which means the lender can look to both the property and the borrower for repayment.

Personal Property Items, called chattels, that do not fit into the definition of real property; movable objects. Any property other than real estate property and fixtures. See Personalty.

Personal Residence The dwelling unit that one claims as one's primary home. This dwelling establishes one's legal residence for voting, tax, and legal purposes.

Personalty Personal property; all property that is not realty. Property that is movable, not fixed to land. See Chattel.

Phantom Gain A sale of real estate in which income is recognized for tax purposes but no money has been received correlating to the gain amount. This can occur when the property's basis has been depreciated below the property's mortgage amount.

Phase I Environmental Site Assessment A preliminary examination of a site to determine the potential for contamination. It includes a review of present and historical land uses and preliminary tests of places that are suspect. A Phase I study is required to support a claim to be an Innocent Purchaser.

PHASE II Environmental Site Assessment A field investigation, when results of a Phase I are positive, to confirm the presence of contamination and estimate the cost of Remediation.

PHASE III Environmental Site Assessment The act of clearing up a contaminated site. See Remediation.

Photovoltaic A term used in solar energy which describes the process of converting light directly into electricity using specially designed silicon cells.

Physical Deterioration A reduction in utility resulting from an impairment of physical condition. For purposes of appraisal analysis, it is most common and convenient to divide physical deterioration into curable and incurable components.

Pieda Terre A building that is not the primary residence of the owner.

Pier A column of masonry that is usually rectangular in horizontal cross section, for supporting other structural members.

Piggyback Loan
1. A combination of the construction loan with the permanent loan commitment.
2. One mortgage held by more than one lender, with one lender holding the rights of the others in subordination.

Pigment A powdered solid used in paint or enamel to give it a color.

Pigtails, Electrical Electric cord that the electrician provides and installs on an appliance like a garbage disposal, dishwasher, or range hood.

Pilot Hole A small diameter hole that is predrilled that guides a nail or screw.

Pilot Light A small, continuous flame used for igniting gas or oil burners when needed.

Pipeline
1. A conduit or network of pipes used to carry liquids such as water, sewage, gasoline, and oil.
2. Used metaphorically of the production or sales process, the course of completion of work in progress.

Pitch The incline slope of a roof determined by the ratio of the total rise to the total run of the given side of the gable. In geometric terms it is the ratio of the horizontal (run) and vertical (rise) portions of the right triangle formed where a given roof line is the hypotenuse of such triangle.

PITI Acronym which stands for principal, interest, taxes, and insurance, and refers to the sum of each of these charges, typically quoted on a monthly basis. These costs are calculated and compared to the borrower's monthly gross income when approving a mortgage loan. A borrowers PITI should generally be less than or equal to 28% of their gross monthly income.

Placement Agent A firm that acts as an intermediary between a fund manager Seeking to raise capital and various investors who may be interested in investing in such a fund.

Plaintiff The person who brings a lawsuit. Contrast with defendant.

Plan Assets The assets of a pension plan.

Plan Sponsor The entity that establishes, contributes to and is responsible for the administration of an employee benefit plan, often used interchangeably to describe staff who administer the plan and trustees or investment board members who govern it.

Plan View Drawing of a structure with the view from overhead, looking down.

Planned Unit Development A planned unit development *(PUD)* is a housing community made up of single family residences, townhomes, and condominiums as well as commercial units. PUDs offer many common areas owned by the HOA and amenities beyond what normal apartment buildings or townhomes offer, including tennis courts and outdoor playgrounds.

Planning Commission A group of citizens appointed by local government officials to conduct hearings and recommend amendments to the zoning ordinance. The planning commission generally oversees the work of a professional planning department, which prepares a comprehensive plan. May also be called a planning board, zoning commission, or zoning board, depending on locality.

Plat A map of a town, section, or subdivision indicating the location and boundaries of individual property. See Rectangular Survey.

Plat Book A book containing recorded subdivisions of land.

Plate Dimensional Lumber that lays horizontally within a framed structure.

Platform Framing The most common type of framing in residential construction in which the framing of the structure rests on a subfloor platform.

Pledged Account Mortgage (PAM) A type of home purchase loan under which a sum of cash contributed by the owner is set aside in an account pledged to the lender. The account is drawn down during the initial years of the loan to supplement periodic mortgage payments. The effect is to reduce the payment amounts in early years. See Graduated Payment Mortgage.

Pledged-Asset Mortgage A mortgage loan, often requiring no cash down

Plenum The main hot air supply duct leading from a furnace.

Plot Plan A diagram showing the proposed or existing use of a specific parcel of land.

Plottage Increased value of a plot of land created by assembling smaller ownerships into one ownership.

Plottage Value Increment in the value of land comprised by assemblage of smaller plots into one ownership.

Plough, Plow T o cut a lengthwise groove in a board or plank. An exterior handrail normally has a ploughed groove for hand gripping purposes.

PLSS See Public Land Survey System.

Plumb Bob A lead weight attached to a string.

Plumb

1. Exactly vertical and perpendicular.

2. The Act of installing plumbing to a structure.

Plumbing Boots A Metal saddle used to strengthen a bearing wall or vertical studs in which a plumbing drain line has been cut through and installed.

Plumbing Ground The plumbing drains and waste lines that are installed beneath a basement floor.

Plumbing Jacks Sleeves that fit around drain and waste vent pipes at, and are nailed to, the roof sheeting. Also called Roof Jacks.

Plumbing Permit A permit needed for new plumbing and larger modifications of existing plumbing systems.

Plumbing Rough Work performed by the plumbing contractor after the Rough Heat is installed. This work includes installing all plastic ABS drain and waste lines, copper, PVC, or PEX water lines, bathtubs, shower pans, and gas piping to furnaces and fireplaces. Lead solder should not be used on copper piping.

Plumbing Stack A plumbing vent pipe penetrating the roof.

Plumbing Trim A work that is performed by a plumbing contractor to get a property ready for a final plumbing inspection.

Plumbing Waste Line Plastic pipe used to collect and drain sewage waste.

Ply A term to denote the number of layers of roofing felt, veneer in plywood, or layers in other built up materials in any finished piece of such material.

Plywood A pane of wood made of three or more layers of veneer, compressed, and joined with glue, and usually laid with the grain of adjoining plies at right angles to give the sheet strength.

PMI Private Mortgage Insurance.

Pocket Card A pocket card is required for salespersons and brokers in most states. Issued by the state licensing agency, it identifies its holder as a licensee and must be carried at all times.

Point A unit of measurement used for various loan charges; one point equals one percent of the amount of the loan. See, Basis Point.

Point Load A point where a bearing/structural weight is concentrated and transferred to the foundation.

Point Of Beginning The starting point of the survey situated in one corner of the parcel in a metes-and-bounds description. All metes-and-bounds descriptions must follow the boundaries of the parcel back to the point of beginning.

Points Points are fees paid to induce lenders to make a mortgage loan. Each point equals 1% of the loan principal. Points have the effect of reducing the amount of money advanced by the lender. See Discount Points.

Police Power The government's right to impose laws, statutes, and ordinances to protect the public health, safety, and welfare, including zoning ordinances and building codes.

Portfolio Holding Collection of properties that is held by an investment company.

Portfolio Income Income derived from assets such as stocks, bonds, and mutual funds, including dividend income, interest, and royalties. Assets are owned by the taxpayer, but usually managed by financial experts.

Portfolio Lender A company that not only originates mortgage loans, but also holds a portfolio of their loans instead of selling them off in the secondary market.

Portfolio Management The portfolio management process involves formulating, modifying, and implementing a real estate investment strategy in light of an investor's broader overall investment objectives. It also can be defined as the management of several properties owned by a single entity.

Portfolio Turnover The average time from the funding of an investment until it is repaid or sold.

Portfolio Value The value of a real estate portfolio, which may exceed the value of the individual assets in the group because of operating cost efficiencies, synergies of management, or overall attractiveness. The portfolio is sometimes valued based on a common theme; that is, one capitalization rate is applied to the aggregate income as

Portland Cement A cement made through the heating of clay and crushed limestone into a brick and then grinding to a pulverized powder state.

Positive Cash Flow See Cash Flow.

Positive Leverage The use of borrowed funds that increases the return on an investment.

Possession The holding, control, or custody of property for one's use, either as owner or person with another right. See Ownership Rights To Realty, Title.

Post A vertical framing member that is designed for carrying a beam.

Post And Beam A building method that make use of just some hefty posts and beams to support an entire structure.

Postconstruction The period after construction during which disturbed areas are stabilized, storm water controls are in place and functioning, and all proposed improvements in the approved land development plan are completed

Post War A building that was built after World War II, Typically between the 1950s and 1970s.

Potential Gross Income The amount of income that could be produced by a real property assuming no vacancies or collection losses. Does not include miscellaneous income.

Potentially Responsible Parties (PRP) Referring to a Superfund site, all owners, operators, transporters, and disposers of hazardous waste are potentially responsible parties. See CERCLA, SARA, SUPERFUND.

Power Center A shopping center with few tenants, most of them anchors.

Power of Attorney A written instrument duly signed and executed by a person who authorizes an agent to act on his/her behalf to the extent indicated in the instrument.

Power of Sale Clause inserted in a mortgage or deed of trust giving the mortgagee (or trustee) the right and power, upon default in the payment of the debt secured, to advertise and sell the property at public auction.

Power Vent A vent, typically found in an attic space, with a fan to speed up air flow. Many times the fan will have a thermostat switch which turns the fan on when the attic reaches a certain temperature.

Prairie House An early-twentieth-century-style house with a long, low roof line, continuous row of windows, and an unornamented exterior. Designed to satisfy the physical and psychological needs of the inhabitants, it is unlike the traditional concept of a house that is a box subdivided into smaller boxes *(rooms)*, each with some doors and windows. Architectural development is credited to Frank Lloyd Wright.

Pre-Approval Before submitting an offer on a home (or even engaging with a real estate agent) you'll likely be required to get pre-approved. This means a lender has checked your credit, verified your information, and approved you for up to a specific loan amount for a period of up to 90 days.

Pre-Approved Or Pre-Qualified Evidence that a potential borrower has passed a preliminary credit screening. A pre-approval from a lender shows that a potential borrower has a solid credit history and is qualified for a mortgage loan of a specified size. In a competitive market, a pre-approval letter can provide greater negotiating influence with a seller, as it can give the seller confidence that borrower is financially capable of completing a purchase.

Preclosing A rehearsal of the closing whereby instruments are prepared and signed by some or all parties to the contract. Used when closings are expected to be complicated.

Preconstruction Method of performing preliminary planning and engineering so as to define the project, identify potential issues, schedule and analyze cost impacts.

Prefabricated
1. Constructed, as building components, in a factory prior to being erected or installed on the construction site.
2. Constructed, as a house, of prefabricated components. See Modular Housing.

Preferred Shares Stocks that have prior claim on distributions and/or assets in the event of dissolution, up to a definite amount before the common shareholders are entitled to anything. As a form of ownership, preferred shareholders fall behind all creditors in dissolutions.

Prelease To obtain lease commitments in a building or complex prior to its being available for occupancy.

Preleased Space in a proposed building that has been leased before the start of construction or in advance of the issuance of a certificate of occupancy.

Premises The specific section of a deed that states the names of the parties, recital of consideration, operative words of conveyance, legal property description, and appurtenance provisions.

Premium
1. The cost of an insurance policy.
2. The value of a mortgage or bond in excess of its face amount.
3. An amount over market value paid for some exceptional quality or feature.

Prepaid Expenses The amounts that are paid prior to the period they cover.

Prepaid Interest The interest paid in advance of the time it is earned.

Prepaids (At Closing) At the time of the closing of a loan, amounts required to be deposited into an escrow account, principally for hazard insurance, taxes, and PMI. May also include interest that will accrue from the closing date until the end of the month.

Prepay (Mortgage) To retire all or a portion of the principal balance before it is due under the mortgage contract.

Prepayment Clause In a mortgage, the statement of the terms on which the mortgagor may pay the entire or stated amount of the mortgage principal at some time prior to the due date.

Prepayment Penalty A charge imposed on a borrower by a lender for early payment of the loan principal to compensate the lender for interest and other charges that would otherwise be lost.

Prepayment Penalty Or Fee A fee assessed by a lender on a borrower who repays all or part of the principal of a loan before it is due. The prepayment penalty compensates the lender for the loss of interest that would have been earned had the loan remained in effect for its full term.

Prepayment Privilege The right of a borrower to retire a loan before maturity.

Prepayment Rights The rights given to the borrower to make partial or full payment of the total principal balance prior to the maturity date without penalty.

Prepayment Terms The terms of agreement for prepayment of a loan. Some loans may require a penalty or extra payment in the event the loan is retired before its' term.

Prepayment The act of paying all or a portion of an outstanding loan balance prior to the contractually agreed date for such payment.

Preplanning A stage of development when financing and government approvals are sought but before architectural drawings are begun.

Pre-qualification Unlike pre-approval, pre-qualification is more of an estimate of how much you can afford to spend on a home. See Pre-approval.

Presale Sale of proposed properties, such as condominiums, before construction begins.

Present Value Of Annuity The value now of a level stream of income to be received finite number of periods. See Ordinary Annuity.

Present Value Of One The value today of an amount to be received in the future, based compound interest rate.

Preservation District A zoning designation covering a sensitive environmental area, or historic districts, and placing especially strict limitations on private landowners to change the essential character of sites within the district.

Preservative Pesticide substance that, for a reasonable period will stop the action of wood destroying fungi, insect borers, and similar destructive agents when the wood has been properly coated or impregnated with it.

Pre-Sold In real estate, a pre-sold home is one that is being sold before completion, during construction, and sometimes even when it is still in the planning stage. Because the home is yet to be built, pre-selling has been likened to buying air or throwing money in a hole yet to be dug. Many Tract Homes in large subdivisions are sold as Pre-Solds.

Pressure Relief Valve (PRV) A device mounted on a hot water heater or boiler which is designed to release any high steam pressure in the tank to prevent tank explosions.

Pressure Treated Wood Lumber that has been saturated with a preservative.

Pretax Income The amount earned from a business or investment before deducting income

PreWar A building that was made before World War II, and usually before 1929, since there were few residential buildings built during the 1930s due to the poor economy.

Price The amount the property would sell for in an arm's length transaction. Both buyer and seller are interested in getting the best terms for themselves. Both parties are knowledgeable about the current marketplace.

Price To Earnings Ratio This ratio is calculated by dividing the current share price by the sum of the primary earnings per share from continuing operations, before extraordinary items and accounting changes, over the past four quarters.

Price-Level-Adjusted Mortgage A loan whose payment is adjusted according to the rate of inflation. The payments are generally quite low, typically 3 to 5% annually of the debt. This type of mortgage is not commonly used in the U.S.

Price-Rent Ratio The average cost of ownership divided by the received rent income or the estimated rent that would be paid if renting.

Price to Earnings Ratio (P/E Ratio) The common metric that is used to assess the relative valuation of equities. To calculate the P/E ratio in the case of a rented house, you have to divide the price of the house by its potential earnings or net income, which is the market rent of the house minus expenses, which include maintenance and property taxes.

Price To Income Ratio It is the basic affordability measure for housing in a given area. It is generally the ratio of median house prices to median familial disposable incomes, expressed as a percentage or as years of income. This ratio, applied to individuals, and also referred to as "attainability", is a basic component of mortgage lending decisions.

Primary Issuance The initial financing of an issuer.

Primary Lease A lease between the owner and a tenant whose interest, all or in part, has been sublet.

Primary Market Area See Market Area.

Primary Market Population The population located within a shopping center's primary trade area.

Primary Metropolitan Statistical Area (PMSA) A geographic entity defined by the federal Office of Management and Budget for use by federal statistical agencies. If an area meets the requirements to qualify as a metropolitan statistical area and has a population of one million or more, two or more PMSAs may be defined within it if statistical criteria are met and local opinion is in favor. A PMSA consists of one or more counties (county subdivisions in New England) that have substantial commuting interchange. When two or more PMSAs have been recognized, the larger area of which they are components then is designated a consolidated metropolitan statistical area. This term was retired in 2003 and is replaced by Metropolitan Division.

Primary Mortgage Market That portion of the credit market that originates mortgage loans, including institutional lenders, such as savings and loan associations and banks, and mortgage bankers and brokers. Contrast with Secondary Mortgage Market.

Primary Residence The place where a person lives most of the time, including a house, a manufactured home, a co-op, a condominium and even a houseboat.

Primary Residence Generally, a primary residence of an owner or renter is one that they occupy the majority of time, usually considered to be 6 months and 1 day out of every year.

Prime Contractor See General Contractor.

Prime Interest Rate The prime interest rate is typically awarded to a U.S. bank's best customers. It's the best-available loan rate and is usually three points above the federal funds rate: the rate banks charge each other for overnight loans.

Prime Rate The lowest commercial interest rate charged by banks on short-term loans to their most creditworthy customers.

Prime Space Typically refers to first-generation space that is available for lease.

Prime Tenant The major tenant in a building, or the major or anchor tenant in a shopping center.

Primer The first, base coat of paint when a paint job consists of two or more coats. A first coating formulated to seal raw surfaces and holding succeeding finish coats.

Principal
1. A sum lent or employed as a fund or investment, as distinguished from its income or profits.
2. The original amount in a loan of the total due and payable at a certain date.
3. A main party to a transaction; the person for whom the agent works.
4. A supervisory and typically part or full owner of a brokerage or Engineering firm.

Principal And Interest Payment (P&I) A periodic payment, usually paid monthly, that includes the interest charges for the period plus an amount applied to amortization of the principal balance. Commonly used with amortizing loans. See Mortgage Constant, Amortization.

Principal Balance The amount owed on a debt, whether the original face amount or the remaining debt on a loan that has been partially amortized.

Principal Broker The licensed broker responsible for the operations conducted by the brokerage firm.

Principal Meridian One of 35 north and south survey lines established and defined as part of the rectangular survey system See Government Rectangular Survey.

Principal Payments The return of invested capital to the lender.

Principal Residence See Primary Residence.

Principal Residence See Primary Residence

Principal, Interest, Taxes And Insurance (PITI) The periodic payment required by an amortizing loan that includes escrow deposits. Each periodic payment includes a Principal And Interest Payment plus a contribution to the escrow account set up by the lender to pay insurance premiums and property taxes on the mortgaged property.

Principle Of Conformity The appraisal theory stating that buildings that are similar in design, construction, and age to other buildings in the area have a higher value than they would have in a neighborhood of dissimilar buildings.

Priority The order of position or time. The priority of liens generally is determined by the chronological order in which the lien documents are recorded; tax liens (like special assessments), however, have priority, even over previously recorded liens.

Private Debt Real Estate One of the four quadrants of the real estate capital markets. Also known as "mortgages" or "whole loan mortgages," but also can refer to participating mortgages, loan participations and loan syndications. Typically refers to commercial loans, but also can refer to direct lending to single family homeowners. Also can refer to privately syndicated mortgage or other real estate-backed debt securities issued by either private or public real estate operating companies. Also See private equity real estate, public equity real estate, and public debt real estate.

Private Equity Fund See Private Equity Real Estate Fund.

Private Equity Manager See Private Equity Real Estate Manager.

Private Equity Real Estate One of the four quadrants of the real estate capital markets. Also known as "equity real estate" or "direct real estate." Typically refers to commercial real estate investments, but also could include such private equity market investments as equity investments in homebuilding projects or properties, or in single family rental home investment programs, as well as private equity investments in real estate operating companies. Private equity investments can be structured in a variety of formats, from direct ownership to joint ventures to limited partnerships, private real estate investment trusts (REITs), group trusts, collective investment trusts, C-corps., limited liability companies and a variety of other legal structures. Also See private debt real estate, public equity real estate, and public debt real estate.

Private Equity Real Estate Fund A pooled fund vehicle targeting institutional investors, individual investors, or both, typically structured as a private real estate investment trust (REIT), or other form of real estate operating company, or through some form of commingling arrangement, that invests in direct equity real estate holdings on behalf of its interest holders. The managers of these funds are called "private equity real estate managers," or simply "real estate investment managers." Private equity funds can be structured either as open-end funds or as closed-end funds.

Private Equity Real Estate Manager (Private Equity Manager) A manager of direct investments in real estate, either for the benefit of the private equity manager's own account, for the benefit of the manager's third party investment management investor clients, or both. Often refers to managers of Opportunity Funds which are funds that typically invest in higher risk, higher return strategies with target returns in the 18% to 20% or higher range, but actually includes all types of managers who invest capital, either for their own accounts of the accounts of other, in direct equity real estate investments. See Private Equity Real Estate, and Private Equity Real Estate Funds.

Private Mortgage Insurance (PMI) Default insurance on conventional loans, provided by private insurance companies. See mortgage insurance. The Homeowner's Protection Act of 1998 allows PMI to be canceled when the amount owed reaches a certain level, particularly when the debt is less than 80% of the home's value, and automatically when the loan principal is less than 78% of its original cost.

Private Offering An investment or business offered for sale to a small group of investors, generally under exemptions to registration allowed by the Securities And Exchange Commission (SEC) and state securities registration laws.

Private Placement A sale of a security in a manner that is exempt from the registration rules and requirements of the Securities and Exchange Commission.

An example would be a REIT directly placing an issue of stock with a pension fund.

Private REIT An infinite or finite life real estate investment company structured as a real estate investment trust. Shares are placed and held privately rather than sold and traded publicly.

Private Sector All economic activity other than that of government.

PRIZM See CLARITAS.

PRM See Permanent reference marker

Pro Forma Statement An analysis of the future of the property and its' potential as opposed to its' current use.

Pro Rata In the case of a tenant, the proportionate share of expenses for the maintenance and operation of the property.

Probate Court Proceeding o establish the will of a deceased person.

Probate Or Prove To establish the validity of the will of a deceased person.

Proceeds From Resale See Resale Proceeds.

Processing The second step in the mortgage application process that involves the verification of information stated on the application.

Procuring Cause The effort that brings about the desired result. Under an open listing, the broker who is the procuring cause of the sale receives the commission.

Production Acres The area of land that can be used in agriculture or timber operations to produce income, not including areas used for crop or machinery storage, or other support areas.

Profit Exemption Current tax rules permit the profit on the sale of a primary residence to be tax exempt for up to $250,000 for an individual, or $500,000 for a married couple.

Pro-Forma Statement From Latin pro forma, meaning "according to form". Financial statements showing what is expected to occur, as opposed to actual results.

Programmatic When a joint venture is formed to acquire multiple assets, some of which may not yet be identified. Multiple assets may be developed or acquired under a single joint venture agreement, or multiple assets may be developed or acquired under a series of joint ventures utilizing a uniform set of documents to create each joint venture.

Progress Payments In construction, loan payments issued to the builder as building is completed. See draw.

Prohibited Transaction ERISA defines the following transactions as prohibited between a pension plan and a party in interest:

1. The sale, exchange or leasing of any property
2. A loan or other extension of credit
3. The furnishing of goods or services

Other prohibited transactions include the transfer of plan assets to a party in interest or use of plan assets by a party in interest, and the acquisition of employer real property in excess of limits set by ERISA.

PRO-JECT Property forecasting and valuation software; a comprehensive lease-by-lease analysis tool for the valuation of income-producing real estate. Users can model any combination of office, industrial, retail, apartment, and mixed-use property types and generate a full range of reports.

Projection Period The time duration for estimating future cash flows and the resale proceeds from a proposed real estate investment.

Promissory Note A promise to pay a specified sum to a specified person under specified terms. See also Note.

Property Condition Disclosure Form A detailed checklist that concerns to the condition of the property including its structure and any environmental issues in and around the property.

Property Description The property description is an accurate, legal description of the land. See Legal Description.

Property Disclosure Acts State mandated seller's property disclosure reports. These reports place the burden of defect disclosure on the seller. Agents are not required to discover property defects but are required to disclose them if they are known.

Property Insurance Protects the physical property and equipment of an insured from a loss that was a result of fire, theft, or other dangers.

Property Line The recorded boundary of a plot of land.

Property Management Report A periodic report that details all income received and disbursed. Typically Produced Monthly.

Property Management The operation of the property of another for compensation. Can Include elements of marketing space; advertising and rental activities; collecting, recording, and remitting rents; maintaining the property; tenant relations; hiring employees; keeping proper accounts; and rendering periodic reports to the owner.

Property Manager The person who is hired and paid to handle the operation of an income producing property.

Property Report Required by the Interstate Land Sale Act for the sale of subdivisions of 50 lots or more, if the subdivisions are not otherwise exempt. Filed with HUD's Office Of Interstate Land Sales Registration *(OILSR)*.

Property Residual Technique In appraisal, a method for estimating the value of property based on estimated future income and the Reversionary Value of the building and land. See Income Approach.

Property Survey A survey is used to determine the boundaries of your property.

Property Tax Taxes levied by the government against either real or personal property. The right to tax real property in the United States rests exclusively with the states, not with the federal government.

Proprietary Lease In a cooperative apartment building, the lease a corporation provides to the stockholders that allows them to use a certain apartment unit under the conditions specified.

Proprietorship Ownership of a business, including income-producing real estate, by an individual, as contrasted with a partnership or corporation.

Pro Rata Share The pro rata share is the apartment's share of the building's underlying mortgage.

Prorate To allocate between seller and buyer their proportionate share of an obligation paid or due; for example, to prorate real property taxes or insurance.

Proration See Pro Rata, Prorate.

Proration The proportional division or distribution of expenses of property ownership between two or more parties. Closing statement prorations generally include taxes, rents, insurance, interest charges, and assessments.

Prospect A person considered likely to buy. A prospective purchaser.

Prospectus A printed advertisement usually in pamphlet form, presenting a new development, subdivision, business venture, or stock issue.

Proxy A person who represents another, particularly in some meeting. Also, the document giving to another the authority to represent.

PRP See Potentially Responsible Parties.

Prudent Man Rule The standard to which a fiduciary is held accountable under ERISA. *"Act with the care, skill, prudence and diligence under the circumstances then prevailing that a prudent man, acting in a like capacity and familiar with such matters, would use in the conduct of an enterprise of a like character and with like aims."*

Public Debt Real Estate One of the four quadrants of the real estate capital markets. Typically refers to Commercial Mortgage Backed Securities *(CMBS)* and Residential Mortgage Backed Securities *(RMS)*, but also can include public bond issues from public and private companies and agencies. Also See private equity real estate, public equity real estate and private debt real estate.

Public Equity Real Estate One of the four quadrants of the real estate capital markets. Typically refers to investments in the securities of publicly traded real estate investment trusts *(REITs)* and other non-REIT publicly traded real estate operating companies. Also See private equity real estate, and private debt real estate.

Public Housing Government-owned housing units made available to low-income individuals and families at no cost or for nominal rental rates.

Public Lands Acreage held by the government for conservation purposes. Public lands are generally undeveloped, and have limited activities attached to them such as grazing, wildlife management, recreation, timbering, mineral development, water development, and/or hunting.

Public Land Survey System (PLSS) Known as the Rectangular Survey System, the PLSS is the surveying system developed and used in the United States to divide and identify real property for sale. It Uses Baselines and Meridians to carve out townships which are typically about 6 miles by 6 miles, square; which are further divided into sections of 1 mile by 1 mile containing 640 acres more or less.

Public Offering Soliciting the general public for the sale of investment units. Generally requires approval by the SEC and/or state securities agencies.

Public Record Usually refers to land transaction records kept at the county courthouse.

Public Sale An auction sale of property with notice to the general public.

Public Sector The portion of the economy run by various levels of government.

Public Utility Easement A right granted by a property owner to a public utility company to erect and maintain poles, wires, and conduits on, across, or under her or his land for telephone, electric power, gas, water, or sewer installation.

Public-Private Partnership (P3) According to the National Council for Public Private Partnerships, a Public-Private Partnership *(P3)* is a contractual agreement between a public agency and a private sector entity. Through this agreement, the skills and assets of each sector both public and private, are shared in delivering a service or facility for the use of the general public. Each party shares in the risks and rewards potential in the delivery of the service and/or facility.

PUD See Planned Unit Development

Pueblo House An early-twentieth-century style of house that is made of adobe brick or some other material made to look like adobe brick. Seen Most often int eh southwestern Unite States. The characteristic projecting roof beams are called vigas.

Puffing The act of overstating the qualities of a property.

Pump Mix Special concrete used in a concrete pump. Generally, the mix has smaller rock aggregate than regular mix.

Punch List An itemized list documenting incomplete or unsatisfactory items after the contractor has notified the owner that the tenant space is substantially complete.

Punch Out For inspection and making a discrepancy list. See Punch List.

Pur Autre Vie Latin, meaning *"for the life of another."* A life estate pur autre vie is a life estate measured by the life of a person other than the grantee.

Purchase and Sales Agreement See Purchase Agreement.

Purchase Agreement A purchase agreement demonstrates a buyer's intent to purchase a piece of property and a seller's intent to sell that property. The document outlines the terms and conditions of a sale and holds each party legally accountable to meeting their agreement. Also called Purchase and Sales Agreement.

Purchase Capital The amount of money used to purchase real estate, regardless of the source.

Purchase Contract See Contract Of Sale, Purchase Agreement.

Purchase Money Mortgage A mortgage given by a grantee *(the buyer)* to a grantor *(the seller)* in part payment of the purchase price of real estate.

Purchase Option The right, but not the obligation, to buy; See Option To Purchase.

Putty A type of dough that is used in sealing glass in the sash, filling small holes and crevices in wood, and for similar purposes.

PVC Also known as CPVC or Poly Vinyl Chloride. A type of white or light gray plastic pipe used sometimes for water supply lines and waste pipe. It should be mentioned the PVC and CPVC are not the same thing, although many times the two acronyms are used interchangeably. The main difference between CPVC and PVC is the range of temperatures each is capable of withstanding. CPVC can handle temperatures up to 200° Fahrenheit, while PVC peaks at 140° Fahrenheit. PVC comes in nominal pipe sizes only, while CPVC is available in both nominal pipe sizes and copper tube sizes.

Q

QI See Qualified Intermediary.

Quadrangle An enclosure with four side surrounded by buildings.

Quadrant A device used to tighten the upper and lower leaves of a Dutch door.

Quadruplex An apartment with four levels.

Qualified Historical Structure A building or collection of building recognized as crucial to the history, the architecture, or the culture of an area by a local or state governmental authority.

Qualified Intermediary (QI) Also called an accommodator or exchange facilitator, someone who oversees a tax-deferred exchange to ensure that the transaction meets the standards of the Internal Revenue Code. All qualified intermediaries must be independent in the transactions they facilitate.

Qualified Plan Any employee benefit plan that is qualified by the IRS as a tax-exempt plan. Among other requirements, the plan's assets must be placed in trust for the sole benefit of the employees covered by the plan.

Qualifying Ratios Estimation that is used to determine if a borrower can qualify for a mortgage.

Qualifying The act of determining a prospect's motivation, then matching his or her needs with the available inventory.

Quality Control The activities done for adequate quality in manufactured products.

Quantity Survey A method used by appraisers to estimate reproduction cost of an improvement; detailed cost estimate of all materials, labor, and overhead required to reproduce a structure. See Cost Approach.

Quarry Bed The side of a piece of building stone that is parallel with the natural strata or veins.

Quarry Tile A man-made or machine-made clay tile that is used in finishing a floor or wall.

Quarter Round A small trim molding that has the cross section of a quarter circle.

Queen Anne House A nineteenth-century Victorian style house that is unique-looking, multistory, and irregular in shape with a variety of surface textures, materials, and colors. The term Queen Anne has come to be applied to any Victorian house that cannot be otherwise classified.

Quiet Enjoyment The right of an owner or a person legally in possession to the use of property without interference of possession.

Quiet Title Suit A suit in court to remove a defect, cloud, or suspicion regarding legal rights of an owner.

Quiet Title To Quiet the title is to bring it through a Quiet title suit in order to provide the owner with marketable title. See Quiet Title Suit.

Quitclaim Deed A quitclaim deed is a document transferring the ownership interest of property from one party to another. It transfers the title of the property, but only transfers what the seller actually owns, without any specific warranty.

R

"Ready, Willing, And Able" Buyer   A buyer who is prepared to buy property on the seller's terms and is ready to take positive steps to consummate the transaction.

R Factor   A colloquialism of R-Value.

R-Value   An insulating material's resistance to conductive heat flow is measured or rated in terms of its thermal resistance or R-value. The higher the R-value, the greater the insulating effectiveness. The R-value depends on the type of insulation, its thickness, and its density. The R-value of some insulations also depends on temperature, aging, and moisture accumulation.

R/W   Right-Of-Way.

Rabbet   A rectangular longitudinal groove cut in the corner edge of a board or plank usually for the purpose of joining that piece of wood with another piece containing a "tongue".

Racial Steering   The unlawful practice of influencing a person's housing choice based on his/her race. See Steering.

Radiant Heating   A way of heating, normally consisting of a forced hot water system with pipes placed in the floor, wall, or ceiling.

Radiation   Energy transferred from a heat source to the air around it.

Radius Clause   In a shopping center tenant's lease, a provision that prevents the tenant from opening another store within a certain distance from the shopping center, which would result in reduced traffic to the existing store and to the shopping center.   Especially important for anchor tenants but also used for Ancillary Tenants.   See also Reverse Radius Clause.

Radon   A naturally occurring radioactive gas that may contaminate water or air in buildings. Studies from mines have indicated a correlation between radon and lung cancer in humans. Homes that are too well insulated and sealed may trap radon gas, increasing its concentration. A pipe that serves to vent radon, especially from the basement to the roof, is often suggested to prevent its buildup.

Radon System   A ventilation system beneath the floor or in a basement designed to fan exhaust radon gas to the outside of the home

Rafter, Hip   A rafter that forms the intersection of an external roof angle.

Rafter, Valley   A rafter that forms the intersection of an internal roof angle.

Rafter   Dimension Lumber that is used to support the roof sheeting and roof loads. The rafters of a flat roof are sometimes called roof joists.

Rail   Cross members of panel doors or of a sash.

Railroad Tie   Creosote and/or preservative impregnated, about 6" X 8" and 6'8' long wooden timber that is used to hold railroad track in place. Also called crosstie and Railway sleeper.

Rake Fascia   Vertical face of the sloping end of a roof eave.

Rake Siding   The practice of installing lap siding diagonally

Rake   Slope or slanted.

RAM Reverse Annuity Mortgage.

Ranch House Originally a low, rambling, one-story house typical of the western United States; now used to describe almost any one-story house. See California Ranch.

Range A six-mile strip of land measured east and west from the meridian lines. See Range Lines.

Range Lines Lines parallel to a principal meridian, marking off the land into 6-mile strips known as ranges; they are numbered east or west of a principal meridian in the Government Rectangular Survey. See Baseline.

Rate Cap The limit on interest rates during the term of an adjustable rate mortgage.

Rate Improvement Mortgage A mortgage loan with a provision that allows the borrower to reduce the interest rate when market rates decline. The provision may be invoked only one time over the life of the loan.

Rate Is established for a much shorter term. The loan may be extended, or rolled over, at the end of the shorter term at the current market interest rate.

Rate Lock A rate lock allows borrowers to lock in an advantageous interest rate before a real estate transaction closes. A rate lock allows the borrower to lock in that interest rate for a specific period of time protecting them from market fluctuations.

Rate Of Interest See Interest Rate.

Rate of Return Annual operating income divided by the amount of capital invested.

Rate Of Return Of Investment See Recapture Rate.

Rating Grade, assigned by a rating agency, designating the credit quality or creditworthiness of the underlying assets.

Rating Agencies Independent firms engaged to rate the creditworthiness of securities for the benefit of investors. The major rating agencies are Fitch Ratings, Standard & Poor's, and Moody's Investors Service.

Ratio
1. The fraction formed by the division of one amount by another.
2. Guidelines that is applied by the lender during underwriting of a mortgage loan application to determine the size a loan to grant an applicant.

Raw Land Unimproved land that remains in its natural state.

Raw Space Unimproved shell space in a building.

Ready Mixed Concrete A Concrete mixed at a plant or in trucks in route to a job and delivered ready for placement.

Real Estate Agent A real estate agent is licensed to negotiate and coordinate the buying and selling of real estate transactions. Most real estate agents must work for and be under the supervision of a realtor or broker with additional training and certification. See Agent.

Real Estate Attorney A lawyer that focuses on property transactions.

Real Estate Board An organization whose members consist primarily of real estate brokers and salespersons. See Board Of Realtors®.

Real Estate Broker Any person, partnership, association, or corporation that sells, or offers to sell, buys, or offers to buy, or negotiates the purchase, sale, or exchange of real estate, or that leases or offers to lease, rents or offers to rent any real estate or the improvements thereon for others and for a compensation or valuable consideration. A real estate broker may not conduct business without a real estate broker's license. See Broker.

Real Estate Brokerage Managers Council An affiliate of the National Association Of Realtors and part of the Realtors National Marketing Institute *(RNMI)*.

Real Estate Capital Resources Association *(RECRA)* A national nonprofit trade organization representing asset managers, investors, and servicers involved in the acquisition, management, and servicing of commercial real estate assets; dedicated to enhancing the value of capital invested in commercial real estate assets through quality asset management and servicing.

Real Estate Commission State agency that enforces real estate license laws.

Real Estate Educators Association A professional organization primarily composed of persons who teach real estate in junior colleges and proprietary license preparation schools.

Real Estate Information Providers Association (REIPA) A nonprofit corporation established to provide a forum for providers of real estate information and/or information technology related to real estate, both commercial and residential.

Real Estate Information Systems (REIS) A large data bank that includes historical rental rates on more than 100,000 properties.

Real Estate Investment Trust (REIT) Ownership of real estate by a group of individual investors who purchase certificates of ownership in a trust. The trust invests in real property and distributes the profits back to the investors free of corporate income tax.

Real Estate Land and/or that which is fixed upon the land. A portion of the earth's surface extending downward to the center of the earth and upward infinitely into space, including all things permanently attached thereto, whether by nature or by man. See Real Property.

Real Estate Market The potential buyers and sellers of real property at the current time, and the current transaction activity for real property. It includes markets for various property types, such as housing market, office market, condominium market, land market.

Real Estate Mortgage Investment Conduit (REMIC) A product of the Tax Reform Act of 1986, REMICs are designed to hold a pool of mortgages for the exclusive purpose of issuing multiple classes of mortgage-backed securities in a way that avoids a corporate double tax.

Real Estate Mutual Fund A regulated investment company *(mutual fund)* that specializes in owning securities offered by real estate related companies, including REITS, real estate development and management companies, and homebuilders.

Real Estate Owned (REO) Property acquired by a lender through foreclosure and held in inventory. Commonly referred to as REO.].

Real Estate Salesperson See Salesperson.

Real Estate Settlement Procedures Act The Real Estate Settlement Procedures Act *(RESPA)* requires lenders to provide disclosures to borrowers informing them of real estate transactions, settlement services, and relevant consumer protection laws. Its goal is to regulate settlement costs, prohibit specific practices such as kickbacks, and limits the use of escrow accounts.

Real Estate Syndicate A partnership formed for participation in a real estate venture. Partners may be limited or unlimited in their liability.

Real Estate Wholesaling See Wholesaling, wholesaler.

Real Property Real property consists of land, anything affixed to it so as to be regarded as a permanent part of the land, that which is appurtenant to the land, and that which is immovable by law, including all rights and interests.

Real Property Tax Lien This type of lien is a tax levied against real property by the local government and has priority over all other liens.

Real Property The rights to use real estate. Sometimes also defined as real estate.

Reality Of Consent An element of all valid contracts. Offer and acceptance in a contract usually are taken to mean that reality of consent also is present. This is not the case, however, if any of the following are present: mistake, misrepresentation, fraud, undue influence, or duress.

Realization Of Gain The taking of the gain or profit from the sale of property. See Realized Proceeds.

Realized Gain In a tax-free exchange, a gain that has occurred financially, but is not necessarily taxed. See Boot, Recognized Gain, Section 1031.

Realized Proceeds. The sales proceeds received by the Taxpayer from sale of the Relinquished Property including the amount used to pay off the mortgage or deed of trust.

Realtist A member of the National Association Of Real Estate Brokers, a group comprised mainly of minority brokers.

Realtor.Com A website of the national association of realtors® at www.realtor.com. Includes a comprehensive list of topics and links.

Realtor® A registered trademark term reserved for the sole use of active members of local Realtors® boards affiliated with the National Association of Realtors®.

Realtors® Land Institute (RLI) An affiliate of the National Association Of Realtors®. It is the only branch of the Realtor® family focused on land brokerage transactions of five specialized types:

1. farms and ranches

2. undeveloped tracts of land
3. transitional and development land
4. subdivision and wholesaling of lots, and
5. site selection and assemblage of land.

Realtors® National Marketing Institute (RNMI) An affiliate of the National Association Of Realtors®; mainly concerned with educational programs and literature for members.

Realty See Real Estate.

Reappraisal Lease A lease where independent appraisers periodically review the rental level. Often, the lessor and lessee will each select an appraiser; if they do not agree on a value, they will choose a third appraiser.

Reassessment The process of revising or updating the value estimate of property for ad valorem tax purposes.

Rebar Reinforcing bar. Ribbed steel bars installed in foundation concrete walls, footers, and poured in place concrete structures designed to strengthen concrete. Rebar comes in various thickness' and strength grades.

Rebate
1. A refund resulting from a purchase or tax.
2. A kickback of a charge, often illegal if done without knowledge of all parties.

Recapture Clause In a contract, a clause permitting the party who grants an interest or right to take it back under certain conditions.

Recapture In the year of sale, all depreciation or cost recovery taken on depreciable property in excess of the amount allowed by the straight-line method is subject to recapture provisions as established by the IRS, which has the effect of taxing the excess at ordinary income rates. Recapture is designed to prevent a taxpayer from taking advantage of both accelerated depreciation and capital gain treatment.

Recapture Of Depreciation See Depreciation Recapture.

Recapture Rate In an appraisal, a term used to describe the rate of recovery of an investment in a Wasting Asset. This rate is added to the discount rate to derive a capitalization RATE in appraisal terminology. May be based on the straight-line, sinking fund, or annuity method.

Recaptured Depreciation An owner may deduct depreciation on a property during its taxable lifetime, once the property is sold the previously deducted depreciation is figured up and "recaptured" or included as taxable income.

Recasting The process of adjusting a loan arrangement, especially under the threat of default. See Workout.

Receiver The court-appointed custodian of property involved in litigation, pending final disposition of the matter before the court.

Receptacle An outlet for electricity that a typical household is going to have many 120 volt receptacles for plugging in lams and appliances and 240 volt receptacles for the range, clothes dryer, air conditioners.

Recession General economic slowdown; officially declared after two consecutive quarters of reduced gross domestic product. Often, there is a shrinkage in the real estate industry without a recession in the general business economy.

Reciprocity Mutual agreement to accept, such as a state's acceptance, as valid the real estate license one has earned in another state.

Recognition Agreement A document that describes the relationship between a lender and the co-op corporation, including in what order each will be repaid in case of a foreclosure.

Recognition Letter A letter used for recognition from the cooperative corporation's board of directors recognizing the secured rights of a lender to the shares of stock and the proprietary lease on a specific apartment.

Recognized Gain In a Tax-Free Exchange, the portion of gain that is taxable. A Realized Gain will generally be recognized to the extent of boot received. See Section 1031.

Recognized Proceeds The portion of the realized proceeds which is recognized as or in.

Reconciliation
1. In an appraisal, the process of adjusting comparables to estimate the value of the subject being appraised.
2. An accounting procedure that balances a trust account by comparing the general ledger with the combined total of the account's individual ledger balances.

Reconfiguration Changing the physical shape of a property.

Reconveyance Occurs when a mortgage debt is retired. The lender conveys the property back to the equity owner, free of the debt.

Record Owner See Owner Of Record.

Recording Fee Money charged for recording the transfer of a property, paid to a city, county, or other appropriate branch of government.

Recording The act of entering or recording documents affecting or conveying interests in real estate in the recorder's office established in each county. Until recorded, a deed or mortgage generally is not effective against subsequent purchases or mortgage liens.

Recourse Borrower is personally liable for repayment of the debt even if the note is in the name of a corporation.

Recovery Fund A fund established in some states from real estate license funds to cover claims of aggrieved parties who have suffered monetary damage through the actions of a real estate licensee. To protect the public, some states mandate errors and omissions insurance as a requirement for licensure.

Rectangular Survey System A system established in 1785 by the federal government that provides for surveying and describing land by reference to principal meridians and base lines. See Government Rectangular Survey, Public Land Survey System.

Red Herring Initial offering plan submitted to the attorney general which, when approved, becomes the *"Black Book"*.

Redeemable Deed Redeemable deed states auction off property deeds, but there is a period during which the delinquent property owner can come back and redeem the property. If a deed is redeemed during that period, it works much like a lien; the property owner must pay what is often a large penalty or interest rate.

Redeemable Deed Sales This is a sale that is called a Tax Deed Sale, but the sale is subject to a right of redemption during a specified time period by the delinquent property owner. For most purposes the sale is very similar to a Tax Lien Sale.

Redeemable Rent In a lease with a Purchase Option, the rent paid that can be applied toward the purchase price.

Redemption Period A period of time established by state law during which a property owner has the right to redeem her or his real estate from a foreclosure or tax sale by paying the sales price, interest, and costs. Many states do not have mortgage redemption laws.

Redemption The right of a mortgagor to redeem the property by paying a debt after the expiration date and before sale at foreclosure; the right of an owner to reclaim the owner's property after the sale for taxes.

Redemption, Equity Of See Equity Of Redemption.

Redevelop The process of demolition of the existing improvements and construction of new improvements on a site. The new improvements are often of a different type from the old.

Rediscount Rate The rate of interest charged to member banks when they borrow from the federal reserve system. Also called Discount Rate.

Redline Blueprints that shows changes; often marked with red pencil or pen.

Redlining The illegal practice of denying loans or restricting their number for certain areas of a community.

Reduced Pressure Zone Device See Backflow Preventer.

Reducer A fitting with different size openings at either end used to go from a larger to a smaller pipe.

Reduction Certificate A document in which the lender acknowledges the sum due on the mortgage loan. Used when mortgaged property is sold and the buyer assumes the debt.

Reentry The legal right of a landlord to possess the property when the term for possession by a tenant has expired.

Reevaluation Lease See Reappraisal Lease.

Referee's Deed Used to convey real property sold pursuant to a judicial order, in an action for the foreclosure of a mortgage or for partition.

Referral Fee A percentage of a broker's commission paid to another broker for the referral of a buyer or seller.

Referral The act of suggesting the use of a certain broker.

Refi Slang for refinance.

Refinance Refinancing replaces an existing loan with a new one. Debt is not eliminated when a borrower refinances. Instead, it typically offers better terms, including a lower interest rate, lower monthly mortgage payments, or a faster loan term.

Reflective Insulation Sheet material with one or both faces covered with aluminum foil.

Refrigerant A substance that remains a gas at low temperatures and pressure and usable to transfer heat. Freon is an example and is used in air conditioning systems.

Regency House An English-style 2 or 3-story symmetrical house with a hip roof. Recognizable by a small octagonal window over the front door is traditional.

Regional Shopping Center A type of shopping center containing from 300,000 to 900,000 square feet of shopping space and at least one major department store.

Register Of Deeds A record of real estate deeds or other land titles that is maintained by a local government official.

Register A grill placed over a heating duct or cold air return.

Registrar The person who is to maintain accurate official records, such as for deeds, mortgages, and other recorded documents.

Reglaze To replace a broken window.

Regression A statistical technique used to estimate mathematical models of economic and other processes. It is used to find a mathematical expression that best fits the relationship between a group of random variables as indicated by a sample of data.

Regulation B The most commonly known rule under the Equal Credit Opportunity Act *(ECOA)*.

Regulation D A regulation of the Securities And Exchange Commission that sets forth conditions necessary for a private offering exemption.

Regulation Z A regulation of the Federal Reserve Board designed to ensure that borrowers and customers in need of consumer credit are given meaningful information with respect to the cost of credit.

Regulations The Internal Revenue Service regulations authorizing and regulating deferred exchanges in which the Taxpayer sells the Relinquished Property to a Buyer and acquires Replacement Property from a different Seller rather than exchanging directly.

Regulatory Taking a situation where the effects of government regulation are deemed so severe as to destroy most of the value of a property. In effect, the government has *"taken"* the property without just compensation.

Rehab See Rehabilitate, Remodel.

Rehabilitate To restore a structure to a condition of good repair.

Rehabilitation Tax Credit The Tax Reform Act of 1986 provides a 20% tax credit for rehabilitating certified historic structures, and a 10% credit for other buildings that were placed in service after 1936. However, there are certain conditions or requirements that are imposed.

Reinforced Concrete Concrete containing adequate reinforcement, typically steel rebar, and designed on the assumption that concrete and steel act together in resisting the forces that would damage or destroy concrete on its own. Further, it is, concrete work into which steel bars have been embedded to impart tensile strength to the member.

Reinvestment Rate The interest rate which an investor is assumed to be able to earn on intermediate cash flow in the projection of a terminal value. See Financial Management Rate Of Return.

REIT See Real Estate Investment Trust

Release Clause A clause found in a blanket mortgage which gives the owner of the property the privilege of paying off a portion of the mortgage indebtedness, and thus freeing a portion of the property from the mortgage.

Release Of Lien To free real estate from a mortgage. See Partial Release.

Release The act or writing by which some claim or interest is surrendered to another.

Reliction Gradual subsidence of waters, leaving dry land.

Relief Valve A device designed to open if it detects excess temperature or pressure. Typically found on a water heater or boiler.

Relinquished Property The property given up by an investor in a 1031 exchange.

Relocation Clause A lease stipulation that allows the landlord to move the tenant within the building.

Relocation Network A geographically diversified group of independent real estate brokerage companies, generally not members of a franchise, that share information with one another concerning potential customers.

Relocation Service An organization that aids a person in not just selling a property in one area and buying another property in another area, but also the moving process itself.

Rem See "In Rem".

Remainder The remnant of an estate that has been conveyed to take effect and be enjoyed after the termination of a prior estate, such as when an owner conveys a life estate to one party and the remainder to another.

Remainderman The person who is to receive the property after the termination of the prior estate

Remediation Remediation is corrective action to clean up an environmentally contaminated site in order to eliminate contamination or reduce the amount to an acceptable level. See CERCLA, Phase I Environmental Site Assessment, Phase II, Phase III, Site Assessment, Stigma.

REMIC See Real Estate Mortgage Investment Conduit.

Remodel To change the appearance and functional utility of a building. This may include painting, repairing, and replacing of fixtures and equipment.

Remodeling Contractor A general contractor who specializes in remodeling work. See Remodeling, Renovation, Rehab.

Remote Remote electrical, gas, or water meter digital readouts installed close to the front of the home in order for utility companies to easily read the homeowners usage of the service.

Rendering A drawing, watercolor, or oil painting giving a perspective view of a proposed building or development to show how it will look when completed, including landscaping; a more artistic representation than the more technical elevation.

Renegotiable Rate Mortgage A mortgage loan that is granted for a term of 3 to 5 years and secured by a long-term mortgage of up to 30 years with the interest rate being renegotiated or adjusted each period.

Renegotiate To legally revise the terms of a contract.

Renegotiated-Rate Mortgage (RRM) A loan whose interest rate is revised at preset intervals but is not pegged to an index.

Renewal Option A clause giving a tenant the right to extend the term of a lease.

Renewal Probability Used to estimate leasing-related costs and downtime, it is the average percentage of tenants in a building that are expected to renew at market rental rates upon the expiration of their leases.

Renovate A general term applied to the process of upgrading an existing improvement. Usually there is an attempt to keep the same general appearance of the building with new materials or to return the building to its original appearance.

Rent A charge for the use of space. See Contract Rent, Economic Rent.

Rent Bid Models A conceptual tool used to explain how land is allocated in competitive markets. This model assumes that space is controlled by the activity that offers the highest bid for the site.

Rent Commencement Date The date on which a tenant begins paying rent.

Rent Concession See Concession.

Rent Control Laws that govern the rate that may be charged for space.

Rent Multiplier See Gross Rent Multiplier.

Rent Roll A list of tenants, generally with the lease rent and expiration date for each tenant.

Rent Schedule A statement of proposed rental rates, determined by the owner or the property manager or both, based on a building's estimated expenses, market supply and demand, and the owner's long-range goals for the property.

Rent Stabilization Usually applies to buildings that is built before 1974 and apartments removed from rent control.

Rentable Area See Net Leasable Area.

Rentable Ratio A building's total rentable area divided by its usable area. It represents the tenant's pro-rata share of the building's common areas and can determine the square footage upon which the tenant will pay rent. The inverse describes the proportion of space that an occupant can expect to actually use.

Rental Building A rental building only has apartments for rent and not for purchase.

Rental Concession What landlords offer tenants to secure their tenancy. While rental abatement is one form of a concession, there are many others such as increased tenant improvement allowance, signage, below-market rental rates and moving allowances.

Rental Growth Rate The expected trend in market rental rates over the period of analysis, expressed as an annual percentage increase.

Rental Rate The periodic charge per unit for the use of a property. The period may be a month, quarter, or year. The unit may be a dwelling unit, square foot, or other unit of measurement.

Rental The possession, but not ownership, of a property for some duration of time under defined terms and conditions.

Rent-Free Period A portion of the term of a lease when no rent is required. It is offered by a landlord as a rental concession to attract tenants.

Rent-Up Period The period following construction of a new building when tenants are actively being sought and the project is approaching its stabilized occupancy.

REO See Real Estate Owned.

Reorientation Changing the market appeal of a property.

Repairs Work performed to return property to a former condition without extending its Useful Life, as distinguished from Capital Improvements. In Income Property, repairs are an Operating Expense for accounting and tax purposes.

Replacement Cost The cost of construction at current prices of a building having utility equivalent to the building being appraised but built with modern materials and according to current standards, designs, and layout. See Reproduction Cost.

Replacement Property. The property being acquired in the exchange.

Replacement Reserves An allowance that provides for the periodic replacement of building components that wear out more rapidly than the building itself and must be replaced during the building's economic life.

Repo Slang term for repossess, Repossession. Also relates to the repurchase of notes.

Repossession Seizure by a lender of property that is collateral for a debt when loan payments are not made; retrieval by a lessor or landlord of rented or leased property.

Reproduction Cost The cost of exact duplication of a property as of a certain date. Reproduction differs from replacement in that replacement requires the same functional utility for a property, whereas reproduction is an exact duplication. See Replacement Cost.

Request For Proposal (RFP) A formal request, issued by a plan sponsor or its consultant, inviting investment managers to submit information on their firms' investment strategy, historical investment performance, current investment opportunities, investment management fees, other pension fund client relationships, etc. Firms that meet the qualifications are requested to make a formal presentation to the board of trustees and senior staff members. Finalists are chosen at the completion of this process.

Resale Price In a projection of real estate investment performance, the assumed selling price a property could fetch at the end of the Projection Period. See Resale Proceeds.

Resale Proceeds The amount a former owner receives upon a sale after paying Transaction Costs, remaining debt, and, sometimes, income taxes. See Proceeds From Resale.

Rescind To withdraw an offer or contract. Regulation Z allows a 3-day period in which to rescind certain credit transactions.

Rescission The termination of a contract by mutual agreement of the parties.

Reservation In A Deed The creation by a deed to property of a new right in favor of the grantor. Usually involves an easement, a life estate, or a mineral interest.

Reserve Account An account that a borrower has to fund to protect the lender. Examples include capital expenditure accounts and deferred maintenance accounts.

Reserve Fund An account maintained to provide funds for anticipated expenditures required to maintain a building. A reserve may be required by a lender in the form of an escrow to pay upcoming taxes and insurance costs. A Replacement Reserve may be maintained to provide for Replacement Cost of short-lived components, such as carpets, heating equipment, or roofing. Deposit of money into such a fund does not achieve a tax deduction.

Reserve Price In an auction or other bidding procedure, an established amount below which the seller is not obligated to accept a winning bid.

Residence The place where one lives, particularly the dwelling in which one lives.

Resident Manager A person who lives in one of the units of an apartment complex while supervising the care of that complex.

Residential Broker One who lists and sells houses or condominiums.

Residential Lead-based Paint Hazard Reduction Act This act stipulates procedures to be followed in disclosing the presence of lead-based paint in the sale or rental of properties built before 1978.

Residential Member (RM) A professional designation once offered by the American Institute Of Real Estate Appraisers. It is being exchanged or phased out in favor of the SRA designation offered by the Appraisal Institute

Residential Pertaining to housing.

Residential Property
1. In real estate brokerage terminology, owner-occupied housing.
2. In income taxation terminology, rental units used for dwelling purposes, not of a transient nature such as a hotel or motel. To qualify as residential, at least 80% of a building's income should be derived from dwelling units.

Residential Sales Council Affiliate of the Realtors® National Marketing Institute of the National Association Of Realtors® that provides educational and promotional materials for members, most of whom are involved in residential real estate sales or brokerage.

Residential Service Contract An insurance contract or home warranty, generally for one year, covering the plumbing, mechanical, and electrical systems of a home. It is available in most areas upon the purchase of an existing home. Either the buyer or seller can pay for the contract.

Residual Income Amount of income that an individual has after all personal debts, including the mortgage, have been paid.

Residual Techniques A method of estimating the value of a building or land, given values of one and Rate Of Return. See Building Residual Technique, Land Residual Technique.

Residual Value or income remaining after deducting an amount necessary to meet fixed obligations.

Resolution Trust Corporation (RTC) The RTC was established by Congress in 1989 to contain, manage and sell failed savings institutions and recover taxpayer funds through the management and sale of the institutions' assets.

Resource Conservation And Recovery Act (RCRA) The U.S. law, passed in 1976, that regulates ongoing operations involving the generation, transport, treatment, storage, and disposal of hazardous waste. Amended in 1984 by the Hazardous and Solid Waste Amendments, which established restrictions requiring the treatment of hazardous waste before disposal in landfills.

RESPA Real Estate Settlement Procedures Act.

Respondeat Superior In terms of the laws pertaining to real estate agencies this is the doctrine that a principal is liable for the acts of an agent.

Restore To return a building to its original quality and appearance. While modern materials are used, the emphasis is on faithful reproduction of the original style.

Restraint Of Trade Business practices designed to restrict competition, create a monopoly, control prices, and otherwise obstruct the free operation of business.

Restraint On Alienation A limiting condition on the right to transfer property. If the condition is against public policy or is unreasonable, courts will void the condition.

Restricted Appraisal Report An appraisal report that contains minimal detail and is intended to be received or relied upon by the client only, not any other party.

Restriction A limitation on the use of real property, generally originated by the owner or subdivider in a deed. See Encumbrance.

Restrictive Covenant A Covenant or Deed Restriction that limits the property rights of the owner.

Retail Gravitation The drawing power of a shopping center; generally, the larger the center, the greater its ability to draw from distant areas

Retail Investor When used to describe an investor, retail refers to the nature of the distribution channel and the market for the services - selling interests directly to consumers.

Retainage In a construction contract, money earned by a contractor but not paid to the contractor until the completion of construction or some other agreed-upon date.

Retaining Wall A vertical partition used to restrict the movement of soil or water.

Retaliatory Eviction T he requirement that a tenant vacate a unit in response to a complaint from the tenant concerning the condition of the building. Landlord-tenant laws in many states forbid such evictions if proper channels are taken to lodge the complaint.

Retention Rate The percent of trailing 12-month earnings that have been ploughed back into the company. It is calculated as 100 minus the trailing 12-month payout ratio.

Retentions Amounts withheld from progress billings until final and satisfactory project completion.

Retire A Debt To pay off the principal on a loan, thereby fulfilling the obligation under the loan contract. See also Amortization.

Return On Assets The income after taxes for the trailing 12 months divided by the average total assets, expressed as a percentage.

Return On Equity The income available to common stockholders for the trailing 12 months divided by the average common equity, expressed as a percentage. See Equity Dividend, Equity Yield Rate.

Return on investment (ROI) The trailing 12-month income after taxes divided by the average total long-term debt, other long-term liabilities, and shareholders equity, expressed as a percentage.

Revaluation Clause See Reappraisal Lease.

Revenue Per Available Room See RevPAR

Revenue Stamps Stamps that are affixed to deeds and, in some states, other documents affecting real estate, and that indicate the payment of the state's deed transfer or other transfer tax. federal revenue stamps have not been used since 1968, but many states have substituted their own.

Revenue Total rent, sales, or earnings of a company; See Gross Income.

Reverse Annuity Mortgage (RAM) A mortgage loan that allows the owner to receive periodic payments based on the equity in the home.

Reverse Exchange When the investor wants to receive the replacement property and then sell the current investment property at a later date.

Reverse Leverage A situation in which financial benefits from ownership accrue at a lower rate than the mortgage interest rate. See Leverage.

Reverse Radius Clause In a shopping center tenant's lease, a clause preventing the shopping center owner from buying or developing a competing mall nearby.

Reversion Capitalization Rate The capitalization rate used to determine reversion value.

Reversion The remnant of an estate that the grantor holds after he or she has granted a life estate to another person; the estate will return or revert to the grantor. Also called a reverter.

Reversion Value A lump-sum benefit that an investor receives or expects to receive at the termination of an investment.

Reversionary Factor The mathematical factor that indicates the present worth of one dollar to be received in the future. See Present Value Of One.

Reversionary Interest The interest which a grantor has in lands or other property upon the termination of the preceding estate.

Reversionary Right An owner's right to regain possession of leased property on termination of the lease agreement.

Reversionary Value The value of property at the expiration of a certain time period.

Review Appraiser One who specializes in Appraisal Reviews.

Revocation An act of recalling a power of authority conferred, as a revocation of a power of attorney, a license, an agency, etc.

RevPAR (Revenue Per Available Room) Total room revenue for the period divided by the average number of available rooms in a hospitality facility.

Rezoning An action to change the designation of a subject parcel or group of parcels on the zoning map. The effect of a rezoning is to change the permitted uses for the affected parcels. See Downzoning.

RFactor or RValue See R-Value.

Ribbon Normally a 1" x 4" board let into the studs horizontally to support the ceiling or second floor joists.

Rider An amendment or attachment to a contract. See Addendum.

Ridge Beam A ridge beam is the highest part of framing in a structure and forms the apex of the roof.

Ridge Board The board placed on the ridge of the roof onto which the upper ends of other rafters are fastened.

Ridge Shingles Shingles used to cover the ridge board.

Ridge The horizontal line at the junction of the top edges of two sloping roof surfaces.

Right Of Assignment The right of assignment allows the lender to sell a mortgage at any time and obtain money invested rather than wait for the completion of the loan term.

Right Of First Refusal If a third party buyer offers to buy or lease a property owner's asset, the right of first refusal ensures the property holder is allowed a chance to buy or lease the asset under the same terms offered by the third party before the property owner accepts the third-party offer.

Right Of Ingress Or Egress The right of egress is a person's legal right to exit a property. The right of ingress is the right to enter a property. It is generally used in rental or easement situations in which the tenant or person to which easement has been granted needs access to a shared driveway, a private road to the property, etc.

Right Of Redemption See Equity Of Redemption.

Right Of Survivorship The right of a surviving joint tenant to acquire the interest of a deceased joint owner; the distinguishing feature of both Joint Tenancy and Tenancy By The Entirety.

Right-of-Way The right to pass over another's land pursuant to an easement or license.

Rim Joist A joist that runs around the perimeter of the floor joist.

Riparian Owner One who owns land bounding upon a river or watercourse. See Riparian Rights.

Riparian Rights An owner's rights in land that borders flowing water, such as a stream or river. These rights include access to and use of the water. See Riparian Owner.

Rise The vertical distance from the eaves line to the ridge. Also the vertical distance from stair tread to stair tread.

Riser And Panel The exterior vertical pipe and metal electric box (panel) the electrician provides and installs at the *"Rough Electric"* stage.

Riser Each of the vertical boards closing the spaces between the treads of stairways.

Risk Management A systematic approach to identifying and separating insurable risks from non-insurable risks and evaluating the availability and costs of purchasing third-party insurance.

Risk Uncertainty or variability. The possibility that returns from an investment will be greater or less than forecast. Diversification of investments provides some protection against risk.

Risk-Adjusted Rate Of Return Used to identify investment alternatives that can be expected to deliver a positive premium, after taking into consideration the expected volatility. The risk-adjusted rate of return is defined as the expected rate of return of a given asset, less the expected return for T-bills, divided by the expected standard deviation of the returns for the assets.

Road Base An aggregate mixture of sand and stone.

Road Show A tour made by executives of a company that plans to go public, where they travel to various cities to meet with underwriters and analysts and make presentations regarding their company and IPO. The road show takes place during the marketing period before the registration statement becomes effective.

Rod A linear unit of measurement used mostly in land surveying equal to 16 1/2 feet.

ROI See Return on Investment.

Roll Roofing Asphalt impregnated roofing products manufactured in roll form. 36inch wide rolls with and 108 square feet of material.

Roll, Rolling To install the floor joists or trusses in their correct place.

Rollback Retroactive claim by a taxing authority of a higher tax rate when property is sold after being taxed at a special use rate or the land is put to a more valuable use.

Rollover Loan A type of mortgage loan, commonly used in Canada, in which the amortization of principal is based on a long term, but the interest rate is established for a much shorter term. The loan may be extended, or rolled over, at the end of the shorter term at the current market interest rate.

Roll-Over Risk The risk that a tenant's lease will not be renewed.

Romex A name brand of nonmetallic sheathed electrical cable that is used for indoor wiring.

Roof Jack Sleeves that fit around the black plumbing waste vent pipes at, and are nailed to, the roof sheeting.

Roof Joist The rafters of a flat roof. Lumber used to support the roof sheeting and roof loads.

Roof Sheathing The wood panels or sheet material fastened to the roof rafters or trusses on which the shingle or other roof covering is laid.

Roof Sheeting See Roof Sheathing

Roof Valley The *"V"* created where two sloping roofs meet.

Rough Opening The horizontal and vertical measurement of a window or door opening before drywall or siding is installed.

Rough Sill The framing member at the bottom of a rough opening for a window. It is attached to the cripple studs below the rough opening.

Roughing-In The initial stage of a plumbing, electrical, heating, carpentry, and/or other area of construction, when all components that won't be Seen after the second finishing phase are assembled.

Round Robin Bidding A fairly simple tax lien bidding process. The bidding goes around the room in a fixed order and each person is given the opportunity to buy a lien. The bidder pays the delinquent taxes plus any penalties, interest and/ or costs for the lien.

Row House Single-family dwelling units attached to one another by common walls, generally with a either a common façade, or a faced that is design to all be of similar style. See Townhouse.

Royalty Money paid to a property owner for extraction of some valuable resource from the land.

RRM See Renegotiated Rate Mortgage.

RPZ See Backflow Preventer.

RTC Resolution Trust Corporation

Rule Of 72 An approximation of the time it takes for money to double when earning Compound Interest. Divide the percentage rate into 72 to derive the number of years to double the principal.

Rule Of 78 A method for computing unearned interest used on installment loans with Add-On Interest. The number 78 is based on the sum of the digits from 1 to 12.

Run With The Land Also referred to as *"Runs with the Land"*. An expression indicating rights or restrictions that affects all current and future owners of a property. Contrasted to an agreement, between a current owner and other parties, that is not passed on to future owners in a deed.

Run, Roof The horizontal distance from the eaves to a point directly under the ridge.

Run, Stair The horizontal distance of a stair tread from the nose to the riser.

Rural Development Nickname for the federal agency of the U.S. Department of Agriculture that channels credit to farmers and rural residents and communities; formerly known as the Farm Service Agency and Farmer's Home Administration *(FmHA)*.

Rural Pertaining to the area outside the larger and moderate-sized cities and surrounding population concentrations. Generally characterized by farms, ranches, small towns, and unpopulated regions. Contrast with suburb.

Rurban Areas On the fringe of urban development, that are in the process of being developed for urban uses.

S

S&L Savings And Loan Association.

S&P Shelf And Pole.

Sack Mix The amount of Portland cement in a cubic yard of concrete mix.

Sacking Removing of defects on a concrete surface through the application of a mixture of sand and cement to the moistened surface and rubbing with a coarse material such as burlap.

Saddle A small second roof built behind the back side of a fireplace chimney to divert water around the chimney.

Safe Harbor Rules that, if followed, will guarantee compliance with the law.

Safe Rate An interest rate provided by relatively low-RISK investments such as high-grade bonds or well-secured first mortgages. See Financial Management Rate Of Return.

Safety Glass Specific type of glass with the ability to withstand breaking into large jagged pieces, usually tempered and laminated.

Sale Pending A real estate transaction for which a contract has been signed but that has not closed. Brokers who are members of Multiple Listing Services may report sales when a contract is signed. Such transactions are not counted as sales until they close, since some sales contracts are never consummated.

Sale Price The sale price, also referred to as the purchase price, refers to the amount of money paid by the purchaser to the seller.

Sale-Leaseback A sale leaseback occurs when a buyer closes on a home and then leases back tenancy to the seller. This usually occurs when the seller needs more time to vacate the home, in which case, the buyer becomes a sort of landlord and receives payment from the seller for every day they remain in the home.

Sales Comparison Approach See Market Comparison Approach.

Sales Comparison Value A value indication derived by comparing the property being appraised to similar properties that have been sold recently.

Sales Contract A contract by which the buyer and seller agree to the terms of sale. See Agreement Of Sale, Earnest Money Contract.

Salesperson A person who performs real estate activities while employed by or associated with a licensed real estate broker.

Saltbox Colonial An early-American-style, 2 or 2 1/2-story house that is square or rectangular with a steep gable roof that extends down to the first floor in the rear.

Salvage Value The estimated value that an asset will have at the end of its useful life.

SAM Shared Appreciation Mortgage.

Sand Float Finish Lime that is mixed with sand, resulting in a textured finish on a wall.

Sandwich Lease A lease held by a lessee who becomes a lessor by subletting. Typically, the sandwich leaseholder is neither the owner nor the user of the property. See Sublease.

Sanitary Sewer A sewer system that is created for the collection of wastewater from the bathroom, kitchen, and laundry drains, and is usually not designed to handle storm water.

SARA Superfund Amendments And Reauthorization Act.

Sash Balance A device usually operated by a spring and designed to hold a single hung window vent up and in place.

Sash A single light frame that has one or more lights of glass.

Satisfaction A document acknowledging the payment of a debt. Once filed, the collateral pledged in the mortgage is returned to the mortgagor for a *"mortgage burning party."*

Satisfaction Of Mortgage See Satisfaction Piece.

Satisfaction Piece An instrument for recording and acknowledging payment of an indebtedness secured by a mortgage.

Saturated Felt A felt which is impregnated with asphalt.

Savings And Loan Association (S&L) A depository institutions that specialize in originating, servicing, and holding mortgage loans, primarily on owner-occupied Residential Property.

Savings Association Insurance Fund (SAIF) The fund that provides deposit insurance for savings and loan associations. It was authorized by FIRREA and is administered by the FDIC.

SBA Small Business Administration.

Scale The proportional relationship between the dimensions of a drawing, plan, or model to the dimensions of the physical object it represents.

Scenic Easement An encumbrance on the title to a property to preserve it in a more-or-less natural or undeveloped state. See Easement.

Schedule A table on the blueprints that list the sizes, quantities and locations of the windows, doors, and mirrors.

Schedule A A list in the offering plan of all the apartments being sold in a newly constructed building or one that is undergoing conversion.

Schedule B The projected cost of operating a cooperative or condominium during its first year of operation and is part of the offering plan.

Scrap Out Usually used in Drywall work but can be any interior work. The removal of all drywall material and debris after the home is *"hung out"*, that is, installed with drywall.

Scratch Coat The first coat of plaster, which is scratched to form a bond for a second coat.

Screed, Concrete To level off concrete to the correct elevation during a concrete pour.

Screed, Plaster A small strip of wood, usually the thickness of the plaster coat, used as a guide for plastering.

Screening Process The process a potential co-op buyer will go through to gain approval from the board of directors, including compiling and submitting the board package for review and sitting down for an interview with the board or a screening committee for the co-op.

Scribing Cutting and fitting woodwork to an irregular surface.

Scupper An opening for drainage in a wall, curb, or parapet.

Scuttle Hole The Access into a crawl space.

Sealer A finishing material, either clear or pigmented, that is usually applied directly over raw wood for the purpose of sealing the wood surface.

Seasoned Loan A loan on which several payments have been collected.

Seasoning Drying and removing moisture from green wood in order to improve its usability.

SEC See Securities and Exchange Commission

Second Home A residence that is not one's Principal Residence. Under current tax law, a taxpayer may deduct interest on two personal residences.

Second Mortgage A second mortgage is when a property owner borrows against the value of their home. They are also commonly referred to as HELOCs and draw on the market value of the home to provide the borrower with funds to use however they wish. They are granted in a lump sum or a line of credit that can be paid back using rate choices that help plan payments.

Secondary Financing A loan on real property secured by a lien junior to an existing first mortgage loan.

Secondary Market See Secondary Mortgage Market.

Secondary Mortgage Market A market for the purchase and sale of existing mortgages, designed to provide greater liquidity for mortgages; also called the secondary money market. Mortgages are originated in the primary mortgage market.

Secondary Offering A stock offering made by an existing public company.

Secondary Space See Second Generation.

Second-Generation Previously occupied space that becomes available for lease, either directly from the landlord or as sublease space.

Section 1031 The section of the Internal Revenue Code that deals with tax-deferred exchanges of certain property. General rules for a tax-deferred exchange of real estate are that the properties must be:

1. Exchanged or qualify as a Delayed Exchange
2. Like-Kind Property; meaning real estate for real estate.
3. Held for use in a trade or business or held as an investment.

Section 121 The section of the Internal Revenue Code that deals with exclusion of gain from the sale of a principal residence after May 6, 1997. An unmarried individual may exclude from income up to $250,000 of gain realized on the sale or exchange of a principal residence. The seller must have owned and occupied the residence for a total of at least two of the five years before the sale. Exclusion may be used on a continuing basis but not more often than once every two years. Exclusion may be up to $500,000 for married individuals who meet certain tests.

Section 1221 The part of the Internal Revenue Code that defines a Capital Asset.

Section 1231 The section of the Internal Revenue Code that deals with assets used in a trade or business.

Section 1245 The section of the Internal Revenue Code dealing with gains from personal property on which depreciation had been claimed. Generally, gains are taxed at the capital gains rate except to the extent of depreciation claimed, which is taxed as ordinary income.

Section 1250 The section of the Internal Revenue Code dealing with gains from real estate on which Accelerated Depreciation had been claimed.

Section 167 The part of the Internal Revenue Code that deals with depreciation.

Section 8 Housing Privately owned rental dwelling units participating in the low-income rental assistance program created by 1974 amendments to Section 8 of the 1937 Housing Act. Sometime referred to simply as *"Section 8"*.

Section
1. A portion of a township under the rectangular survey system (government survey method). A township is divided into 36 sections numbered 1 to 36. A section is a square with mile-long sides and an area of one square mile, or 640 acres.
2. It is a *"cut-through"* representation of the internal composition of a building or its structure. Normally showing how the building is constructed, from foundation to roof.

Section, Block, And Lot Number A method used for land description that refers to a number of section, block, and lot which appears on maps and plats of recorded subdivided land.

Secured Loan A secured loan is backed by the borrower's assets, including cars, a second home, or other large items that can be used as payment to a lender if the borrower is unable to pay back the loan.

Securities And Exchange Commission (SEC) The federal agency that supervises and oversees the issuance and exchange of public securities.

Securitization The process of converting an illiquid asset, such as a mortgage loan, into a tradable form, such as mortgage-backed securities.

Security
1. Property that serves as collateral for a debt.
2. A document that serves as evidence of ownership.

Security Agreement A document granting a lender the right to execute against certain specified real and/or personal property as collateral for a loan or other obligation.

Security Deposit A deposit of money by a tenant to a landlord to secure performance of a lease. It also can take the form of a letter of credit or other financial instrument.

Security Instrument In the simplest of terms, this is a mortgage. An interest in real estate that allows the property to be sold upon a default on the obligation for which the Security Interest was created. The security instrument is more specifically described as a security deed, a mortgage, or a Trust Deed.

Security Interest The interest granted to a lender by a borrower in a security agreement.

Seed Money The amount needed to begin a real estate development, prior to being able to borrow under a mortgage loan. Required costs include those for a Feasibility Study, Loan Application and Loan Commitment fees, attorney and accountant fees, land option costs, and others. See Front Money.

See-Through Building A vacant building. See Shell.

Seisen Possession of real property under claim of freehold estate.

Seizen See Seisen.

Seizing The possession of land by one who claims to own at least an estate for life therein.

Self-Administered REIT When members of the management are employees of the REIT or an entity having essentially the same economic ownership as the REIT.

Self-Amortizing Mortgage A mortgage that will retire itself through regular principal and interest payments.

Self-Contained Appraisal Report A written appraisal report that contains all the information required by USPAP, with extensive detail.

Self-Help The efforts of a landlord to cure a default on the lease without aid of legal proceedings. In most states, self-help remedies are not considered a legitimate substitute for a legal eviction.

Self-Managed REIT An REIT whose employees are responsible for performing property management functions.

Self-Proving Will A will in which the witnesses give their testimony at the time of signing. This testimony is preserved in a notarized affidavit to eliminate the problem of finding the witnesses at the maker's death and to assist in the probating procedure.

Self-sealing Shingles A type of shingle containing factory applied strips or spots of self-sealing adhesive. Most shingles sold in the US these days are self sealing.

Seller Carry-Back A seller carry-back is financing in which the seller acts as a bank or financial institution financing some or all of the transaction. The buyer will sign a promissory note agreeing to pay a specific amount to the seller, and the seller transfers the title to the new owner. If the buyer is unable to make their monthly payments at any time, the seller can legally foreclose and take back the property.

Seller Contribution The seller contribution is a payment by the seller of a property of some, or all, of the buyer's closing costs.

Seller Financing A debt instrument taken back by the seller as part of the purchase price for a property. Such financing is used as an inducement to a sale when normal third party financing is expensive or unavailable and in situations where the existing, first-lien loan may be assumed by the buyer but the difference between the existing debt and sales price exceeds the cash resources of the buyer. Seller financing may be in the form of a senior mortgage or a junior mortgage.

Seller. The person selling a property.

Seller's Agent A seller's agent is the listing agent that works in the best interests of the seller.

Seller's Market An economic condition that favor sellers, reflecting rising prices and market activity.

Selling Broker (Agent) The licensed real estate Broker that brings forth the buyer.

Semiannual Twice a year.

Semigloss Paint A paint or enamel made so that its coating, when dry, has some luster or sheen but is not very glossy. Bathrooms and kitchens are often painted semigloss.

Senior Classes With regard to securities, describes the classes with the highest priority to receive the payments from the underlying mortgage loans.

Senior Mortgage See First Mortgage.

Senior Residential Appraiser See SRA.

Sensitivity Analysis technique of investment analysis whereby different values of certain key variables are tested to see how sensitive investment results are to possible change in assumptions. It is a method of evaluating the riskiness of an investment.

Separate Account A relationship where a single pension plan sponsor retains an investment manager or adviser to source real estate product under a stated investment policy exclusively for that sponsor.

Separate Property The real property owned by a husband and wife prior to their marriage.

Septic Permit A health department authorization to build or modify a septic system.

Septic System A form of onsite sewage treatment in areas with no connection to public sewers

Service Drop A service drop is the aboveground electrical cables that come from the nearest electrical pole connecting the electrical service of the house.

Service Entrance Panel Main power cabinet where electricity enters a home wiring system.

Service Equipment Main control gear at the service entrance, such as circuit breakers, switches, and fuses.

Service Lateral Underground power supply line.

Service Panel See Service Entrance Panel.

Servicer An organization that acts on behalf of a trustee for the benefit of security holders. A mortgage servicer manages the daily administrative work around a loan, including processing loan payments, responding to borrower inquiries, and tracking principal and interest paid.

Servicing The term that describes all of the administrative tasks that must be completed to successfully hold a tax lien portfolio through the redemption period and, if necessary, perfect your interest in the property if there is no redemption.

Servient Tenement The land on which an easement exists in favor of an adjacent property; also called a servient estate.

Setback The amount of space local zoning regulations require between a lot line and building line. The distance from a curb, property line or other reference point, within which building is prohibited.

Setback Thermostat A thermostat with a clock which can be programmed to come on or go off at various temperatures and at different times of the day/week.

Settlement See Closing

Settlement Shifts in a structure's foundation.

Settlement Statement See Closing Statement.

Severally Separately, individually; same as *"In Severalty."*

Severalty The ownership of real property by one person only; also called sole ownership.

Severance Damages An element of value arising out of a condemnation to which a tract was a part.

Sewage Ejector A pump used to *"lift"* wastewater to a gravity sanitary sewer line. Usually used in basements and other locations which are situated below the level of the side sewer.

Sewer A system of pipes, containments, and treatment facilities for the disposal of plumbing wastes.

Sewer Lateral The portion of the sanitary sewer which connects the interior wastewater lines to the main sewer lines. The side sewer is usually buried in several feet of soil and runs from the house to the sewer line. It is usually owned by the sewer utility, must be maintained by the owner, and may only be serviced by utility approved contractors.

Sewer Stub The junction at the municipal sewer system where the home's sewer line is connected.

Sewer Tap The physical connection point where the home's sewer line connects to the main municipal sewer line.

Shake A wood roofing material, normally cedar or redwood.

Share Loan A loan used to finance the purchase of shares in a co-op corporation.

Shared Appreciation Mortgage (SAM) A residential loan with a fixed interest rate set below market rates, with the lender entitled to a specified share of appreciation in property value over a specified time interval. Loan payments are set to amortize the loan over a long-term maturity, but repayment is generally required after a much shorter term. The amount of appreciation is established by sale of the home or by appraisal if no sale is made.

Shared Equity Mortgage A home loan in which the lender is granted a share of the equity, thereby allowing the lender to participate in the proceeds from resale. After satisfying the unpaid balance of the loan, the borrower splits the residue of the proceeds with the lender. Shared equity plans often require the lender to buy a portion of the equity by providing a portion of the down payment.

Shares When purchasing in a cooperative building, the apartment is not actually purchased directly as real estate but rather shares in the cooperative corporation are purchased.

Shear Block Plywood that is face nailed to short wall studs *(above a door or window, for example)*. This is done to prevent the wall from sliding and collapsing.

Sheathing The structural wood panel covering, usually OSB or plywood, used over studs, floor joists or rafters/trusses of a structure.

Sheeting See Sheathing.

Shed Roof One having a single, sloped side.

Sheet Metal Duct Work The heating system usually round or rectangular metal pipes and sheet metal and installed for distributing air from the furnace to rooms in the home.

Sheet Metal Work All components of a house employing sheet metal, such as flashing, gutters, and downspouts.

Sheet Rock A manufactured panel made out of gypsum plaster and encased in a thin cardboard.

Shell The frame of a building. Generally, the builder has stubbed out utilities, built entrances, and provided the HVAC unit.

Sheriff's Deed Evidence of ownership given by a court in the sale of property for unpaid taxes.

Shim A small piece of scrap lumber or shingle, usually wedge shaped, which when forced behind a furring strip or framing member forces it into position.

Shingles
1. Used over sheathing for exterior wall covering of a structure.
2. Roof covering of asphalt.

Shopping Center A collection of retail stores with a common parking area and generally one or more large department, discount, or food stores; sometimes including an enclosed mall or walkway. See Urban Land Institute, Institute Of Real Estate Management, National Retail Merchants Association. See also Anchor Tenant.

Short Circuit A situation that occurs when hot and neutral wires come in contact with each other. Fuses and circuit breakers protect against fire that could result from a short.

Short Form An instrument, seldom more than two pages, that refers to another document. The short form is often recorded in lieu of a cumbersome longer document.

Short Sale A short sale occurs when a homeowner sells their property for less than what's owed on the mortgage. A short sale allows the lender to recoup some of the loan that's owed to them but must be approved by the lender before the seller moves forward.

Short-Term Capital Gain Profit on the sale of a capital asset that was held, generally, for less than 12 months.

Shutter Usually lightweight louvered decorative frames in the form of doors located on the sides of a window. Some shutters are made to close over the window for protection.

Side Sewer The portion of the sanitary sewer which connects the interior wastewater lines to the main sewer lines.

Sidecar Fund Or Investment A sidecar or over-allocation fund is a blind-pool co-investment vehicle under common sponsorship with a private equity fund. The sidecar fund has a right of second opportunity to participate in larger investments where there is a need for additional equity capital to complete the deal brought by the fund sponsor to the lead private equity fund.

Siding Materials used to weatherproof outside walls, typically made of wood or wood products, vinyl, or aluminum, often in the form of or made to resemble clapboards or shakes.

Sill Cock An exterior water faucet.

Sill Plate Bottom horizontal member of an exterior wall frame which rests on top a foundation, sometimes called mudsill.

Sill Seal Fiberglass or foam insulation installed between the foundation wall and sill *(wood)* plate.

Sill The wood plate framing member that lays flat against and bolted to the foundation wall with anchor bolts and upon which the floor joists are installed.

Simple Interest A method of calculating the future value of a sum assuming that interest paid is not compounded, i.e., that interest is paid only on the principal. See also Compound Interest.

Simulate Artificially replicate the behavior of a system for purposes of analysis. The simulation may be less complex than the actual system, allowing the analyst to focus on certain variables that are of interest. See Sensitivity Analysis.

Simultaneous Exchange A straight 1031 exchange in which the property closings happen on the exact same date, and the investors relinquish and receive their respective properties in, typically, back-to-back closing sessions.

Single Hung Window A window with one vertically sliding sash or window vent.

Single Purpose Entity An entity, usually but not always a limited liability company, designed to provide bankruptcy-remote protections for a lender.

Single REOC Fund A fund offered by a fully or partially vertically integrated real estate operating company. The fund doesn't enter into joint ventures with third party operators, because the REOC sponsoring the fund IS the operator of the assets. Example: Carmel Partners' fund series.

Single-Family Housing A type of residential structure designed to include one dwelling. Adjacent units may share walls and other structural components but generally have separate access to the out-side and do not share plumbing and heating equipment. Examples of Single-family housing include detached housing units, and zero lot line homes.

Sinking Fund An account that, when compounded, will equal a specified sum after a specified time period. See Compound Interest.

SIOR Society Of Industrial And Office Realtors®.

Site A plot of land prepared for or underlying a structure or development. The location of a property.

Site Analysis Determines the suitability of a specific parcel of land for a specific use.

Site Assessment (Environmental) See Environmental Site Assessment.

Site Development The installation of all necessary improvements made to a site before a building or project can be constructed on the site.

Site Plan A detailed plan that depicts the location of improvements on a parcel.

Site-Built Home A home that is constructed primarily on its site. Although some components may be prefabricated off-site, the home is erected, framed, and finished by workers on location using stock materials.

Situs The personal preference of people for one area of land over another, not necessarily based on objective facts and knowledge.

Skirting This is a strip of material that covers the joint between the floor and wall in a room.

Skylight A more or less horizontal window located on the roof of a building.

Slab The exposed wearing surface laid over the structural support beams of a building to form the floor of the building.

Slab On Grade A type of foundation with a concrete floor which is placed directly on the soil. The edge of the slab is usually thicker and acts as the footing for the walls.

Slab, Door A rectangular door without hinges, frame, or, most often light.

Slag Concrete cement that sometimes covers the vertical face of the foundation void material.

Sleeper A wood member embedded in concrete, as in a floor, that serves to support and to fasten the subfloor or flooring.

Sleeve Installed under the concrete driveway or sidewalk, used to run a sprinkler pipe or low voltage wire.

Slope The incline angle of a roof surface, given as a ratio of the rise in inches to the run in feet. See pitch.

Slump The wetness of concrete. A 3 inch slump is dryer and stiffer than a 5 inch slump.

Small Business Administration (SBA) A federal government agency in Washington, D.C., that encourages small business.

Smart Building See Intelligent Building.

SMSA Standard Metropolitan Statistical Area.

Social Investing Investments driven in whole or in part by social or political objectives; meaning non-real estate objectives. Under ERISA, social investing is economically justified only if proper real estate fundamentals are considered first.

Socialize

1. To place under government or group ownership or control.
2. To make fit for companionship with others.
3. To convert or adapt to the needs of society.
4. To take part in social activities.
5. To engage others in a particular discussion or plan about a specific topic.

Society Of Industrial And Office Realtors® (SIOR) An organization, affiliated with The National Association Of Realtors®, whose members are mainly concerned with the sale of warehouses, factories, and other industrial property. Confers SIOR designation.

Soffit The underside of a roof that extends beyond the exterior walls. The soffit covers the eaves.

Soft Cost The portion of an equity investment other than the actual cost of the improvements themselves that may be tax-deductible in the first year.

Soft Market A market in which demand has shrunk or supply has grown faster than demand and in which sales at reasonable prices have become more difficult. See Buyer's Market.

Soft Money

1. In a development or an investment, money contributed that is tax-deductible.
2. Sometimes used to describe costs that do not physically go into construction, such as interest during construction, architect's fees, legal fees, etc.

Soil Bank Land held out of agricultural production in an effort to stabilize commodity prices and promote soil conservation. Subsidies to farmers participating in the soil bank program are provided by the U.S. Department of Agriculture.

Soil Pipe A large pipe that carries liquid and solid wastes to a sewer or septic tank.

Soil Stack A plumbing vent pipe that penetrates the roof.

Solar Heating See Active Solar Heating, Passive Solar Heating.

Sole Plate Bottom horizontal member of a frame wall.

Sole Proprietorship Ownership of a business, with no formal entity as a vehicle or structure.

Solid Bridging A solid member placed between adjacent floor joists near the center of the span to prevent joists or rafters from twisting.

Solid Waste a general term for all types of waste material, whether or not hazardous.

Sonotube Round A large cardboard tubes designed to hold wet concrete in place until it hardens.

Sound Attenuation The process of using fiberglass insulation to soundproof a wall or subfloor.

Southern Colonial A large, early-American-style, 2 or 3-story frame house with a characteristic colonnade extending across the front. The roof extends over the colonnade, and the colonnade typically has a minimum four columns.

Sovereign Wealth Fund (SWF) A sovereign wealth fund *(SWF)* is a state-owned investment fund composed of financial assets such as stocks, bonds, property, precious metals, or other financial instruments. Sovereign wealth funds invest globally. Most SWFs are funded by foreign exchange assets.

Sovereignty Of The Soil The beginning of the record of ownership of land by conveyance from the sovereign or the state. Historically, this is known also as a patent.

Space Heat The heat supplied to the living space, for example, to a room or the living area of a building.

Space Plan A graphic representation of a tenant's space requirements, showing wall and door locations, room sizes and sometimes furniture layouts.

Spacing The distance between individual units, shingles, or members.

Span The clear distance that a framing member carries a load without support between structural supports.

Spanish Villa A Latin-style, asymmetrical, 1- to 3-story house with painted stucco exterior walls and red tile roof.

SPE See Single Purpose Entity.

Spec Home A house built before it is sold. The builder speculates that he can sell it at a profit.

Spec Speculative; built without a tenant or buyer/user.

Special Agent One who is engaged to act for another, with limited authority.

Special Assessment A tax or levy customarily imposed against only those specific parcels of real estate that will benefit from a proposed public improvement, such as a street or sewer.

Special Assessment District A geographic area designated to pay for the cost of specific public improvements which will benefit the properties in that geographic area.

Special Purpose Entity See Single Purpose Entity.

Special Servicer A firm that is employed to work out mortgages that are either delinquent or in default.

Special Use Permit A permit which allows a specific exception to an existing zoning ordinance for a particular parcel of land. It is also known as a conditional use permit

Special Warranty Deed A deed in which the grantor warrants or guarantees the title only against defects arising during the period of his or her tenure and ownership of the property and not against defects existing before that time, generally using the language *"by, through, or under the grantor but not otherwise."*

Special-Purpose Property A building with limited uses and marketability, such as a church, theater, school, or public utility.

Specialty Center Shopping Center Typically anchored by restaurants, a theater, or other entertainment venues rather than the traditional supermarket or department store.

Specialty Contractor Licensed to perform a specialty task

Specific Lien A lien affecting or attaching only to a certain, specific parcel of land or piece of property.

Specific Performance A remedy in a court of equity compelling a defendant to carry out the terms of an agreement or contract

Specific Performance Suit A legal action brought in a court of equity in special cases to compel a party to carry out the terms of a contract. The basis for an equity court's jurisdiction in breach of a real estate contract is that land is unique, and mere legal damages would not adequately compensate the buyer from the seller's breach.

Specifications Detailed instructions provided in conjunction with plans and blueprints for construction. Specifications may stipulate the type of materials to be used, special construction techniques, dimensions, and colors.

Specified Assets When a joint venture is formed specifically to acquire or develop a pre-defined asset.

Specified investing Investment in individually specified properties or portfolios, or investment in commingled funds whose real estate assets are fully or partially specified prior to the commitment of investor capital.

Speculation Investment or other decision whose success depends on an event or change that is not certain to occur.

Speculative Building Land development or construction with no formal commitment from the end users of the finished product. The speculative builder anticipates that a demand exists or will form for the product when it is put on the market. See Spec Home.

Speculative Space Any tenant space that has not been leased before the start of construction on a new building.

Speculator One who invests with the anticipation that an event or series of events will occur to increase the value of the investment.

Spendable Income Same as After-Tax Cash Flow.

Splash Block Portable concrete channel generally placed beneath an exterior sill cock or downspout in order to receive roof drainage from downspouts and to divert it away from the building.

Split-Level Also called tri-level; a popular style of home, best suited for side-to-side slopes, in which a 1-story wing is attached between the levels of a 2-story wing.

Sponsor Creator and developer responsible to file all of the initial paperwork, write bylaws, gather investors, and ultimately sell the units *(or shares)* for a condominium or co-op community.

Sponsoring Broker A duly licensed real estate broker who employs a salesperson. Under law, the broker is responsible for the acts of her or his salespeople.

Spot Zoning The act of rezoning a parcel of land where all surrounding parcels are zoned for a different use, in particular where the rezoning creates a use that is incompatible with surrounding land uses. Spot zoning is generally disallowed in the courts.

Spread
1. The difference between the bid price and asking price.
2. The difference between the cost of money and the earnings rate.

Spreading Agreement An agreement that extends the collateral of a loan to include several properties.

Square Footage The area measured in square feet of a certain property. Square footage can be measured in different ways and is usually considered approximate.

Square A unit of measure that totals 100 square feet usually applied to roofing and siding material. Also, a situation that exists when two elements are at right angles to each other.

Squaretab Shingles Shingles on which tabs are all the same size and exposure.

Squatter See Estate By Sufferance, Adverse Possession.

Squatter's Rights Those rights acquired through adverse possession. By *"squatting"* on land for a certain statutory period under prescribed conditions, one may acquire title by limitations. If an easement only is acquired, instead of the title to the land itself, one has title by prescription, or easement by prescription. See Estate By Sufferance, Adverse Possession.

Squeegie Fine pea gravel used to grade a floor before concrete is poured.

SRA Senior Residential Appraiser, a designation granted by the Appraisal Institute For Residential Appraisers. An SRA may refer to himself as a member of the Appraisal Institute, though not an MAI.

Stabilized Budget A forecast of income and expenses that can reasonably be expected for a certain period of time; usually 5 years.

Stabilized Net Operating Income Projected income less expenses that are subject to change but have been adjusted to reflect equivalent, stable property operations.

Stabilized Occupancy The optimum range of long-term occupancy that an income-producing real estate project is expected to achieve after exposure for leasing in the open market for a reasonable period of time at terms and conditions comparable to competitive offerings.

Stable Mortgage A mortgage loan instrument that combines fixed and adjustable rates in the same loan. The rate applied to the loan is a blend of a fixed rate and a rate that varies according to an index. The loan is a creation of General Electric Capital Mortgage Service, Inc., and FNMA.

Stachybotrys Chartarum See Black Mold.

Stack To position trusses on the walls in their correct location.

Stacking Plan Arrangement of tenants on floors in a high-rise office building.

Stagflation Term coined in the 1970s to describe an economic situation of stagnant economic condition with inflation.

Stair Carriage Supporting member for stair treads.

Stair Landing A platform between flights of stairs or at the termination of a flight of stairs.

Stair Rise The vertical distance between stairs treads.

Stakeholder Anyone who may be affected by a decision. Someone who has a stake in the outcome of a decision involving land or real property. Generally used to justify government regulations that affect rights to private property.

Standard Metropolitan Statistical Area (SMSA) See Metropolitan Statistical Area.

Standard Practices A term used to define the basic and minimum construction standards.

Standby Commitment A commitment by a lender to make available a sum of money at specified terms for a specified period. A standby fee is charged for this commitment. The borrower retains the option of closing the loan or allowing the commitment to lapse.

Standby Fee The sum required by a lender to provide a standby commitment. See Standby Loan. The fee is forfeited should the loan not be closed within a specified time.

Standing Mortgage A standing mortgage is an interest only mortgage with no principal reduction over time.

Starker Exchange Also known as a 1031 Tax-Deferred Exchange or tax-free property exchange. Allows a property owner to defer paying federal and some state income taxes by trading one business type property for another, as long as both are like/kind properties

Starker Transaction See Starker Exchange.

Starter Strip Asphalt roofing applied at the eaves that provide protection by filling in the spaces under the cutouts and joints of the first course of shingles.

Starts See Housing Starts.

State Rule A method for determining just compensation for condemnation in many states.

State-Certified Appraiser See Certified General Appraiser, Certified Residential Appraiser.

Static Vent A vent without a fan.

Statute A law established by an act of the Legislature.

Statute Of Frauds The part of a state law that requires certain instruments, such as deeds, real estate sales contracts, and certain leases to be in writing to be legally enforceable.

Statute Of Limitations That law pertaining to the period of time within which certain actions must be brought to court.

Statutory Dedication The owners of a subdivision or other property file a plat that results in a grant of public property, such as the streets in a development.

Statutory Foreclosure A foreclosure proceeding not conducted under court supervision.

Statutory Lien A lien imposed on property by statute, for example, a tax lien; in contrast to a voluntary lien, which an owner places on his or her own real estate, for example, a mortgage lien.

Statutory Right Of Redemption The legal right of a mortgagor to redeem the property after it has been sold at a foreclosure sale. This right is granted BY state law for a limited period of time, depending on the state.

STC Sound Transmission Class. The measure of sound stopping of ordinary noise.

Steel Inspection An inspection of the concrete foundation wall conducted before it is poured into the foundation panels.

Steering The illegal practice of channeling home Seekers to particular areas or avoiding specific areas, either to maintain or to change the character of an area, or to create a speculative situation. See, Racial Steering.

Step Flashing Flashing application method that is used where a vertical surface meets a sloping roof plane.

Step Loan A type of Adjustable-Rate Mortgage for which the interest rate is adjusted only once during the term of the loan. Therefore, the loan shares some of the features of both fixed-rate and adjustable-rate loans.

Stepped-Up Basis An income tax term used to describe a change in the Adjusted Tax Basis of property, allowed for certain transactions. The old basis is increased to market value upon inheritance, as opposed to a Carry-Over Basis in the event of a Tax-Free Exchange.

Step-up Lease A lease specifying set increases in rent at set intervals during the term of the lease.

Stick Built A dwelling built without prefabricated components. Also called conventional building.

Stick-Style House A nineteenth-century-style house with exposed framing members, high steep roofs, complex silhouettes, diagonal braces, and a large amount of ginger-bread trim. Also called Carpenter Gothic

Stigma A negative image of property, after its environmental problem was remediated.

Stigmatized Property A property regarded by some as undesirable because of events that have occurred on the property, like murder or suicide, or present paranormal activities. Sometimes, proximity to undesirable property causes a property to become stigmatized, too.

Stile An upright framing member in a panel door.

Stipulations The terms within a written contract.

Stool The flat molding fitted over the windowsill between jambs and contacting the bottom rail of the lower sash.

Stop Box A cast iron pipe with a lid, providing emergency water shut off to a property.

Stop Clause In a lease, stipulates an amount of operating expense above which the tenant must bear. Often the base amount is the amount of expense for the first full year of operation under the lease.

Stop Order An official, written notice to a contractor to terminate some or all work on a project for reasons such as safety violations, defective materials or workmanship, or termination of the contract.

Stop Valve A device installed in a water supply line, usually near a fixture, that permits an individual to shut off the water supply to one fixture without interrupting service to the rest of the system.

Stops Moulding along the inner edges of a door or window frame. Also valves used to shut off water to a fixture.

Storm Sash See Storm Window.

Storm Sewer A pipe system designed to collect storm water and separate it from the wastewater system.

Storm Window A second window providing additional protection against cold weather.

Story That part of a building between any floor or between the floor and roof.

Straight Lease A lease specifying a fixed amount of rent that is to be paid periodically, typically monthly, during the entire term of the lease.

Straight Lease See Flat Lease.

Straight Line Depreciation See Straight Line Method.

Straight-line Method A method of calculating depreciation for tax purposes computed by dividing the adjusted basis of a property less its estimated salvage value by the estimated number of years of remaining useful life.

Straight-Line Recapture Rate The part of a Capitalization Rate that accounts for the annual erosion of a Wasting Asset by assuming an equal amount of loss in value each year of the Useful Life of the asset.

Straw Man One who purchases property that is, in turn, conveyed to another for the purpose of concealing the identity of the eventual purchaser.

Strict Foreclosure A foreclosure proceeding in which the mortgagee has the right to possess the mortgaged property directly upon default on the mortgage agreement. This type of foreclosure is rarely used in contemporary markets.

Strict Liability An owner's responsibility for cleaning up a contaminated site, even though the owner was not negligent. See Innocent Purchaser, Lender Liability.

Strike The door frame plate that engages a latch or dead bolt.

String, Stringer A timber or other support for cross members in floors or ceilings. In stairs, the supporting member for stair treads.

Strip Center Any shopping area comprised of a row of stores but smaller than a neighborhood center anchored by a grocery store.

Strip Development See Strip Shopping Center.

Strip Flooring Wood flooring consisting of narrow, matched strips.

Strip Shopping Center A form of commercial land use in which each establishment is afforded direct access to a major thoroughfare; generally associated with intensive use of signs to attract passers-by. Generally without an Anchor Tenant.

Structural Floor A framed lumber floor, installed as a basement floor.

Stub, Stubbed To push through.

Stucco An outside plaster finish made with Portland cement as its base.

Stud Framing A building method that distributes structural loads to each of a series of relatively lightweight studs.

Stud Shoe A metal structural bracket that reinforces a vertical stud.

Stud A vertical wood framing piece, attached to the horizontal sole plate below and the top plate above.

Subagency An agent appoints a subagent to help the agent in a specified transaction and to act on the principal's behalf.

Subagent An agent of a person already acting as an agent of a principal.

Subchapter S Corporation A type of corporation with a limited number of stockholders that elects not to be taxed as a regular corporation and meets certain other requirements. There are 75 or fewer Stockholders in this type of company. Shareholders include, in their personal tax return, their pro-rata share of Capital Gains, Ordinary Income, Tax Preference Items, and so on. See Passive Income.

Subcontractor A contractor working under and being paid by the general contractor, often a specialist in nature, such as an electrical contractor, cement contractor, etc.

Subdivider One who partitions a tract of land for the purpose of selling the individual plots. If the land is improved in any way, the subdivider becomes a developer.

Subdividing Dividing a tract of land into smaller tracts.

Subdivision A tract of land divided by the owner, known as the subdivider, into blocks, building lots, and streets according to recorded subdivision plat that must comply with local ordinances and regulations.

Subfloor The framing components of a floor to include the sill plate, floor joists, and deck sheeting over which a finish floor is to be laid.

Subject Property In appraisal, the property being appraised.

Subject To Acquiring property with an existing mortgage, but not becoming personally liable for the debt.

Subject To Financing A clause in the contract of sale for a cooperative apartment stipulating that the agreement is conditioned upon the buyer's obtaining financing from a financial institution in an agreed upon amount.

Subject To Mortgage Circumstance in which a buyer takes title to mortgaged real property but is not personally liable for the payment of the amount due. The buyer must make payments in order to keep the property; however, with default, only the buyer's equity in that property is lost.

Sublease A lease from a lessee to another lessee. The new lessee is a sublessee or subtenant. See Sandwich Lease.

Sublessee A person or identity to whom the rights of use and occupancy under a lease have been conveyed, while the original lessee retains primary responsibility for the obligations of the lease.

Sublet A sublet is when the owner of an apartment or the main lease holder decides to rent the apartment to a subtenant. See Sublease.

Subletting The leasing of premises by a lessee to a third party for part of the lessee's remaining term.

Submortgage An arrangement in which a mortgage lender pledges a mortgage as collateral for his/her own loan.

Subordinate Mortgage A second or third mortgage that has a lower priority in the event of a default than the first mortgage.

Subordinate The Fee The act of a landlord property owner granting to the tenant's lender a right to foreclose the landlord's interest, upon default of the tenant under its loan agreements, sometimes in return for a fee.

Subordinated Classes With regard to CMBS, describes those classes with the lowest priority to receive payments from the underlying mortgage loans.

Subordinated Ground Lease A lease where the mortgage has priority over the ground lease.

Subordination
1. The process of sharing the risk of credit losses disproportionately among two or more classes of securities.
2. A relegation to a lesser position usually in respect to a right or security. The concept of agreeing to make an otherwise senior interest junior *(or subordinate)* to an interest which otherwise would be a junior interest.

Subordination Agreement An agreement that changes the order of priority of liens between two creditors.

Subordination Clause A clause which permits the placing of a mortgage at a later date which takes priority over an existing mortgage.

Subordination, Non-Disturbance And Attornment Agreement A document providing for subordination, non-disturbance and attornment obligations by parties with diverse interests in the same property.

Sub-Prime Loans An industry term used to describe loans with less stringent lending and underwriting terms and conditions. Due to the higher risk; sub-prime loans charge higher interest rates and fees.

Subprime Mortgage See Sub-Prime Loans.

Subrogation The substitution of one creditor for another, with the substituted person succeeding to the legal rights and claims of the original claimant. Subrogation is used by title insurers to acquire the right the sue from the injured party to recover any claims they have paid.

Subscribing Witness One who writes his/her name as witness to the execution of an instrument.

Subsequent Taxes Subsequent taxes are the future taxes that are due after a tax is held.

Substitution An appraisal principle stating that the maximum value of a property tends to be set by the cost of purchasing an equally desirable and valuable substitute property, assuming that no costly delay is encountered in making the substitution.

Substitution Of Collateral A situation where a lender allows the borrower to transfer the mortgage that the borrower signed on a subject property to another, different property that the borrower has that is of equal or greater value

Subsurface Rights See Mineral Rights.

Suburb A town or unincorporated developed area in close proximity to a city. Suburbs, largely residential, are often dependent on the city for employment and support services; generally characterized by low density development relative to the city.

Suit For Possession A court suit initiated by a landlord to evict a tenant from leased premises after the tenant has breached one of the terms of the lease or has held possession of the property after the expiration of the lease.

Suit For Specific Performance A legal action brought by either a buyer or a seller to enforce performance of the terms of a contract.

Suit To Quiet Title A legal action intended to establish or settle the title to a particular property, especially when there is cloud on the title.

Summary Appraisal Report A written appraisal report that contains a moderate amount of detail.

Summary Possession See Eviction, Actual.

Summation Appraisal An approach under which value equals estimated land value plus reproduction costs of any improvements after depreciation has been subtracted.

Sum-Of-Years-Digits Depreciation In tax and accounting, a method of allocating the cost of an asset over its useful life. It requires a fraction to be computed each year, which is applied against the depreciable amount. The numerator is the number of years left to be depreciated. The denominator is the sum of the year's digits of the depreciable life.

Sump As part of a drainage system, a pit in the basement to collect excess moisture and liquids. to avoid flooding, a sump pump may be installed to remove accumulated water in the sump pit.

Sump Pump A submersible pump in a sump pit that pumps any excess ground water to the outside of a building.

Sunk Cost A sunk cost refers to money that has already been spent and which cannot be recovered.

Sunken Room A Room in a home that one must walk down usually one or two steps to enter. a room into which a person must step down to enter. .The area lies lower than other areas of the dwelling within that floor. A sunken living room would be a good example.

Sunset Clause A provision in a sales contract that sets a date after which the agreement is no longer in effect.

Sunspace A room, generally with glass walls and roof, designed to collect solar heat.

Super Jumbo Loan A loan more than $1,000,000.

Super Regional Center Shopping Center A shopping center that is larger than a typical regional mall.

Superadequacy A component of real estate that is beyond what is needed in the structure.

Superfund Amendments And Reauthorization Act (SARA) The law that confirmed the continued existence of Superfund. SARA put more *"teeth"* into CERCLA in terms of both fault and penalty, though SARA provides an innocent landowner defense, for a buyer who conducted a Phase I environmental study before the acquisition, with negative results.

Superfund The commonly used name for CERCLA, the federal environmental cleanup law. If a site is on the Superfund list, it is required to be cleaned up by any and all previous owners, operators, transporters, and disposers of waste to the site. The federal government will clean such sites, requiring the responsible parties to pay the cleanup costs. Imposes strict liability. See *Comprehensive Environmental Response Compensation And Liability Act (CERCLA)*.

Superstructure The portion of a building that is above the ground.

Supply The amount of goods available in the market to be sold at given price. The term often is coupled with demand.

Surety One who voluntarily binds himself to be obligated for the debt or obligation of another.

Surety Bond An agreement by an insurance or bonding company to be responsible for certain possible defaults, debts, or obligations contracted for by an insured party; in essence, a policy insuring one's personal and/or financial integrity. In the real estate business, a surety bond generally is used to ensure that a particular project will be completed at a certain date or that a contract will be performed as stated.

Surface Rights A right or easement granted with mineral rights, enabling the possessor of the mineral rights to drill or mine through the surface.

Surrender The cancellation of a lease by mutual consent of the lessor and the lessee.

Surrogate's Court A court having jurisdiction over the proof of wills, the settling of estates and of citations. See Probate.

Survey The process by which boundaries are measured and land areas are determined. The on-site measurement of lot lines, dimensions, and positions of buildings, structures, and areas on a lot, including the determination of any existing encroachments or easements. Also called a Land Survey.

Surveyor One who prepares Surveys.

Survivorship The right of a joint tenant or tenants to maintain ownership rights following the death of another joint tenant. Survivorship prevents heirs of the deceased from making claims against the property. See Joint Tenancy.

Suspended Ceiling A ceiling system supported by hanging it from the overhead structural framing.

Sway Brace Diagonal bracing installed to prevent a wall from falling over.

Sweat Equity A value added to a property due to improvements as a result of work performed personally by the owner.

Sweetener Something included in a transaction to make it more acceptable.

SWF See Sovereign Wealth Fund.

Swing Loan A short-term loan that allows a homeowner to purchase a new home before selling the former residence. See Bridge Loan, Gap Loan.

Swiss Chalet A Swiss-style 1 1/2- to 2 1/2-story, gable roof house with extensive natural decorative woodwork on the exterior.

Switch An electrical device that completes or disconnects an electrical circuit.

SYD Sum-Of-Years-Digits.

Syndicate A combination of two or more persons or firms to accomplish a joint venture of mutual interest.   Syndicates dissolve when the specific purpose for which they were created has been accomplished. See syndication, syndicator.

Syndication A method of selling property whereby a sponsor or syndicator sells interests to investors. May take the form of a Partnership, Limited Partnership, Tenancy In Common, Corporation, or Subchapter S Corporation.

Syndicator A person in business who sells an investment in shares or units.

Synthetic Lease A transaction that appears as a lease from an accounting standpoint but as a loan from a tax standpoint.

T

T & G Tongue And Groove. A joint made by a tongue that fits into a corresponding groove in the edge of another board to make a tight flush joint.

T Bar Ribbed with a *"T"* shape with a flat metal plate at the bottom that is driven into the earth. Used chain link fence poles, and to mark locations of a water meter pit.

T Hinge A surface hinge with the short member attached to the jamb and the long member attached to the door.

T & M Time and Material.

Tab The exposed portion of strip shingles defined by cutouts, such as *"three tab shingles"*.

Taber Abrader An instrument used to test the abrasion resistance of a material.

Table Funding The practice of originating mortgage loans with internal capital, until enough loans have been packaged for sale in the Secondary Market. Sale of the package allows the lender to recoup capital for further lending.

Table Saw A type of power saw in which the saw motor and blade remains stationary on a table and the material to be cut is passed through it, on the table.

Tack Weld A small weld to hold steel pieces together temporarily.

Tacking Adding on to a time period.

Tag-Along Rights See Drag-Along Rights.

Tail Beam A short beam, joist, or rafter, supported by a header joist at one end and a wall at the other.

Tail Joist See Tail Beam.

Take Off a Listing and often pricing of the material necessary to complete a job.

Takedown The time when a borrower actually accepts money from a lender under a line of credit or loan commitment.

Takeout Financing A commitment to provide permanent financing following construction of a planned project. The takeout commitment is generally predicated upon specific conditions, such as a certain percentage of unit sales or leases, for the permanent loan to *"takeout"* the Construction Loan. Most construction lenders require takeout financing.

Takeout Loan See Takeout Financing.

Taking Most often used as a common synonym for condemnation, or any interference with private property rights, but it is not essential that there be physical seizure or appropriation. Also used in a *"Subject To"* purchase, as in: *"taking the home, subject to the financing in place"*.

Tangible Property Real estate and other valuables that can be seen and/or touched.

Taping The procedure of covering drywall joints with paper or fiberglass tape.

Target Date Fund Target date funds are based on the premise that the younger the investor, the longer the time horizon he or she has to retirement or some other goal and the greater the risk he or she can take to potentially increase returns.

Tax A charge levied upon persons or things by a government.

Tax Abatement A financial incentive offered by a local or municipal government to stimulate development in a particular area.

Tax And Insurance Escrow An account required by a mortgage lender to fund annual property tax assessments and hazard insurance premiums for the mortgaged property. Funded through monthly contributions by the mortgagor. See PITI.

Tax Assessor Local government official, who is either appointed or elected depending upon the municipality; whose primary function is to estimate the value of all real property within the municipality in which they serve. See Assessor.

Tax Base The assessed valuation of all real property that lies within a taxing authority's jurisdiction. When multiplied by the tax rate, it determines the amount of tax due.

Tax Basis See Basis *(Tax)*; See Adjusted Tax Basis.

Tax Bracket Marginal rate for income taxes; the percentage of each additional dollar in income required to be paid as income taxes.

Tax Credit A reduction against income tax payments that would otherwise be due.

Tax Deductible A tax deductible expense helps to reduce taxable income. The tax deductible expenses related to real estate are interest payments on mortgages and real estate taxes.

Tax Deduction One that can be used to reduce taxable income. See Tax Deductible.

Tax Deed Sale A tax deed sale give the buyer immediate ownership of the property. This ownership often requires the filing of a quiet title action to have marketable title, but it is not subject to redemption by the delinquent taxpayer.

Tax Deed The type of instrument given to a grantee by a government that had claimed the property for unpaid taxes. Not to be confused with a Warranty Deed or Quit Claim Deed.

Tax Defaulted Land Sale These are lands that have gone through a sale and were not purchased by a tax sale buyer. They instead were purchased by the taxing jurisdiction or the state and are available for purchase on a negotiated purchase. In some cases these lists may be called *"Lands Available"*, *"Assignment Lists"*, *"OTC lists"*, or *"Lands for Sale"*.

Tax Depreciation An accounting procedure that allows an owner to take a business deduction for a property's annual depreciation according to tax laws, instead of basing the depreciation on the property's actual gain or loss of value in the market. This method also shelters income generated by a property from taxation.

Tax Foreclosure The process of enforcing a lien against property for nonpayment of delinquent property taxes. Taxing authorities hold a superior lien against all taxable property to enforce the payment of their taxes. See Foreclosure.

Tax Grievance Complaint filed by a taxpayer to challenge their property's assessment.

Tax Levy Amount of money that a taxing authority needs to raise through property taxes.

Tax Lien An In Rem proceeding, in which the taxing authority places a claim against a property due to the non-payment of taxes. If the taxes are not paid, the taxing authority has the right to take the property.

Tax Lien Sale A tax lien sale does not give the lien buyer ownership of the property. It gives the buyer a claim for money that is superior to almost all other liens, including mortgages and is secured by the real estate. If this claim for money is not satisfied the lien holder can apply for and receive the property, subject to the conditions set by the statutes for the jurisdiction.

Tax Map An official map showing the dimensions of the properties in a municipality

Tax On Home Sale See Section 121.

Tax Preference Items Certain types of income or deductions that are added to adjusted Gross Income to calculate the Alternative Minimum Tax.

Tax Rate The ratio or percentage at which a property is taxed which is often multiplied by a property's assessed value to determine the property tax.

Tax Roll A list or record containing the descriptions of all land parcels located within the county, the names of the owners or those receiving the tax bill, assessed values and tax amounts.

Tax Sale A court-ordered sale of real property to raise money to cover delinquent taxes.

Tax Shelter An investment made especially for the purpose of creating income tax deductions in order to reduce taxes resulting from other taxable income sources.

Tax Stop A clause in a lease that stops a lessor from paying Property Taxes above a certain amount. See Escalator Clause, Stop Clause.

Tax Taking The taxing jurisdiction *"takes"* the property and becomes the owner. The property is later sold, either through a negotiated sale or an auction.

Taxable Value See Assessed Value.

Taxation The process by which a government or municipal quasi-public body raises monies to fund its operation.

Tax-Deferred Exchange See Starker.

Tax-Exempt Property Real Property that is not subject, in whole or in part, to Ad Valorem property taxes.

Tax-Free Exchange Same as tax-deferred exchange. See Section 1031.

Taxpayer The person or entity carrying out the exchange.

Tax-Sheltered Income Cash flow received from rental property that is not taxable; See Tax Shelter.

TDR Transferable Development Rights.

Teaser Rate A contract interest rate charged on an adjustable-rate mortgage for the initial adjustment interval that is significantly lower than the fully indexed rate at the time. It is an incentive to encourage borrowers to accept adjustable-rate mortgage loans . In general, the interest rate reverts to the fully indexed rate at the first adjustment date. See Fully Indexed Rate.

Technical Risk Ratios There are five statistical measures or technical risk ratios used in applying modern portfolio theory *(MPT)*: alpha, beta, standard deviation, R-squared, and the Sharpe ratio. All of these indicators collectively are intended to help investors determine the risk-reward profile of a managed portfolio of equities or alternatives.

Teco Metal Straps that are nailed and secure the roof rafters and trusses to the top horizontal wall plate.

Tee A *"T"* shaped plumbing fitting.

Tempered Strengthened Tempered glass will not shatter nor create shards but will *"pelletize"* like an automobile window.

Tenancy At Sufferance The tenancy of a lessee who lawfully comes into possession of a landlord's real estate but who continues to occupy the premises improperly after her or his lease rights have expired.

Tenancy At Will

1. An estate that gives the lessee the right to possession until the estate is terminated by either party; the term of this estate is indefinite.
2. One who holds possession of premises by permission of the owner or landlord. The characteristics of the lease are an uncertain duration and the right of either party to terminate on proper notice.

Tenancy By The Entirety The joint ownership, recognized in some states, of property acquired by husband and wife during marriage. On the death of one spouse, the survivor becomes the owner of the property.

Tenancy For Life See Life Estate.

Tenancy For Years Created by a lease for a fixed term, such as 2 months, 3 years, 10 years, and so on.

Tenancy From Year To Year See Leasehold.

Tenancy In Common A form of co-ownership by which each owner holds an undivided interest in real property as if he or she were the sole owner. Each individual has the right to partition. Unlike a joint tenancy, there is no right of survivorship between tenants in common, and owners may have unequal interests.

Tenancy In Severalty Ownership of property by one person or one legal entity; corporate ownership.

Tenancy The right of possession of real property. May refer to owner-ship or occupancy. See Tenancy In Common, Joint Tenancy.

Tenant Fixtures Fixtures added to leased real estate by a lessee that, by contract or by law, may be removed by the lessee upon expiration of the lease.

Tenant Improvement (TI) Improvements made to the leased premises by or for a tenant.

Tenant Improvement (TI) Allowance Defines the fixed amount of money contributed by the landlord toward tenant improvements. The tenant pays any of the costs that exceed this amount.

Tenant Mix A phrase used to describe the quality of a property's income stream. In multi-tenanted properties, institutional investors typically prefer a mixture of national credit tenants, regional credit tenants and local non-credit tenants.

Tenant One who rents real estate from another and holds an estate by virtue of a lease. See Leasee.

Tender
1. An offer to perform an obligation, together with actual performance or evidence of present ability to perform.
2. To perform under a contract.
3. To pay or deliver.

Tenement Everything that may be occupied under a lease by a tenant.

Tenure In Land The mode in which a person holds an estate in lands.

Tenure The nature of an occupant's ownership rights; an indication of whether one is an owner or a tenant.

Term The lifetime of a loan.

Term Loan One with a set maturity date, typically without amortization.

Term Mortgage A term mortgage is a mortgage with interest payments only during the mortgage term, with the principal due at the end of the term.

Term, Amortization The amortization term is the period of time in which the interest and principal payments of a loan must be made.

Termination (Lease) The cancellation of a lease by the action of either party. A lease may be terminated by expiration of the term, surrender and acceptance, constructive eviction by lessor, or option, when provided in the lease for breach of covenants.

Termination (Listing) The cancellation of a broker-principal employment contract. A listing may be terminated by death or insanity of either party, expiration of listing period, mutual agreement, sufficient written notice, or the completion of performance under the agreement.

Termite Clause A provision in a sales contract that allows the buyer to have the property inspected for termite infestation. In general, if termites are discovered, the buyer may require the seller to treat the property or the buyer may cancel the contract. Most clauses now use the term wood-destroying insects to protect against other types of insects that harm structures, such as the Powder Post Beetle and Old House Borer.

Termite Inspection An examination of a structure by qualified personnel to determine the existence of infestation by termites. See Wood-Destroying Insect.

Termite Shield A shield, usually of galvanized metal, placed in or on a foundation wall or around pipes to prevent the passage of termites.

Termites Wood eating insects.

Terms The conditions and arrangements specified in a contract.

Terra Cotta A ceramic material molded into masonry units.

Testament A Will. Generally to dispose of personal property. Common usage employs the words Will, Testament, and Last Will And Testament as synonyms.

Testamentary Trust A trust created by a will, which comes into effect only after the testator's death.

Testate Having made and left a valid Will.

Testator A Will maker.

Testatrix A woman who makes a Will.

Testimonium A clause that cites the act and date in a deed or other conveyance. Before signing a deed, the grantor should make sure that everything is in order, e.g., the spelling of names and legal descriptions. This is the testimonium clause.

Thermoply™ A laminated protective casing attached to the side of external walls.

Thermostat A device which relegates temperature by switching AC and heating equipment on or off.

Third Party One who is not directly involved in a transaction or contract but may be involved or affected by it.

Three-Dimensional Shingles An Architectural laminated shingles with additional tabs or layers.

Threshold The bottom metal or wood plate of an exterior door frame. Generally they are adjustable to keep a tight fit with the door slab.

Tie-in Arrangement A contract where one transaction depends upon another.

TIL Truth-In-Lending Law. See Regulation Z.

Time And Materials Contract A construction contract which specifies a price for different elements of the work such as cost per hour of labor, overhead, profit.

Time Is Of The Essence A phrase in a contract that requires the performance of a certain act within a stated period of time.

Time Value Of Money The passage of time has an impact on money through its growth due to earning of interest or appreciation, or loss due to inflation.

Timeshare A form of property ownership under which a property is held by a number of people, each with the right of possession for a specified time interval. Time-sharing is most commonly applied to resort and vacation properties.

Time-Weighted Average Annual Rate Of Return The constant annual return over a series of years that would compound to the same return as compounding the actual annual returns for each year in the series.

Tinner A name for the heating contractor.

Tipup Gutter Extensions The downspout extension that directs water away from the property's gutter system.

Title

1. A property's title represents the rights to the property. Those rights are transferred from the seller to the buyer during a real estate transaction and give the buyer legal rights to the property upon closing.
2. The means whereby the owner has the just and full possession of real property.

Title Abstract See Abstract Of Title.

Title Binder Temporary title insurance expected soon to be replaced by a title insurance policy.

Title Company One in the business of examining title to real estate and/or issuing Title Insurance.

Title Defect An unresolved claim against the ownership of property that prevents presentation of a marketable title. Such claims may arise from failure of the owner's spouse, or former part owner, to sign a deed, current liens against the property, or an interruption in the title records to a property. See Cloud On The Title.

Title Evidence Certificate or deed of a person's legal right to ownership of a property.

Title Insurance A policy issued by a title company that insures against loss resulting from defects of title to a specifically described parcel of real property, or from the enforcement of liens existing against it at the time the title policy is issued.

Title Policy Endorsement Specific individual agreements by a title insurance company adding to or altering the basic provisions of a title policy.

Title Report A document indicating the current state of the title, such as easements, covenants, liens, and any defects. The title report does not describe the Chain Of Title. See Abstract Of Title.

Title Search A review of all recorded documents affecting a specific piece of property to determine the present condition of title.

To Have And To Hold Clause See Habendum Clause.

Toenailing To drive a nail in at a slant. Method used to secure floor joists to the plate.

Top Chord The upper or top member of a truss.

Top Plate Top horizontal member of a frame wall supporting ceiling joists, rafters, or other members.

Topography The state of the surface of the land; may be rolling, rough, flat, etc.

Torrens Certificate A certificate showing ownership of property. They are issued by government agencies in some states.

Torrens System A method of evidencing title by registration with the proper public authority, generally called the registrar. See, Torrens Title.

Torrens Title System of title records provided by state law; it is a system for the registration of land titles whereby the state of the title, showing ownership and incumbrances, can be readily ascertained from an inspection of the *"registrar of titles"* without the necessity of a search of the public records.

Tort A wrongful act, wrong, injury or violation of a legal right.

Total Acres All land area contained within a real estate investment.

Total Assets The sum of all gross investments, cash and equivalents, receivables, and other assets presented on the balance sheet.

Total Commitment The full mortgage loan amount that is obligated to be funded if all stated conditions are met.

Total Inventory The total square footage of a type of property within a geographical area, whether vacant or occupied.

Total Principal Balance The total amount of debt, including the original mortgage amount adjusted for subsequent fundings, principal payments and other unpaid items *(e.g., interest)* that are allowed to be added to the principal balance by the mortgage note or by law.

Total Retail Area Total floor area of a retail center less common areas. It is the area from which sales are generated and includes any department stores or other areas not owned by the center.

Total Return The sum of quarterly income and appreciation returns.

Town Charter A legal document establishing a municipality, such as a city or town.

Townhouse A townhouse is a private residence where at least one wall is shared with another residence.

Township Lines The horizontal lines running at six-mile intervals parallel to the base lines in the rectangular survey system.

Township The principal unit of the rectangular survey system. A township is a square with six-mile sides and an area of 36 square miles.

Toxic Black Mold See Black Mold.

Toxic Mold See Black Mold.

Track Record A developer's or builder's reputation for producing on a timely and economical basis. A good track record can be helpful in arranging financing or attracting investors for a new project.

Tract A parcel of land, generally held for Subdividing; A Subdivision.

Tract House A dwelling that has a similar style and floor plan to those of all other houses in a development.

Trade Area See Market Area.

Trade Fixtures Personal property that is attached to a structure that is used in the business. Because this property is part of the business and not deemed to be part of the real estate, it is typically removable upon lease termination.

Trading Up Buying a larger, more expensive property.

Tranche A class of securities. CMBS offerings are generally divided into rated and unrated classes, or tranches, according to seniority and risk. Higher-rated tranches allow for internal credit enhancements; lower-rated classes offer higher yields.

Transaction Costs The costs associated with buying and selling real estate.

Transfer of Ownership The transfer of ownership refers to transfer of a property's deed and title from the seller to the buyer at closing.

Transfer Tax Transfer tax is a transaction fee charged upon the transfer of a property's title. It is imposed by the state, county, and municipal authority where the transaction is taking place and is based on the property's value and classification. Typically, the seller is responsible for paying real estate transfer tax, unless otherwise agreed upon during the transaction.

Transferability The ease with which possession and/or use will be conveyed from one party to another.

Transferable Development Rights The permission to increase the intensity of development for a parcel in exchange for decreasing the density of an adjacent parcel.

Transmitter A device that causes the garage door or gate to open and close.

Trap A plumbing fitting that holds water to prevent air, gas, and vermin from backing up into a fixture.

Tread The walking surface board in a stairway on which the foot is placed.

Treasury Index The treasury index is published by the Federal Reserve Board and based on the average yield of Treasury securities. Financial institutions often use this index as the basis for mortgage notes.

Treated Lumber A wood product which has been impregnated with chemical pesticides such as CCA *(Chromated Copper Arsenate)* to reduce damage from wood rot or insects.

Trespass Unlawful entry or possession of property.

Tri-Level See Split-Level.

Trim (Plumbing, Heating, Electrical) The work that the *"mechanical"* contractors perform to finish their respective aspects of work, and when the home is nearing completion and occupancy.

Trim Interior The finish materials in a building, such as moldings applied around openings like window trim, door trim, or at the floor and ceiling of rooms such as baseboard, cornice, and other moldings.

Trim The final tasks performed by the contractor or subcontractors when the project is nearing completion but typically before occupancy.

Trimmer The vertical stud that supports a header at a door, window, or other opening.

Triple Mint Triple mint condition is a residence that is in immaculate condition.

Triple Net Lease A lease that requires the tenant to pay all expenses of the property being leased in addition to rent. Typical expenses covered in such a lease include taxes, insurance, maintenance, and utilities.

Trophy Building A landmark property that is well known by the public and highly sought by institutional investors such as pension funds and insurance companies. Generally one-of-a-kind architectural designs, with the highest quality of materials and finish, expensive trim. These properties are more desirable than Class A buildings.

True Lease A specific type of multiyear lease which does not pass on ownership rights of the asset to the lessee.

Truss An engineered and manufactured roof support member with *"zigzag"* framing members. A truss does the same job as a rafter but is designed to have a longer span than a rafter.

Trust Account A separate bank account segregated from a broker's own funds, in which the broker is required by state law to deposit all monies collected for clients. In some states called an Escrow Account.

Trust An arrangement whereby property is transferred to a trusted Third Party *(the trustee)* by a grantor *(the trustor)*. The Trustee holds the property for the benefit of another who is the Beneficiary.

Trustee In general, a manager of a trust.

1. The trustee oversees the flow of funds through the CMBS structure on behalf of the bondholders.
2. The trustee is typically responsible for collecting principal and interest from the servicer, distributing payments to bondholders, and reporting to bondholders.
3. The trustee manages a trust to the benefit of the beneficiary.

Trustee's Deed A deed executed by a trustee conveying land held in a trust to the beneficiary.

Trustee's Sale A foreclosure sale conducted by a trustee under the stipulations of a Deed Of Trust.

Truth In Lending See Regulation Z.

Tub Trap A "U" shaped section of a bathtub drainpipe that holds a water seal to prevent sewer gasses from entering the home through tubs water drain.

Tudor An English-style imposing-looking house with fortress lines. Siding is chiefly stone and brick with some stucco and half timbers. Windows and doors have molded cement or stone trim around them.

Turnkey Project A development in which a developer completes the entire project on behalf of a buyer; the developer turns over the keys to the buyer at completion.

Turnkey Term used when the contractor or subcontractor provides all materials and labor for a job.

Turpentine Petroleum, volatile oil used as thinner in paints and as a solvent in varnishes

Two Step Mortgage A mortgage that offers an initial fixed interest rate for a period of time after which, at a predetermined date, the interest rate adjusts according to current market rates.

U

U Bolt A *"U"* shaped, bent iron bar that has bolts and threads at both ends.

U Stirrup An open top, U-shaped loop of steel bar used as reinforcing against diagonal tension in a beam.

U.S. Department of Housing and Urban Development (HUD) A federal agency that administers funding for projects related to housing

UBC See Uniform Building Code.

UCC See Uniform Commercial Code.

UCC1 Statement One of the standard mortgage documents listed in the Uniform Commercial Code.

UF Cable Underground Feeder Cable.

UHF Cable Cable that is designed for ultrahigh frequency.

ULI Urban Land Institute.

Ultimate Compressive Strength The stress at which a material crushes. Typically Used when discussing Concrete.

Ultimate Load The absolute maximum magnitude of load which a structure can sustain, limited only by ultimate failure.

Ultimate Strength Maximum strength that can be developed in a material. Typically Used when discussing Concrete.

Umbrella Partnership Real Estate Investment Trust Organizational structure where a REIT's assets are owned by a holding company for tax purposes.

Umbrella Policy Coverage over and above what the policyholder would have in their regular liability insurance.

Unbuffed End An untrimmed, serrated factory cut end.

Under Construction The period of time after construction has started but before the certificate of occupancy has been issued.

Under Contract This term describes the period of time after a seller has accepted a buyer's offer to purchase a property and during which the buyer is able to perform its due diligence and finalize financing arrangements. Some refer to it as being "in escrow". During this time, the seller is precluded from entertaining offers from other buyers. A home is under contract when a seller has accepted an offer from a buyer, but the transaction has not yet closed.

Undercapitalized Having too little capital for efficient operation.

Undercoat A preparatory coating layer put on a surface before painting. Also known as the Prime coat and/or Primer.

Underfloor Duct A round or rectangular metal pipe placed under a wood floor construction or in a concrete floor to distribute warm air from a heating or air conditioning system.

Underground Plumbing Waste lines and plumbing drains installed beneath a basement floor.

Underimprovement A structure or development of lower cost than the Highest And Best Use of the site.

Underlay A thin layer added underneath the carpeting to provide a smooth surface, comfort and to reduce wear on the carpet. It is also used as a means of insulating sound, heat, and moisture.

Underlayment

1. A secondary water resistant layer added beneath the roof's shingles
2. A layer between a subfloor and a finished floor that facilitates leveling and adhesion.

Underlying Cost Any cost that can be expected within the following budget period. Underlying costs are costs that the company knows it will have to pay out throughout the budget period.

Underlying Mortgage Refers to the first mortgage when there is a Wraparound Mortgage.

Underpinning The process of strengthening the foundation of an existing building or other structure.

Underwater Mortgage A home purchase loan with a higher balance than the free-market value of the home.

Underwater A slang term used to refer to a property whose debt exceeds its value. Also known as *"upside-down"*.

Underwrite

1. Assume liability for certain events.
2. Guarantee the sale of certain securities.
3. Assess the risk of a situation.

Underwriter A company, usually an investment banking firm, that guarantees or participates in a guarantee that an entire issue of stocks or bonds will be purchased.

Underwriters' Laboratories A testing agency that works to benchmark certain electrical devices and test components for possible safety hazards.

Underwriting The process by which a lender decides whether a potential debtor is creditworthy and should receive a loan.

Undivided Interest An ownership right to use and possession of a property that is shared among co-owners, with no one co-owner having exclusive rights to any portion of the property.

Unearned Increment An increase in the value of a property caused by increased population, development, or demand for which the owner is not responsible.

Unencumbered Property that is free of liens and other encumbrances.

Unencumbered Property Unencumbered property is property that is free of any lien.

Unfaced Insulation A fiberglass blanket insulation product without a vapor barrier.

Uniform Commercial Code (UCC) A codification of commercial law, adopted in most states, that attempts to make uniform laws relating to commercial transactions, including chattel mortgages and bulk transfers. Security interests in chattels are created by an instrument known as a security agreement. Article 6 of the code regulates bulk transfers, that is, the sale of a business as a whole, including all fixtures, chattels, and merchandise.

Uniform Residential Appraisal Report (URAR) Standard Fannie Mae Form 1004 used by appraisers.

Uniform Residential Loan Application Report (URLA) Standard Fannie Mae Form 1003 used by loan originators.

Uniform Settlement Statement The form prescribed by the Real Estate Settlement Procedures Act for Federally Related Mortgages, which must be prepared by whoever handles a closing, must contain certain relevant closing information, and must be given to buyer and seller.

Uniform Standards Of Professional Appraisal Practices (USPAP) A set of requirements covering ethics, record keeping, research and reporting promulgated by the Appraisal Foundation, and adhered to by its members.

Unilateral Contract A one-sided contract by which one party makes a promise to induce a second party to do something. The second party is not legally bound to perform; if the second party does comply, however, the first party is obligated to keep the promise.

Unimproved Land Land that is in a natural state and has not yet had the necessities such as water, sewer, electric, and telephone lines brought to the property. It has not yet been graded and is not ready for building.

Unimproved Property See Raw Land, Unimproved Land.

Unincorporated Association An organization formed by a group of people. If the organization has too many characteristics of a corporation, it may be treated like one for income tax purposes.

Union A plumbing fitting that joins pipes end-to-end to allow quick and convenient detachment of pipes without the need for welding. A standard union pipe comes in three parts consisting of a nut, a female end, and a male end.

Unit In multifamily residential property, a suite of rooms making up a residence for 1 tenant. It is generally characterized by a private entrance and some method of individuality from other units in the building or complex.

Unities The four characteristics required to create a Joint Tenancy:
1. Unity Of Interest
2. Unity Of Possession
3. Unity Of Time
4. Title

Unit-In-Place Method A technique used by appraisers to estimate the Reproduction Cost of a structure. The method involves estimating the cost of producing and installing individual components, such as the foundation, exterior walls, and plumbing. Similar methods include the trade-breakdown method and segregated-costs method. See Cost Approach.

Unity of Interest Unity of interest occurs when co-owners all have the same percentage of ownership in a property.

Unity of Ownership The four unities traditionally needed to create a joint tenancy; unity of title, time, interest, and possession.

Unity of Possession Unity of possession occurs when all co-owners have the right to possess any and all portions of the property owned, without physical division.

Unity of Time Unity of time occurs when co-owners receive title at the same time in same conveyance.

Unqualified Buyers a potential buyer who does not meet underwriting guidelines due to insufficient income, length of employment, lack of traditional credit lines, not enough money down, or other factors determined by the underwriter.

Unrated Classes Typically the most subordinated classes of CMBS.

Unrealized Gain The excess of current market value over cost for an asset that is unsold.

Unrecorded Deed An instrument that transfers title from the grantor to the grantee without providing public notice of change in ownership. Recording is essential to protect one's interest in Real Estate.

Unrelated Business Taxable Income (UBTI) A special federal tax levied on investment income generated from property held in a pension plan in which there is a mortgage.

UPREIT See Umbrella Partnership Real Estate Investment Trust.

Upside-Down See Underwater.

Upset Price See Reserve Price.

URAR See Uniform Residential Appraisal Report.

Urban Area Defined by the U.S. Bureau of the Census as a community with a population of 2,500 or more. Contrast with Rural.

Urban Land Institute (ULI) A nonprofit organization providing research and information on land use and development. Among the many publications of the ULI are the periodicals, *Urban Land*, and several development guides for specific types of land use.

Urban Plan A technical and political process concerned with the use of land and design of the urban environment, including air and water and infrastructure passing into and out of urban areas such as transportation and distribution networks.

Urban Property City property; closely settled, usually densely populated property.

Urban Renewal The acquisition of run-down city areas for purposes of redevelopment.

Urea Formaldehyde Foam Insulation An effective insulating material that can be injected into a wall through a small opening. The foam expands within the cavity to fill it. However, the insulation may release formaldehyde gas, which may be hazardous.

URLA See Uniform Residential Loan Application Report

Usable Area The occupiable part of an office or a building floor; generally measured from *"paint to paint"* inside the permanent walls and to the middle of partitions separating one tenant's space from that of other tenants on the same floor. There is no deduction for interior beams or columns. See BOMA Measurements, Efficiency Ratio, Gross Leasable Area.

Usable Ratio A building's total rentable area divided by its usable area. It represents the tenant's pro-rata share of the building's common areas and can determine the square footage upon which the tenant will pay rent. The inverse describes the proportion of space that an occupant can expect to actually use.

Usable Square Footage The area contained within the demising walls of the tenant space that equals the net square footage multiplied by the circulation factor.

USDA United State Department of Agriculture. The federal department that administers programs providing services to farmers.

Use The specific purpose for which a parcel or a building is intended to be used or for which it has been designed or arranged.

Use Variance The permission to use the land for a purpose which, under the current zoning restrictions, is prohibited.

Useful Life In real estate investment, the number of years a property will be useful to the investors.

USPAP Uniform Standards Of Professional Appraisal Practices, promulgated by the Appraisal Foundation. These are requirements for research and reporting with which a professional appraiser is to comply.

Usufructuary Rights Interests That provide for the use of property that belongs to another.

Usury The practice of charging more than the rate of interest allowed by law. In the United States it is up to each state to determine what rate, if any is to be considered usury.

Utilities
1. Services, such as water, sewer, gas, electricity, and telephones, that are generally required to operate a building.
2. The periodic charges for such services.

Utility Ability of the property to fill a need.

Utility Easement The legal right which gives a utility company permission to use and access an area of a property.

V

VA Guaranteed Loan A mortgage loan in which the loan payment is guaranteed to the lender by the Department of Veteran Affairs. See VA Mortgage.

VA Mortgage Service members, veterans, and eligible surviving spouses can receive home loan guarantees provided by private lenders. The Department of Veteran's Affairs guarantees a portion of the loan, which leads to more favorable terms for the borrower.

VA See Veterans Administration.

Vacancy Factor The amount of gross revenue that pro forma income statements anticipate will be lost because of vacancies, often expressed as a percentage of the total rentable square footage available in a building or project.

Vacancy Rate The Ratio of the total amount of available space in relation to the total inventory of space and expressed as a percentage.

Vacant Land Land not currently being used. May have utilities and Off-Site Improvements.

Vacant Space Existing tenant space currently being marketed for lease excluding space available for sublease.

Vacate To move out.

Vacation Home A dwelling used by the owner occasionally for recreational or resort purposes. It may be rented to others for a portion of the year. Income tax deductions pertaining to vacation homes depend on the frequency of use by the owner. Generally, a business loss cannot be claimed on a vacation home. See Second Home.

Vacuum Piping The pipe from the suction side of a pump connected to a vacuum fitting located at the pool and below the water level to which underwater cleaning equipment may be attached.

Valid Contract A contract that complies with all the essential elements on a contract and is binding and enforceable on all parties to it.

Valid Having force, or binding force; legally sufficient and authorized by law.

Valid Lease An enforceable lease that has the following essential parts: lessor and lessee with contractual capacity, offer and acceptance, legality of object, description of the premises, consideration, signatures, and delivery. Leases for more than one year also must be in writing.

Valley Flashing An aluminum water barrier installed at the valley to keep water from entering.

Valley A "*V*" shaped area of a roof formed when two sloping portions of the roof meet at an angle.

Valuable Consideration A type of promised payment upon which a promisee can enforce a claim against an unwilling promisor. Includes money, extension of time, and other equivalents for the grant. It should be distinguished from good consideration, which may be love and affection toward a relative, generosity, and the like. Typically the two terms are used together as in: *"For Good and Valuable Consideration"*

Valuation Estimated worth or price. The act of valuing, normally by appraisal.

Valuation Fee The fee paid by a borrower to cover the cost of property inspection.

Value Engineering Method of analyzing the cost versus the value and alternative materials, equipment, and systems.

Value In Use The worth of a property in a certain use, typically as it is currently being used. This amount may be greater or less than its market value.

Value The present worth of future benefits arising from the ownership of real property. To have value, a property must have utility, scarcity, effective demand, and transferability.

Value-Added
1. A phrase generally used by advisers and managers to describe investments in underperforming and/or undermanaged assets that possess some type of upside potential. NOI and property value can be positively affected through a change in marketing, operating, or leasing strategy; physical improvements; and/or a new capital structure.
2. The amount by which the value of an article is increased at each stage of its production, not including initial costs of production.
3. The amount of any goods, services, or property having features added to a basic line or model for which the buyer is prepared to pay extra.

Vapor Barrier A product used to prevent moisture damage caused by wall condensation.

VARA A measurement or unit of length.

Variable Expense Property operating expenses that increase with occupancy.

Variable Interest Rate An amount of compensation to a lender that is allowed to vary over the maturity of a loan. The amount of variation is generally governed by an appropriate index. See Variable Rate Mortgage, Renegotiated Rate Mortgage.

Variable Rate Mortgage A mortgage loan that contains an interest rate provision related to a selected index. Under this provision, the interest rate may be adjusted annually either up or down.

Variable Rate An interest rate that will vary over the term of the loan. They are usually based on a benchmark rate such as a country's prime rate.

Variable-Maturity Mortgage A long-term mortgage loan, under which the interest rate may be adjusted periodically. Payment levels remain the same, but the loan maturity is lengthened or shortened to achieve the adjustment.

Variable-Payment Plan Any mortgage repayment schedule that provides for periodic change in the amount of monthly payments.

Variance An exception from the zoning ordinances; permission granted by zoning authorities to build a structure or conduct a use that is expressly prohibited by zoning ordinance.

Vendee A buyer. Generally used for real estate; one who purchases personal property is usually called the buyer.

Vendee's Lien A lien against property under contract of sale to secure deposit paid by a purchaser.

Vendor A seller, usually of real estate. The term seller is commonly used for personal property.

Vendor's Affidavit Document signed under oath by the seller stating that the seller has not encumbered title to real estate without full disclosure to the purchaser.

Vendor's Lien See Purchase Money Mortgage.

Veneer Generally a thin decorative covering over a rougher one.
1. On an exterior it is wood or brick that covers a less attractive and less expensive surface.
2. To cover something such as furniture with a thin decorative layer of fine wood.

Vent (Pipe) A pipe allowing air and gasses to flow.

Venture Capital Money raised for high-risk investments.

Verification Sworn statements before a duly qualified officer that the contents of an instrument are correct.

Vermiculite A hydrous mineral that expands when heated. Used in construction.

Vest To create an entitlement to a privilege or right.

Vesting Options Choices buyers have in how to acquire property.

Veterans Administration (VA) An agency of the federal government that provides services for eligible veterans. Generally, a veteran who has served beyond basic training, more than 120 days active duty in the armed forces is eligible for a home loan with no down payment.

Vicarious Liability The responsibility of one person for the acts of another.

Violations Acts, deeds, or conditions contrary to law or permissible use of real property.

Virtual Storefront An online business presence for sales.

Visqueen A polyethylene plastic sheeting that is used for covering concrete as it sets along with many other uses.

Void
1. To have no force or effect; that which is unenforceable.
2. Cardboard box used when dealing with expansive soils to form the void space between the bottom of grade beams and slabs. Also known as void boxes.

Voidable That which is capable of being adjudged void but is not void unless action is taken to make it so.

Voltage A measure of electrical potential.

Voluntary Alienation A legal term that describes a sale or gift made by the free will of the seller or donor.

Voluntary Foreclosure A voluntary foreclosure is a foreclosure proceeding that is done by the borrower, rather than the lender, in an attempt to avoid further payments.

Voluntary Lien a debt that the property owner agrees to have recorded. Typically a mortgage.

VRM See Variable-Rate Mortgage.

W

W/C Ratio In concrete work, this is the water to cement ratio. It is a unitless number expressed in both decimals and as a percentage.

Waferboard A wooden panel that is used as an alternative to plywood. Made from small pieces of scrap as oppose to plywood which consists of organized wood layers.

Waiting Period The time between the initial filing of a registration statement and its effective date.

Waiver Of Tax Lien A form to be signed by a taxing authority stating that it will not file a lien. This form is typically needed when real estate is sold by an estate.

Waiver The renunciation, abandonment, or surrender of some claim, right or privilege.

Walk-Through Inspection An inspection of premises by a buyer or tenant prior to closing or taking possession.

Walk Through Colloquial term for Walk-Through Inspection.

Walkup Building A walkup building is a building that does not have an elevator and are usually four or five stories.

Wall Out When a painter spray paints the interior of a home.

Warehousing (Loan) The packaging of a number of mortgage loans for sale in the Secondary Mortgage Market by a financial institution or mortgage banker who has originated the loans.

Warping Distortion that causes a material to bend or twist out of shape.

Warranty (Labor) A warranty issued to by the developer or contractor to pay the costs of labor required to exchange or replace damaged materials

Warranty (Material) A warranty issued to by the company manufacturing construction materials such as roofing material or siding.

Warranty A promise contained in a contract.

Warranty Deed A conveyance of land in which the grantor warrants the title to the grantee. See General Warranty Deed and Special Warranty Deed.

Warranty Of Habitability An implied assurance given by a landlord that an apartment offered for rent is free from safety and health hazards.

Waste Often found in a mortgage or lease contract, or in a Life Estate, this term refers to property abuse, destruction, or damage *beyond normal wear and tear*. The possessor causes unreasonable injury to the holders of other interests in the land, house, garden, or other property. The injured party may attempt to terminate the contract or sue for damages.

Waste Pipe A plumbing pipe created to carry waste or excess fluids.

Wastewater Water that has been used by people or in manufacturing that contains waste.

Wasting Asset Something of value that deteriorates over time.

Water Closet Another name for a bathroom.

Water Meter Pit The iron or PVC bonnet and concrete rings containing the water meter.

Water Rights The right of a property owner to use water on, under or adjacent to the land for such purposes as irrigation, power, or private consumption. See Riparian Rights, Usufructuary Rights.

Water Table The upper level at which underground water is normally encountered in a particular area.

Water Tap (Valve) Valve which controls the release of liquids or gas. It marks the point connecting a water line with the main municipal water system.

Water-repellent Water repellents and sealers are used as a natural finish that increase the wood's resistance to water, adding a finish coat of wax that enables the wood to repel water and moisture.

Water-resistant Drywall Resistant to moisture and is generally installed in showers, bathrooms, and basement walls. Sometimes called *"Green Board"*.

WCR See Women's Council Of Realtors®.

Wear And Tear The physical deterioration of property as the result of use, weathering, and age.

Weatherization The process of protecting buildings from the elements *(weather, wind, rain)* and reducing cooling or heating energy consumption.

Weatherstripping A method of installing weatherstrips. This is a materials designed to seal a door or a window for air leaks and water penetration.

Weep Holes Small openings located at the bottom of window frames or weep bricks designed to allow moisture and water to escape, thus preventing moisture damage.

Weighted-Average Coupon The weighted average of the gross interest rates of the mortgages underlying a pool as of the issue date, with the balance of each mortgage used as the weighting factor.

Weighted-Average Equity The denominator of the fraction used to calculate investment-level income, appreciation, and total returns on a quarterly basis, consisting of net assets at the beginning of the period adjusted for weighted contributions and distributions.

Weighted-Average Rental Rates The average proportion of unequal rental rates in two or more buildings within a market.

Western Row House A nineteenth-century-style-house usually built to cover an entire street or block. It has common side walls with the house on either side.

Western Town House See Western Row House.

Wet Loan A mortgage in which the funds are obtained before all required documentation is completed. It allows the borrower to purchase property in a timelier fashion and complete the required paperwork after the transaction.

Wetlands Federal and/or state protected transition areas between uplands and aquatic habitats that provide flood and storm water control, surface and groundwater protection, erosion control, and pollution treatment.

White Elephant A property that is too expensive to maintain or generates too little rent to pay for itself.

Whole House Fan A type of ceiling fan created to circulate air inside a building.

Wholesale a term used in real estate investing which describes the act of getting a home under contract to buy and then selling the contract to some other investor or end user.

Wholesaler One who flips homes at deep discounts or one who flips the contract to buy such a home. See Wholesale.

Will The disposition of one's property to take effect after death. See Testament.

Williamsburg Georgian An English-style house built in Williamsburg and representative of the early Georgian houses built in America throughout the early 1700s. They had simple exterior lines and generally fewer of the decorative devices characteristic of the later Georgian houses. Most were 2 or 3-story rectangular houses with two large chimneys rising high above the roof at each end.

Wind Bracing Diagonal braces made of wood or metal, which are installed to prevent a wall from tracking, twisting, bending, or falling over.

Window An opening in the wall of a building to let in light and air. Most are made of transparent material and have the ability to be opened and closed.

Window Buck A wooden frame installed within a concrete foundation or block wall to define the space which will later be used to install a window.

Window Frame A part of a window unit that consist of the head, jambs, and sill which forms a precise opening in which a window sash fits.

Window Sash A part of a window unit. it is a single assembly of stiles and rails made into a frame for holding the glass. See Sash.

Window Well See Area Well..

Winged Ant See Termite.

Wire Nut A device used to splice together two or more wires securely.

Without Recourse Words used in endorsing a promissory note or bill to denote that the holder is not to look to the debtor personally in the event of nonpayment: the creditor has recourse only to the property. A form of exculpation. Same as Nonrecourse. See endorsement, exculpatory clause.

Women's Council Of Realtors® (WCR) An organization, affiliated with the National Association Of Realtors®, devoted to preparing women in real estate for their emerging roles in society, to encouraging members to a productive career in real estate, and to developing leadership potential. Publishes *The Real Estate Scene (monthly)* and the *WCR Communiqué (quarterly)*.

Wonderboard ™ A cement based backer board generally used on bathtub decks as a tile backing material.

Wood Decking Plywood, lumber, or glued laminated member that is placed on a roof or floor structural members for structural rigidity of building frame and to provide a surface for traffic or substrate for roofing or flooring system.

Wood-Destroying Insect A term used in certain home inspection forms; as a condition for purchase, the property must be free of these insects. See Termite.

Woodwork A higher than average quality feature of finish work using wood for ornamental design. In general, the interior trim of a home.

Words Of Conveyance Words of conveyance is a stipulation in a deed demonstrating the definite intent to convey a specific title to real property to a named grantee.

Work Triangle The total distance of the sides of the *"triangle"* connecting the refrigerator, range, and sink in a home kitchen; experts say that this distance should be between 15 and 21 feet for maximum efficiency.

Working Capital The difference between current assets and current liabilities.

Working Drawings The set of plans for a building or project that comprise the contract documents that indicate the precise manner in which a project is to be built.

Working Mortgage A mortgage loan in which payments are made more frequently than once a month and are timed to coincide with the borrower's pay period. Typically, the payments are deducted directly from the borrower's paycheck.

Workout The process by which a borrower attempts to negotiate with a lender to restructure the borrower's debt rather than go through foreclosure proceedings.

Workout (Agreement) A mutual effort by a property owner and lender to avoid foreclosure or bankruptcy following a default; generally involves substantial reduction in the debt service burden during an economic depression. See Cash Flow Mortgage, Distressed Property.

Workout Assumption The assumption of an existing mortgage by a qualified, third party borrower from a financially distressed borrower.

Wraparound Loan See Wraparound Mortgage.

Wraparound Mortgage A mortgage that includes in its balance an underlying mortgage. Rather than having distinct and separate first and second mortgages, a wraparound mortgage includes both.

Wrapped Drywall Areas that get complete drywall covering, as in the doorway openings of bifold and bi-pass closet doors.

Writ Of Attachment The method by which a debtor's property is placed in the custody of the law and held as security, pending the outcome of a creditor's suit.

Writ Of Ejectment See Ejectment.

Write-down The accounting procedure used when the book value of an asset is adjusted downward to better reflect current market value.

Write-off The accounting procedure used when an asset has been determined to be uncollectible and is therefore charged as a loss.

X

Y

Y A plumbing fitting with a Y shape.

Yard

1. The open grounds of a property.
2. A unit of measurement equal to three feet.

Yield The effective return on an investment, as paid in dividends or interest.

Y Strainer Device with a Y shape that is used in pipelines for withholding undesired substances from flowing into the pumped materials, usually liquid or gas.

Yield (Concrete) The total volume of net concrete made for use in a project.

Yield (Investment) The ratio of cash flow produced by an investment property divided by the price of acquiring and maintaining the property.

Yield Curve A graph of current interest rates of similar obligations, arranged by maturity.

Yield Maintenance A prepayment premium that allows investors to attain the same yield as if the borrower made all scheduled mortgage payments until maturity.

Yield Maintenance Fee A component of a prepayment penalty, stated to be designed to replace interest earnings a lender would have received on a loan if the borrower had not prepaid the loan.

Yield Maintenance Premium A penalty, paid by the borrower, designed to make investors whole in the event of early redemption of principal.

Yield Spread The difference in yield between a debt instrument or other investment and a benchmark value, typically U.S. Treasuries of the same maturity.

Yield To Maturity (YTM) The Internal Rate Of Return on an investment. Considers all inflows and outflows of investment returns and their timing.

Yoke The location where a home's water meter is sometimes installed between two copper pipes and located in the water meter pit in the yard.

YUPCAP A slang term for a young urban professional who cannot afford property.

Z

Z-Bar Flashing A galvanized metal flashing for the prevention of water from penetrating through the horizontal joints between sheets of plywood siding.

Zero Ice Another name for dry ice.

Zero Lot Line A form of cluster housing development in which individual dwelling units are placed on separately platted lots. They may be attached to one another, but not necessarily.

Zero Lot Line House A piece of residential real estate in which the structure comes up to or very near to the edge of the property line.

Zero Slump Concrete A stiff or dry concrete showing no measurable slump after the removal of the cone.

Zombie Title A title to real property that happens when a lender initiates foreclosure proceedings by issuing a notice of foreclosure and then unexpectedly dismisses the foreclosure.

Zone An area set off by the proper authorities for specific use; subject to certain restrictions or restraints.

Zone A room or part of a building requiring concentrated air conditioning so it can maintain a desired temperature.

Zone Valve A type of valve that is controlled by a thermostat and placed near a cooler or heater. Used for controlling the flow of water and steam in hydronic systems to different parts of the building.

Zoned Air Conditioning The practice of warming or cooling an area of a building where residents spend the most time, instead of heating or cooling the entire property.

Zoning The division of a city or town into zones and the application of regulations having to do with the architectural design and structural and intended uses of buildings within such zones.

Zoning A method used by a governing authorities for the restriction of the permitted use of a region within a mapped land.

Zoning Map A map which shows the different zoning districts in the state.

Zoning Ordinance The set of laws and regulations controlling the use of land and construction of improvements in a given area or zone.

Zoning Permit Document permitting a specific land use and purpose.

1031 See Starker

80-10-10 MORTGAGE A type of Piggyback Mortgage, in which a first mortgage covering 80% of the value of the home is combined with a Second Mortgage that covers 10% of value. The remaining 10% is a cash down payment. The purpose of this combination of loans is to avoid the use of Mortgage Insurance. An 80-15-5 mortgage is set up in a similar manner, and obtains the same results, except the down payment is only 5% of value.